Figures, Tables, and Textboxes

CW01499156

Figures

Tables

Textboxes

Archival Arrangement
and Description

Archival Arrangement and Description

Analog to Digital

Lois Hamill

ROWMAN & LITTLEFIELD
Lanham • Boulder • New York • London

Published by Rowman & Littlefield
A wholly owned subsidiary of The Rowman & Littlefield Publishing Group, Inc.
4501 Forbes Boulevard, Suite 200, Lanham, Maryland 20706
www.rowman.com

Unit A, Whitacre Mews, 26-34 Stannary Street, London SE11 4AB

British Library Cataloguing in Publication Information Available

Library of Congress Cataloging-in-Publication Data Available

ISBN 9781442279155 (hardback : alk. paper)
ISBN 9781442279162 (pbk. : alk. paper)
ISBN 9781442279179 (electronic)

∞™ The paper used in this publication meets the minimum requirements of American National Standard for Information Sciences—Permanence of Paper for Printed Library Materials, ANSI/NISO Z39.48-1992.

Printed in the United States of America

Contents

Acronyms and Abbreviations

AACR	*Anglo-American Cataloging Rules*
AACR2	*Anglo-American Cataloging Rules*, 2nd edition
AHA	American Historical Association
AIIM	Association for Information and Image Management
AIMS	*An Inter-Institutional Model for Stewardship*
AIP	archival information package
APPM	*Archives, Personal Papers, and Manuscripts: A Cataloging Manual for Archival Repositories, Historical Societies, and Manuscript Libraries*
CAN/MARC	Canada machine-readable cataloging
CSV	comma-separated values
DACS	*Describing Archives: A Content Standard*
DC	Dublin Core
DIP	dissemination information package
DMS	document management system
DTD	document-type definition
DVD	digital video disc
EAC-CPF	*Encoded Archival Content—Corporate Bodies, Persons, and Families*
EAD	encoded archival description
ECM	enterprise content management system
EGAD	Experts Group on Archival Description (an ICA committee)
FTP	file transfer protocol
HRS	Historical Records Survey
HTML	hyper-text markup language
ICA	International Council on Archives
ILS	integrated library system
IR	institutional repository
ISAAR(CPF)	*International Standard Archival Authority Record for Corporate Bodies, Persons, and Families*
ISAD(G)	*General International Standard Archival Description*
ISDF	*International Standard for Describing Functions*
ISO	International Organization for Standardization
IT	information technology
LC	Library of Congress
LCNAF	Library of Congress Registry of Name Authority Files

LOD	linked open data
MARC	machine-readable cataloging
MARC AMC	MARC format for archives and manuscript collections
METS	metadata encoding and transmission standard
MPLP	"More Product, Less Process"
NA	National Archives (1935–December 11, 1949)
NARA	National Archives and Records Administration (1985–present)
NDSA	National Digital Stewardship Alliance
NISTF	National Information Systems Task Force
NUCMC	*National Union Catalog of Manuscript Collections*
OAC	Online Archive of California
OAI-PMH	Open Archives Initiative Protocol for Metadata Harvesting
OAIS	open archival information system
OCLC	Online Computer Library Center (originally Ohio College Library Center)
OhioLINK	Ohio Library and Information Network
OPAC	online public access catalog
PDF	portable document format
PDF/A	portable document format—archival
PDI	preservation description information
PII	personally identifiable information
POWRR	Preserving (Digital) Objects with Restricted Resources
PREMIS	Preservation Metadata Implementation Strategies
RAD	*Rules for Archival Description*
RDA	resource description and access
RIM	records and information management
RLG	Research Libraries Group
RLIN	Research Libraries Information Network
SAA	Society of American Archivists
SC&UA	special collections and university archives
SGML	standardized general markup language
SIP	submission information package
SNAC	Social Networks and Archival Context
SQL	structured query language
UID	unique identification number
USMARC	U.S. machine-readable cataloging
USMARC AMC	U.S. machine-readable cataloging for archives and manuscripts control
XML	extensible markup language

Acronyms and Abbreviations

Preface

I believe that archivists need technical skills to be able to work with digital materials at a variety of levels. At the same time, they need [a] strong grasp of archival principles to be able to translate and adapt those concepts into new ways of working.—Richard Pearce-Moses, sixty-first president, Society of American Archivists[1]

I have learned a lot in the last eighteen months while researching and writing this book. Arrangement and description has been one of my specialties since graduate school, but this book is about building on the known and familiar, practices and theory, to extend ourselves to the newest format: digital. Some archivists may work exclusively with digital records, but no archives will give up its rich cultural history of medieval to modern analog treasures to go exclusively digital. It is a hybrid world, so we add skills for digital records to our tool belt.

This book is about taking the practice and theory we know, which has worked for analog records, and modifying it as needed to adapt to the unique qualities of digital objects. As for analog records, which tasks to perform in which sequence are often at the discretion and experience of the archivist, balanced with her or his archives' practices, standards, and resources.

During my research I kept encountering sources that focused on only one aspect of digital records yet overlapped other sources, a little here and a little there. I tried to reconcile them with each other and my own perspective. This evolved into an eighty-row, seven-column spreadsheet to capture the digital workflow. Being a practical person, it was intended as a cheat sheet of not just the sequence of tasks but also where to record information, to reconcile archival functions with OAIS functions, connect tasks to types of metadata gathered and created, identify standards (mostly DACS) governing the task, link the task to the digital software my department preferred for performing the task and add notes. Most of this is shared in the tables throughout the book, but the columns for standards and software were cut due to page size constraints.

Take this tool and build on it. Add the column for software and complete it. Customize it for your practice and archives. This is not intended as a list of what *must* be done. It is an effort to reconcile multiple voices into a sequential workflow of all the tasks that could be performed in their appropriate sequence if one had the ability to perform everything it was said should be done. Not all tasks will be necessary, depending on the source of the files, the storage medium by which they arrive, the file formats, the information content, your skill level, and the resources available to you.

Further tools to help your practice include a glossary, an appendix of dates to help date digital materials you encounter and better understand recent standards and software development, and an appendix with suggestions of software tools for processing digital files. These are strictly offered as a resource for your assessment; I do not endorse any of them.

The qualities of authenticity, integrity, reliability, and usability are important to the long-term preservation of digital records. These are largely qualities inherent in the files received by the archives, although archivists will strengthen and hopefully maintain them by the actions they take. The ⚕ symbol on the tables identifies tasks supporting these four qualities. This means files can also be appraised for these qualities. No one else has framed technical appraisal this way.

There are many facets to working with digital records, from technical appraisal to preservation, description, standards, impact on users, legal implications, and possibilities of what could be done with the power of the web. There is too much for anyone to master it all, and the pace of technological change makes some knowledge obsolete in five or ten years. If newcomers to the profession were to look back fifteen to twenty years ago to the topics we specialized in then, there were not as many as there are today. The SAA Archival Fundamentals Series of the 1990s focused on five core functions. Compare that with today's SAA bookstore offerings. Conference presentations and journal articles give the impression that the topic under discussion needs to be performed to a very detailed level every time it is done. It is unrealistic to imagine that an archivist could execute all the functions she performs to the in-depth level that a specialist might perform just a few tasks. When working with digital records, assess the risk; make decisions; document them in policies, processing plans, or finding aids; do your best; and move on. Doing something is better than nothing, which clearly results in loss. The intention behind what I have written is to present how to perform certain archival tasks with some level of specificity. The explanation is provided in case the task needs to be done, not to say that the task *must* be done.

The final contribution I make is to raise questions about where archival description is going and how inclusive that direction will be. Efficient implementation of an OAIS model to preserve digital files involves automation. Automation means software. Although there are no silver bullets, hopefully the profession can develop a limited number of requisite applications to develop an OAIS system rather than one for each task. The semantic web currently relies on linked (open) data, also more easily created with software. These require resources that may not be equally available to all. Tiered levels of application (like DACS's required, optimum, and added-value fields) will make advances that rely on technology more accessible to a greater percent of archives.

This volume is for new archivists in training, for new archivists who may be the only professional in their archives, and for those experienced archivists who may just be starting to tackle the challenge of digital records or to develop a program at their institution. Some chapters build on the topic discussed, with further considerations or potential policy decisions if a more intentional program is being considered. While I am most familiar with the academic environment, most of what I have written should fit archives managed by a professionally trained archivist. Even within the academic environment, there are differences. Each archivist will need to adjust to the specifics of her or his setting.

And here is the fine print:

1. The term *digital file* is intended to be a broad, generic reference, regardless of information content and whether born digital or scanned from analog.

2. A *folder* is a paper or electronic container that holds individual items, whether analog or digital.

3. The difference in vocabulary for *record group* and *collection* refers primarily to the circum-stances of or reason for their creation—an individual or private person versus a business or organizational transaction (in the broad sense of interaction, not a financial transaction). The term *organizational records* is intended as a broadly inclusive one, including for-profit, nonprofit, church, civic, social, and sporting groups and clubs or other groups of people who come together in an intentional way for some common activity.

4. After about 1977, the term *archivist* is meant to be inclusive of all archivists, regardless of the materials they manage, their job title, or type of employing institution.

5. I use the term *preservation*, not *conservation*, for tasks within the education of most archivists for both analog and digital materials. Preservation tasks help protect and extend the life of archival records.

6. In chapter 1, *archival records* means they are archival materials that have been appraised and meet criteria for permanent retention versus items that have not been appraised yet and may not merit keeping. I use *materials* as a broad term that includes all formats or types of records. The word *classification* is used in the library sense.

Note

1. Richard Pearce-Moses, *Archives in the Digital Era*, accessed July 8, 2016, http://archivesinthedigitalera .blogspot.com.

Acknowledgments

Thank you to the NKU Faculty Senate for the time afforded by the summer fellowship and the stipend that allowed me to take additional training on digital resources. This new knowledge definitely informed my thinking. Thank you Provost Ott-Rowlands, President Mearns, and members of the board of regents, who approved my fall 2015 sabbatical, which enabled additional research and time to start writing. Thank you to Arne Almquist, associate provost for learning sciences and technologies and dean of the library, and my supervisor, Lois Schultz, associate dean for collections, for supporting my scholarship, especially with extra time to meet deadlines.

Thank you to my editor, Charles Harmon, for the opportunity to write this book. Thanks also to the Kentucky Library Association's Academic Section for a professional development grant that I used to attend one last workshop; to Steely Library's Source Finder staff, who obtained materials from near and far for my many requests; to Meg Miner for her support and service on my editorial board; to Lisa Perna for editorial support; and to Seth Shaw for his assistance.

Thanks to my great staff, especially Vicki Cooper, who shouldered a lot of additional responsibility during my fellowship and sabbatical, and Anne Ryckbost, who called my attention to informative, recent professional literature.

And to Kiki, who faithfully met me at the door every night, patiently kept me company for endless hours of writing, and sometimes successfully persuaded me to take a break and play with her.

1

A Brief History of Arrangement and Description

Arrangement and description are core functions that all archivists need to understand and be able to perform. The manner in which archivists organize the information and records they manage, whether they exist physically or only intellectually, is at the heart of what makes the archival profession unique. The archival principles developed for arrangement and description are based on the unique qualities of the records themselves. Archival records are distinctive from published materials and objects, yet despite the wide range of form, format, and content, as a body they share much in common. It took American archivists nearly a century to reach this conclusion and agree on consistent practices.

French archivist and historian Natalis de Wailly is credited in 1841 with defining *respect des fonds*, or provenance, as American archivists know it today. De Wailly said, "[A]ll documents which come from a body, an establishment, a family, or an individual form a *fonds*, and must be kept together." He referred to records *by* a creator, not *about* a creator. *Respect des fonds* was quickly recognized in Europe as the only sound basis for archival arrangement. Around 1880, German archivists at the Royal Archives of Prussia developed the corollary principle of original order that they called *Strukturprinzip*.[1]

Pre-1895

The American archival profession, as well as its history of arrangement and description, has its roots in the American Historical Association, founded in 1884. Before then, civil authorities and settlers colonizing the New World brought record-keeping practices with them. Vital records and legal matters concerning wills and estates were recorded in New England in the 1620s. Colonists expected authorities to maintain records of import to the community and to access them for the protection of their legal rights. Writing in the late 1980s, James M. O'Toole, then an archival educator, credits these government records as the beginning of the public records tradition in the United States.[2] During the eighteenth and nineteenth centuries, a number of private individuals began amassing collections of historical books, manuscripts, pamphlets, private letters, and government records to further their own historical writing. This was the beginning of the second strand in American archival history, the historical manuscripts tradition.

The United States was the last major modern country to develop its archival profession and build a national archives, not taking significant steps until the 1930s. The library profession in America developed much earlier than the archival field. Cutter's cataloging rules, the Dewey decimal subject classification system, and the American Library Association all existed by 1876. By the end of the nineteenth century, most manuscript collections were managed by libraries or the library unit of historical societies.[3]

The earliest archival records collected were fragmented remains of the colonial, revolutionary, and subsequent eras. The records that still existed or were collected were not typically large bodies of related records, whether of private or public origin. They were predominantly random, not strongly related to one another, and of limited quantity. These qualities made it easy to treat individual documents as discrete items, a library principle.[4] Whether a document was originally a public government record or a personal paper was unimportant to private and institutional collectors alike. The difference between the two types of records was further blurred because both were described as historical manuscripts. Both tended to be organized in the same manner regardless of their owner.[5] They were classified using prevailing library techniques. Individual items were classified separately, even to the point of separating pages in a document or letters from their enclosures or attachments. Archivist Richard Berner, writing about the evolution of archival arrangement and description, said that, until the beginning of the twentieth century, "variations on the chronological-topical/geographical classification" scheme were applied "without serious challenge" to archival records.[6]

Historical Manuscripts, 1895–1936

From its founding in 1884, the American Historical Association (AHA) was concerned with the preservation and use of historical records. American historians traveling to Europe to conduct research discovered archives, saw records being preserved there, and learned how they were organized. The AHA established the Historical Manuscripts Commission in 1895 to focus on preserving historical material "of an essentially personal character" and the Public Archives Commission in 1899 to address public government records. Unfortunately, two separate commissions were established, implying that historical manuscripts and public records were different. This led to the conclusion that they needed to be managed differently, essentially dividing manuscript curators from archivists.[7]

As a major national institution, the Library of Congress (LC) held a lot of influence with manuscript custodians. In 1904, Worthington C. Ford, head of the Manuscripts Division, wrote the first American codification for archival manuscripts, published in Charles A. Cutter's *Rules for a Dictionary Catalog*.[8] In 1913, John C. Fitzpatrick, assistant chief of the Manuscripts Division, published his manual *Notes on the Care, Cataloguing, Calendaring and Arranging of Manuscripts*, in which he recommended a chronological-geographical arrangement and cataloging directly from manuscripts instead of their finding aids. Both were library practices. The former separated materials related by provenance.[9] The latter treated individual documents as discrete, failing to provide collective description or address relationships among documents.

Public Archives, 1895–1936

Meanwhile, in 1898, the New York State Library hired Dutch archivist Arnold Van Laer as head of its Manuscript Division. Following the European practice of provenance, he reclassified records that had previously been arranged chronologically to arrange them according to their record-creating agency. The Public Archives Commission actively worked for the establishment of a federal archives and a state archives for each state, among other goals. Alabama established the first state archives in 1901 and organized its archives according to provenance from its founding.[10]

The Public Archives Commission held the first conference of archivists in 1909, continuing them until 1936, when the Society of American Archivists (SAA) was founded. The 1909 conference was likely the first time provenance was discussed at a professional gathering of American archivists. Keynote speaker Waldo Leland, the leading American archival theoretician, argued for adoption of provenance over the application of library subject classification methods to archival documents.[11] At subsequent conferences, public records archivists examined how they did their work and debated the thinking behind it.

"The 1930s brought major change to the American archival scene." The National Archives (NA) opened in 1935.[12] Just as the Library of Congress led in matters of historical manuscripts, the National Archives quickly began to dominate in matters of government records. In 1936, archivists left the AHA and formed their own professional organization. That same year the Survey of Archives of the Federal Government outside the District of Columbia began as another Works Progress Administration (WPA) program to cope with high unemployment. As its name indicates, this survey collected detailed information about federal records located outside Washington, DC. Although funded by the WPA, National Archives staff managed the project. "The Survey of Federal Records was an important training ground for future archivists as well as for experimentation in archival methods."[13] The volume of records to be surveyed required collective description, not item-level description, a notable point of difference between archival and library perspectives for archival records. Both the Survey of Federal Records and the Historical Records Survey (HRS) systematically applied collective description to the records they inventoried. *The Manual of the Survey of Federal Archives* explicitly instructed field workers on how to identify series, to describe each series separately, and to ignore records below the series level.[14] HRS field workers completed a single collection level form per collection. The same form was successfully used for both government and historical manuscript records.[15] This demonstrated the "applicability of archival concepts to the description of manuscripts."[16] These two projects, initiated simultaneously, were likely the first systematic application of collective description in the American archival field.

Between 1909 and 1940, the public archives field developed in a different direction than historical manuscripts did. Archivists working with government records felt that their purpose, clientele, and records were different from manuscript curators and their historical manuscripts. They organized records to facilitate retrieval for government needs, which led to different classification methods than those used for historical manuscripts. The first classification plan based on provenance was presented in 1906 and implemented at the Iowa state archives by 1914.[17] By 1938, Illinois state archivist Margaret Cross Norton was arguing for the use of the series as the level for "cataloging" archival records. Although trained as both a historian and a librarian, Norton pragmatically foresaw that it would be difficult to justify founding a national archives and state archival programs if they existed solely for scholarly research.[18]

Historical Manuscripts, 1936–1956

Despite forty years of membership overlap between historical and library associations and archival commissions and committees, by 1940, the break between historical manuscript curators and public records archivists was complete. There had been some cooperation between librarians, manuscript curators, and archivists while working on the Historical Records Survey of the Works Project Administration, but by 1940, the American Library Association was more interested in developing a national cataloging code.[19]

Even though public archives made progress toward development of theory and practice, the historical manuscript tradition dominated the field until about 1960. Collecting emphasized papers of the remote past, until the Minnesota and Wisconsin state historical societies took the lead in the 1930s and began to collect twentieth-century papers. This trend became typical after World War II and dominant by the 1970s. The shift to collecting modern papers was the key factor in eventually reuniting the historical manuscripts and public archives traditions. As modern collections increasingly resembled public records in size, complexity, and degree of relatedness, manuscript curators began to borrow practices from public archives.[20]

In 1940, the Library of Congress was reorganized. The cataloging function remained in the Manuscripts Division, but cataloging policy and rules formation was split off and transferred to the Descriptive Cataloging Division of the Processing Department. This functional separation led to the conclusion that manuscript cataloging could be separated from both arrangement and the creation of registers, a tool like the card catalog to help discover pertinent material. The split was significant because of its impact on the eventual development of a cataloging code and subsequent impact on the rules for entries in the *National Union Catalog of Manuscript Collections* (NUCMC).[21] The second factor leading to creation of a cataloging code resulted from reforms implemented by Solon J. Buck, who resigned as second archivist of the United States in 1948 to become chief of the Manuscripts Division of the Library of Congress. At the National Archives, he helped develop the record group concept and recommendations to replace classification and cataloging with inventories as the basic finding aid for record groups.[22] Definition of the record group resolved the problem of how to arrange related records and also enabled collective description. As the first Manuscripts Division chief with archival experience, Buck initiated reforms for processing and description that replicated the reforms accomplished at the National Archives. The manuscript group system was established as the parallel to the record group system and the register as the equivalent of the inventory. Provenance was used to identify manuscript collections. Development of the register gave catalogers an information source from which to catalog, but they only used the "Scope and Contents" note, omitting series descriptions and box lists, as rich potential sources of cataloging terms. Berner criticized this decision because it resulted in disconnecting the card catalog from the other finding aids instead of integrating all collection registers.[23]

The AHA suggested creating a national register listing all manuscript collections using information gathered by the HRS as the basis for creating a comprehensive guide. A committee was formed in 1949 with representatives from SAA, the American Association for State and Local History, and the Library of Congress. Initially the National Archives was excluded but then added from 1952 to 1953, when federal and state records were to be included. National Archives staff repeatedly objected to the proposed rules for description from concern that the rules would be used not just for submissions to NUCMC but also for all other manuscript description performed at participating institutions, meaning their own internal descriptive system. The NUCMC rules described items at the collection level and the item level.[24] Item-level description was consistent with library practice but counter to public archivists' practice of collective description and the series as the cataloging unit. It was a step backward, even for the LC. The solution chosen was to omit government records and the National Archives' participation.

As desire for a national cataloging code grew and progress was made on the NUCMC descriptive rules, it became increasingly difficult to separate creation of a national guide to historical manuscripts from development of a standardized library cataloging code. Assumptions that the NUCMC project needed approval by the American Library Association and the LC began to drive decisions instead of sound archival theory or practice. Historical manuscript repositories were being pushed toward usage of library techniques for book cataloging instead of practices more appropriate for archival manuscripts. The suitability of item-level description was not questioned. The role of cataloging was not examined in light of the interrelated processes of archival arrangement and description.[25]

Although initial testing in 1955 revealed problems, NUCMC was given to the LC Manuscripts Division to start implementation. The initial plan was for both a book and catalog card format. The Manuscripts Division proposed a name and subject index for the book version, hoping to avoid use of the cataloging rules. The LC was one of the developers of the description rules, yet its own Manuscripts Division was unhappy with them and sought to avoid using them.[26] Recall that the cataloging policy and rules formation function had been transferred out of the Manuscripts Division in 1940. Despite using the manuscript group concept and collective description itself, the LC did not guide the description rules development in a direction more compatible with manuscripts, even when National Archives' staff argued for the same.

Because the goal was to produce a union catalog, the intention was that participating institutions would collect all cards produced. What happened was that, except for nine, each institution only took cards for their own holdings or perhaps nearby institutions, thus destroying the union quality. It was only after this failure that publication of the bound volumes started. Book subscribers received the complete union version describing all holdings nationally for all names and subjects in the index. The National Archives staff's fears about the card catalog were realized. Because repositories only collected cards for their holdings, the cards became an internal finding aid, and the entry rules became the institution's de facto cataloging code for historical manuscripts. The NUCMC description rules ultimately served as the basis for the *Anglo-American Cataloging Rules* (AACR) published in 1967. AACR and AACR2 inherited all of NUCMC's weaknesses: item-level description instead of collective description; cataloging and describing items instead of series; separation of one step, cataloging, from a process of accessioning, arranging, and describing; and nonintegrated finding aids. Finally, in 1983, the LC allowed modified description rules for archives and manuscript collections as approved in Steven L. Hensen's *Archives, Personal Papers, and Manuscripts: A Cataloging Manual for Archival Repositories, Historical Societies, and Manuscript Libraries* (APPM).[27] APPM only revised chapter 4 of AACR2; all the other rules still applied and were used to create thousands of U.S. machine-readable cataloging (USMARC) and U.S. machine-readable cataloging for archives and manuscripts control (USMARC AMC) catalog records, which still exist today in the OCLC WorldCat database. Too many archivists still seem comfortable with using library cataloging for archival materials. The unsuitability of library standards for archival records and collections does not seem to be a concern for most in discussions of national bibliographic networks for archives.

Public Archives, 1936–1966

Illinois state archivist Margaret Cross Norton, influential in the 1930s and 1940s, worked to establish a model public archives program. In 1937, as chair of SAA's Cataloging and Classification Committee, she led the committee's revision of the Illinois State Library's cataloging code for the archives. The revisions were based on lessons already learned from work at the National Archives and systematic refinement of the series concept by the HRS. The revised code identified the series as the cataloging unit for archives. This was the first serious treatment of the record series concept.[28]

By early 1941, the National Archives realized its initial approach to government records was not working. It concluded that the library practice of cataloging didn't work and abolished the Cataloging and Classification Divisions. The inventory became the primary finding aid providing collective description at the record group level, replacing library-style cataloging of each accession. Responsibility for writing description was assigned to the division that processed that body of records, not a separate unit. Description was generally only to the series level. Any inherent weaknesses in the NA's descriptive system were spread to the LC when Buck reproduced the system there. As alluded to earlier, the record group was defined and recognized as the basis for arrangement and description in February 1941. The record group and inventory concepts gradually spread from the National Archives to repositories across the United States.[29]

In the early 1950s, a number of *Staff Information Circulars* written for the NA's staff provided more specific guidance on arrangement and description. T. R. Schellenberg, assistant archivist of the United States and noted archival theoretician, actively wrote about arrangement and description during the 1950s and 1960s for both public records and historical manuscripts. By the time he wrote *The Management of Archives* in 1965, he had concluded that public archives practices for arrangement and description were also applicable to historical manuscripts. Oliver Wendell Holmes's influential article "Archival Arrangement—Five Different Operations at Five Different Levels" was published in 1964. In 1966, Frank B. Evans summarized the current state of archival arrangement as being grounded on provenance, original order, and the record group concept of five hierarchal levels yet still being diverse in application.[30]

Blending Two Traditions, 1956–1984

In 1956, Lester J. Cappon asked what the difference was between historical manuscripts and archives. The lack of commonly accepted professional vocabulary with commonly accepted definitions of archives, archival records, and archival functions and processes has been problematic. Its lack contributed to difficulty in defining our profession, distinguishing archivists from other information specialists, and in identifying common ground. Cappon said the historian would call government records or public records "official" while describing everything else as private, unofficial, or personal. Archivists managed government records, while manuscript curators managed the rest. If "official" versus "unofficial" was to be the distinction between the two, then the line was exceedingly thin, as Cappon pointed to examples of personal papers mixed with official government or business papers created by the same person. Conversely, papers that had once been government documents were taken by that official when he departed, eventually being donated by descendants to an institution.[31]

Lucile M. Kane, curator of manuscripts at the Minnesota Historical Society, an early collector of modern twentieth-century manuscript collections, recommended practices in her 1960 work *A Guide to the Care and Administration of Manuscripts* consistent with those of public records archivists. By the time Schellenberg wrote his second book, *The Management of Archives*, published in 1965, he had concluded that archival theory also applied to private manuscripts. As mentioned before, Solon Buck brought the record group concept developed by the National Archives to the Library of Congress when he directed the Manuscripts Division there. These two leading institutions influenced the practices implemented by other institutions nationally. In 1976, the SAA Committee on Finding Aids published their report comparing inventories and registers, the predominant finding aid for archives and manuscript collections, respectively.[32] This element-by-element comparison of their use revealed that the two finding aids were actually very similar. The implied conclusion was that the records themselves had many similar qualities, consequently making it possible to use similar arrangement and description methods for both types of records. The next year, the first modern American manual on arrangement and description, *Archives and Manuscripts: Arrangement and Description*, was published. It was directed toward both archivists and manuscript curators.

Data have to be organized in order to manage them using computers; the more uniform their organization, the easier to work with large quantities of data. System compatibility between institutions enables automation. SPINDEX 1 was an experimental project by the LC in 1966 to describe the scope and contents of the papers reported to it for entry into NUCMC. It was designed as an alternative to cataloging manuscripts because it could accept data from all record levels. The project revealed dissimilarities in arrangement, description, and finding aid formats, all symptoms of the then lack of standards for arrangement and description. Awareness of the state of automation in the library field in the mid-1970s joined foresight by some archivists that the archival profession needed to participate in the development of a feasible national information exchange system for archival records and collections.[33] This was the start of standards development by archivists for archivists.

SAA Council formed the National Information Systems Task Force (NISTF) in 1977. Charged with technically analyzing two existing national information systems to determine which was "best suited to archival needs," the task force quickly recognized that this was a political dilemma. It redefined its charge to "explore how the Society and the profession should be involved in constructing the best feasible national information system for archives and manuscript collections."[34] Archivists and manuscript curators had vastly different opinions regarding national information systems. This was not surprising considering manuscript curators had a history of a closer relationship with library practices. By 1977, NUCMC had been cataloging manuscripts for nearly twenty years. The standardization developed in the creation of the NUCMC description rules led to the *Anglo-American Cataloging Rules* (AACR) in 1977 and standardization of how manuscripts were at least described. Identification of pertinent descriptive information and how it was to be organized resulted in the development of the machine-readable cataloging (MARC) standard for books, released in late 1968.

Archivists and manuscript curators had developed practices that were somewhat separate yet parallel. Even within their own strand, many believed that their institution was too unique to arrange and describe archival records the same way as its peers. This was the problem the NISTF faced. The development of MARC demonstrated that computers could transmit and share data that was standardized. Although it was difficult in the mid-1970s to envision future uses for a national information exchange system, it was clear to some that the archival profession needed to develop standards for itself. If it didn't, it would be done for them.

Showing great political astuteness, NISTF commissioned a study to conclude that there were "no systematic differences" between practices at institutional, public archives, and historical manuscript repositories. With the goal of forging a political consensus that would support archival information exchange, the task force sidestepped earlier deal-breaking questions to focus on facilitating such an exchange by establishing standards of practice. Development of a descriptive standard seemed feasible—a data elements dictionary of descriptive information created by archives, manuscript repositories, and records centers. In order to gain the greatest political support, the task force included whatever descriptive elements were potentially available for exchange, meaning any elements then currently in use in any type of descriptive forms or paperwork. Everything was accepted into the data dictionary and was going to be approved as a standard. There were no minimum criteria for inclusion. The archival community needed a process for approving whatever standard NISTF might develop and to feel the process had been inclusive. The working group creating the data dictionary included representatives from the National Archives and Records Administration, the LC, the National Historical Publications and Records Commission, and the Research Libraries Group. Because inclusivity of data elements was a ground rule, participants in the working group were asked up front to agree to support the resulting standard. They did. The final data dictionary was published in October 1982, but the first draft was presented in the spring of 1982 at negotiations that led to the new MARC format for Archives and Manuscript Collections (MARC AMC).[35] The data dictionary was a standard in its own right, but MARC AMC was designed to work with it.

Although no institution wanted to give up any autonomy in managing its processing program, the reality is that, in order to transmit descriptive data via computers, compile it into a shared database, or machine-automate metadata or finding aids, creating a common exchange format is required, meaning standardization. The task force was urged to use existing standards to facilitate the development process, specifically those used for the bibliographic MARC standard. Those members representing institutions who were also Research Libraries Group (RLG) members particularly argued for MARC because they hoped to use the Research Libraries Information Network (RLIN) to exchange catalog records for archival records. The LC had previously developed its own MARC format for manuscripts, but it was strongly rejected by the archival profession. In 1983, MARC AMC received final approval and replaced the earlier version. SAA was made co-owner of the format, meaning that it couldn't be revised without SAA's approval.[36] All separate MARC formats, including AMC, were integrated by 1995, which was harmonized with the Canada machine-readable cataloging (CAN/MARC) and published in 1999 as MARC21.[37]

The first version of *Archives, Personal Papers, and Manuscripts*, a data content standard, was approved by SAA in 1983. As in the 1950s, with the NUCMC descriptive rules, the LC Manuscripts Division found AACR2 unworkable for archival records. Department member and NISTF member Steve Hensen revised chapter 4 of AACR2 to produce APPM. RLG quickly adopted the new AMC format and APPM in order to start adding archival records to its RLIN network. Many RLG members owned significant archives and manuscript collections. OCLC adopted MARC AMC in late 1984, having previously been one of the few users of the old LC MARC Format for Manuscripts.[38] The period between 1977 and 1984 saw the start of archival development of descriptive standards and a very fertile period of results from that activity.

The Internet was invented in 1989. What had been developed as a private network to share scientific research evolved into a network for public use. In 1993, Mosaic released the first web browser that accommodated graphics. At the end of 1994, only a small number of websites existed. The next wave of descriptive standards development, 1994–2004, began with the Berkeley Finding Aids Project headed by Daniel Pitti. Started in 1993, the goal was to develop a "prototype encoding standard for finding aids" for delivery via the Internet.[39] The encoding standard would enable the creation of longer-lasting finding aids freed of dependency on proprietary software or hardware. The prototype was developed using standardized general markup language (SGML), a standard for developing markup languages that define classes of documents in a document-type definition (DTD). Through identification of the common elements of finding aids and definition of the relationships between those elements, the project developed the FINDAID DTD and the markup language to describe it. A 1995 assessment by archival experts determined the prototype was successful. They recommended further refinements and renamed it encoded archival description (EAD). EAD was publicly released in late 1996 and has replaced MARC as a data structure standard.[40] Note that EAD aligns with the *General International Standard Archival Description* [ISAD(G)] standard published in 1994.

The 2001 to 2003 Canadian–U.S. Task Force on Archival Description attempted to reconcile APPM, the Canadian *Rules for Archival Description*, and ISAD(G) to create a data content standard compatible with EAD and MARC21. Although significant differences in practice failed to produce a common standard, American representatives left with a collaborative document that became a national standard, *Describing Archives: A Content Standard* (DACS).[41] The first edition of DACS was published in 2004, the second in 2013, and the latest revisions in 2015. DACS replaced APPM as the accepted data content standard.

The most recent descriptive standard, *Encoded Archival Content—Corporate Bodies, Persons, and Families* (EAC-CPF), was adopted in 2011. It is the American version of the *International Standard Archival Authority Record for Corporate Bodies, Persons, and Families* [ISAAR(CPF)] first adopted in 1996, with a second edition also released in 2011. EAC-CPF is a data structure standard designed to create and share archival authority records for organizations, individuals, and families who create, collect, or are the subject of archival records or collections. EAC-CPF allows for more complete authority records than the Library of Congress Name Authority Control File does. Removing names from finding aids and putting them into name authority files enables data linkage not previously possible.[42] Person A can be linked to multiple sets of records located in diverse repositories or to which she relates in different roles, creator or correspondent. Person A can be linked to relative B in different relationships, like spouse or sister-in-law, so that records for the same or related families can be located within or across repositories. Recording biographic information or corporate history in the archival authority record reduces information redundancy for all finding aids related to a specific archival authority record, assuming the use of software that will retrieve the specified archival authority record and insert it in finding aids where appropriate. Eventually archival authority records should increase staff efficiency.

Conclusion

New archivists need to understand the history of archival arrangement and description in the United States, especially development of standards in order to evaluate current and proposed new practices, tools, and standards. The library field was established and developed and started standards development before the archival profession. Librarians were motivated to develop bibliographic standards and, as technology evolved, to automate them out of a desire for economic benefits. The very nature of library resources, intentionally created and mass produced, made standardization possible.

Archivists argued for their first fifty to seventy-five years that their collections were unique, and many considered discussions of standardization to be absurd. Archival records are unique, organically created pieces of a larger body, intentionally produced to document transactions or incidentally made to meet personal needs, generally unpublished, often undated, and frequently by an unknown creator. These qualities are much more challenging to standardize. Archivists weren't motivated to standardize for economy. Their motive was to improve access to their collections, intellectually at first, then, as the World Wide Web and technology developed, through digital replicas of the records themselves.

Development of the first archival descriptive standard must have been like herding cats. Those who managed historical documents initially worked with discrete documents or small bodies of related documents owned by libraries and used by historians for research. Archivists working with government records quickly had to deal with large volumes of organically created records that routinely received accruals. Records were used by the office of origin and others to perform the functions of their office, with secondary usage by nongovernment researchers. These differences made it difficult to see what they shared in common.

The first "standard," the data dictionary, accepted all submissions in order to encourage buy-in and support from all constituencies involved. Its companion standard, MARC AMC, was heavily based on standards for bibliographic description. They were developed in the void of consensus among American archivists on descriptive practices, elements of description, and vocabulary. There were no international archival descriptive standards to use as a starting point. Networked online library catalogs were the sole method available for computerized search and access to nationwide information about archival collections.[43] It is understandable that, for political expediency, a bibliographic-dependent solution seemed like the best choice at the time. Through this early work, arrangement and description practices for archives and manuscripts became unified. APPM was also closely aligned with bibliographic practices because librarians were asked to approve it as an alternative to AACR2. Since the 1990s, descriptive practices and standards have developed that are more consistent with the nature of archival records and archival principles.

As recently as 2011, archivist William E. Landis, who has spent most of his career developing, applying, or teaching descriptive standards, cautioned that today's archivists still "rely too heavily on *bibliographic* benchmarks and yardsticks as means of shaping and measuring our professional *archival* practice." Archivists themselves still use the term *cataloging* instead of *arrangement and description*. The newest bibliographic standard, resource description and access (RDA), focuses on a framework of production and distribution of works that does not fit the organic method by which archival records are created. Landis points to DACS and ISAD(G), an international standard he argues has been largely ignored by American archivists, as not only more appropriate to archival practice but also as going beyond mere description to the challenge of "capturing and recording salient information" throughout the process of managing archival records.[44] Archivists need to consider what this significant information is that will help future generations understand the organizations, people, and activities that our archival records document and take action to ensure that our descriptive practices, systems, and standards capture it.

Notes

1. Michel Duchein, "The History of European Archives and the Development of the Archival Profession in Europe," *American Archivist* 55 (Winter 1992): 19. Luciana Duranti, "Origin and Development of the Concept of Archival Description," *Archivaria* 35 (Spring 1993): 50, also cites Naples in 1812, the Grand Duchy of Tuscany in 1822, and the Papal State in 1839 as describing and adopting *respect des fonds* before France. She cites Francesco Bonaini in the Grand Duchy of Tuscany in 1869 and Max Lehmann in Germany in 1882 for formulating the principle of original order. Richard C. Berner, *Archival Theory and Practice in the United States: A Historical Analysis* (Seattle: University of Washington Press, 1983), 3, uses the term *Registraturprinzip*, which refers to the registry system the Prussians developed to establish the original order for government records.

2. James M. O'Toole, *Understanding Archives and Manuscripts*, Archival Fundamentals Series (Chicago: Society of American Archivists, 1990), 30.

3. Richard C. Berner, "Arrangement and Description: Some Historical Observations," *American Archivist* 41 (April 1978): 181.

4. Berner, *Archival Theory*, 11; Berner, "Arrangement and Description," 169.

5. Berner, *Archival Theory*, 11; Lois D. Hamill, "Provenance and Original Order: The Evolution of Their Acceptance as Principles of Arrangement and Description" (master's thesis, University of Massachusetts Boston, 1997), 13-14.

6. See Berner, *Archival Theory*, 13. Library classification schemes of the period included topical/subject, alphabetic, chronologic, and geographic. Individual documents or pieces of documents were arbitrarily given unity by the person classifying them into the same classification category, not based on who created the records, as required by archival application of provenance.

7. T. R. Schellenberg, *The Management of Archives* (New York: Columbia University Press, 1965), 21, 23, 23-24. Richard Berner, *Archival Theory*, 17-18, cites the Historical Manuscripts Commission's interest in publication over development of a manual or guidelines for organizing and describing private papers. Some thought the Conference of State and Local Historical Societies (now the American Association for State and Local History) created by the AHA was the more appropriate body to address the concern of a manual. AHA support for archival activities started to flag during World War I and never revived. Finally, Berner also cites the cross-membership between the Public Archives Commission, the Historical Manuscripts Commission, and the AHA by noted public records archivists who never expressed the opinion that what was valid for public records was also valid for private records.

8. Berner, *Archival Theory*, 2. Cutter, librarian at the Boston Athenaeum, first published his *Rules for a Dictionary Catalog* in 1876. This work lays out the rules for cataloging library materials in order to produce a dictionary catalog. Per Schellenberg, *Management of Archives*, 15, dictionary catalogs list the author, subject, and title entries in alphabetic order and are essentially a repository guide to a library's holdings.

9. Schellenberg, *Management of Archives*, 39.

10. Berner, *Archival Theory*, 13, 3. The Prussian State Archives formalized the practice of original order when they developed a registry system and office. Records leaving active use in government offices passed through the Registry Office before going to the archives. The Registry Office recorded the creating government agency information, arranged, managed, and retrieved the records on that basis. The Prussian method focused on the administrative function of the records in contrast to the French system, which focused on research. The Prussian method was adopted by the Netherlands, where the first modern archival manual was written to explain these principles of arrangement and description. Van Laer was familiar with these methods and applied them in New York.

11. Berner, *Archival Theory*, 15; Hamill, "Provenance and Original Order," 20-21; Schellenberg, *Management of Archives*, 43. Richard C. Berner, "Historical Development of Archival Theory and Practices in the United States," *Midwestern Archivist* 7, no. 2 (1982): 104, is definitive that it was the first time.

12. Hamill, "Provenance and Original Order," 25. The National Archives was so named from 1935 to December 1949, the National Archives and Records Service from December 1949 to 1985, and the National Archives and Records Administration from 1985 to the present.

13. Donald R. McCoy, *The National Archives: America's Ministry of Documents, 1934-1968* (Chapel Hill: University of North Carolina Press, 1978), 64-66; Hamill, "Provenance and Original Order," 25.

14. Work Projects Administration, Survey of the Federal Archives, *The Manual of the Survey of Federal Archives* (Washington, DC: Works Progress Administration, 1936), 23, 23-25, 28.

15. Work Projects Administration, Historical Records Survey, *Preparation of Inventories of Manuscripts: A Circular of Instructions for the Use of the Historical Records Survey Projects*, preliminary ed. (Washington,

DC: Federal Works Agency, Work Projects Administration, Division of Professional and Service Projects, Research and Records Projects Subdivision, 1940), 23; Berner, "Arrangement and Description," 171–72. The 1940 version of Work Projects Administration, Historical Records Survey, *Preparation of Inventories of Manuscripts*, is a revised and expanded version of the original Works Progress Administration, Historical Records Survey, *The Preparation of Guides to Manuscripts* ["Supplement 6 to the *Manual of the Historical Records Survey*" (Washington, DC: WPA, Division of Women's and Professional Projects, September 10, 1937)].

16. Berner, "Arrangement and Description," 172.

17. Ethel B. Virtue, "Principles of Classification for Archives," in *Annual Report of the American Historical Association for the Year 1914: In Two Volumes*, vol. 1 (Washington, DC: Government Printing Office, 1916), 381, 376–80.

18. Berner, "Arrangement and Description," 171; Thornton W. Mitchell, introduction to *Norton on Archives: The Writings of Margaret Cross Norton on Archival and Records Management*, by Margaret Cross Norton (Carbondale: Southern Illinois Press, 1975), xvii.

19. William F. Birdsall, "The American Archivists' Search for Professional Identity, 1909–1936" (PhD diss., University of Wisconsin, Madison, 1973), 203; Berner, *Archival Theory*, 103.

20. Berner, *Archival Theory*, 1, 23; Hamill, "Provenance and Original Order," 32; Schellenberg, *Management of Archives*, 28–31; Fredric M. Miller, *Arranging and Describing Archives and Manuscripts*, Archival Fundamentals Series (Chicago: Society of American Archivists, 1990), 22.

21. Berner, *Archival Theory*, 39.

22. McCoy, *National Archives*, 106.

23. Berner, *Archival Theory*, 40; Schellenberg, *Management of Archives*, 56; Library of Congress, *Departmental and Divisional Manuals No. 17 Manuscripts Division* (Washington, DC: Library of Congress, 1950): 19, 25. The manual uses the terms *preliminary* and *definitive inventory*, not *register*. Schellenberg, *Management of Archives*, 56–57, credits Katherine Brand for the development of the register in about 1953. *Departmental and Divisional Manuals No. 17,* 7, 19–20. Berner, *Archival Theory*, 41, makes this claim, but in 1955, Katherine Brand discusses using the register to catalog for the NUCMC project and says parts 3 to 5 will be the source for the catalog entries [Katherine Brand, "The Place of the Register in the Manuscripts Division of the Library of Congress," *American Archivist* 18 (January 1955): 60, 64–66]. These sections of the register are the "Description of Series," "Container List," and an optional section naming correspondents. This seems to contradict Berner, but he may have used a different source.

24. Berner, *Archival Theory*, 42; Robert H. Land, "The National Union Catalog of Manuscript Collections," *American Archivist* 17 (April 1954): 196; Berner, *Archival Theory*, 42; Berner, "Arrangement and Description," 173–74.

25. Berner, *Archival Theory*, 43–44.

26. Berner, *Archival Theory*, 43–44.

27. Berner, *Archival Theory*, 78, 44–45, 78–81; Richard Pearce-Moses, *A Glossary of Archival and Records Terminology* (Chicago: Society of American Archivists, 2005), s.v. "archives, personal papers, and manuscripts," accessed January 3, 2017, http://www2.archivists.org/glossary/terms/a/archives-personal-papers-and-manuscripts.

28. Berner, *Archival Theory*, 31. Per Berner, "Historical Development," 116n3, the revised code was Illinois State Library, *Catalog Rules: Series for Archives Material* (Springfield: Secretary of State and State Librarian, 1938). This is a published book.

29. McCoy, *National Archives*, 106–7; Berner, *Archival Theory*, 27-28.

30. Frank B. Evans, "Modern Methods of Arrangement of Archives in the United States," *American Archivist* 29 (April 1966): 241–63.

31. Lester J. Cappon, "Historical Manuscripts as Archives: Some Definitions and Their Application," *American Archivist* 19 (April 1956): 101, 105–7. The first SAA-published glossary didn't appear until 1974: Frank Evans, Donald Harrison, and Edwin Thompson, "A Basic Glossary for Archivists, Manuscript Curators, and Records Managers," *American Archivist* 37 (July 1974): 415–33.

32. Society of American Archivists' Committee on Finding Aids, *Inventories and Registers: A Handbook of Techniques and Examples* (Chicago: Society of American Archivists, 1976).

33. Berner, *Archival Theory*, 87, 85; David Bearman, *Towards National Information Systems for Archives and Manuscript Repositories: The National Information Systems Task Force (NISTF) Papers 1981-1984* (Chicago: Society of American Archivists, 1987), 2.

34. Bearman, *Towards National Information Systems*, 2.

35. Bearman, *Towards National Information Systems*, 3–6. The Research Libraries Group, Inc. (RLG), was a library consortium comprised of leading university and special libraries dedicated to supporting scholarly research, hence its interest in archival materials. Founded in 1974, RLG created its own networked catalog, Research Libraries Information Network (RLIN). In 2006, it merged with OCLC. The data dictionary was published as "Data Elements Used in Archives, Manuscripts, and Records Repository Information Systems: A Dictionary of Standard Terminology," in *MARC for Archives and Manuscripts: The AMC Format*, by Nancy Sahli (Chicago: Society of American Archivists, 1985). The data dictionary was a separate standard that SAA was responsible for maintaining.

36. Bearman, *Towards National Information Systems*, 7, 8; Victoria Irons Walch, comp., chap. 3 in *Standards for Archival Description: A Handbook* (Society of American Archivists, 1994), accessed November 24, 2015, http://www.archivists.org/catalog/stds99/chapter3.html; Bearman, *Towards National Information Systems*, 8–9.

37. Ed Glazier, "As the Formats Integrate . . . ," *RLG Focus*, no. 5 (December 1993), accessed November 25, 2015, http://worldcat.org/arcviewer/1/OCC/2007/07/09/0000068851/viewer/file60.txt; "MARC21 Harmonized USMARC and CAN/MARC," *Library of Congress*, 1998, accessed November 25, 2015, http://www.loc.gov/marc/annmarc21.html.

38. "Report of the Working Group on Standards for Archival Description," *American Archivist* 52 (Fall 1989): 448, 449, n. 15. Approximately 40,000 OCLC records for archival materials were entered using the old MARC format.

39. Mark Frauenfelder, "Computing Sir Tim Berners-Lee," *MIT Technology Review* (October 1, 2004), accessed December 18, 2016, https://www.technologyreview.com/s/403095/sir-tim-berners-lee; Tim Berners-Lee, James Hendler, and Ora Lassila, "The Semantic Web," *Scientific American* (May 2001): 4; "World Wide Web," *Wikipedia*, accessed November 27, 2015, https://en.wikipedia.org/wiki/World_Wide_Web; Daniel V. Pitti, "Encoded Archival Description: The Development of an Encoding Standard for Archival Finding Aids," *American Archivist* 60 (Summer 1997): 279.

40. Pitti, "Encoded Archival Description," 276, 280, 281.

41. Pearce-Moses, *Glossary*, s.v. "Canadian–United States Task Force on Archival Description," accessed December 1, 2015, http://www2.archivists.org/glossary/terms/c/canadian-united-states-task-force-on

-archival-description; Planning Committee on Descriptive Standards, *Canadian Archival Standard Rules for Archival Description* (Ottawa, Canada: Bureau of Canadian Archivists, 2008), xiii, accessed December 1, 2015, http://www.cdncouncilarchives.ca/rad/radcomplete_july2008.pdf.

42. Sibyl Schaefer and Janet M. Bunde, "Module 1: Standards for Archival Description," *Archival Arrangement and Description*, Trends in Archives Practice series (Chicago: Society of American Archivists, 2013), 30–31.

43. William E. Landis, "Overcoming the Bibliographic Conundrum in Archival Description," *American Archivist* 74 (Supplement 2011): 13–14. This paper was originally part of session 706 at the 2011 SAA annual meeting.

44. Landis, "Overcoming the Bibliographic Conundrum," 16–17, 18, 17. Among other responsibilities, Landis was a member of SAA's Encoded Archival Description Working Group and the Canadian–U.S. Taskforce on Archival Description that helped develop DACS. Earlier in his presentation, Landis, 12, stated he was using "*bibliographic* in its broadest sense to include all types of published and distributed resources."

Additional Reading and Resources

Bearman, David. *Towards National Information Systems for Archives and Manuscript Repositories: The National Information Systems Task Force (NISTF) Papers 1981–1984*. Chicago: Society of American Archivists, 1987. This report highlights the politics of the task force's work and includes several working papers in which Bearman identifies professional educational gaps, the impact of patron expectations, and potential policy directions.

Berner, Richard C. *Archival Theory and Practice in the United States: A Historical Analysis*. Seattle: University of Washington Press, 1983. See pages 39–45 for more specifics on the development of NUCMC and the descriptive rules.

——. "Archivists, Librarians, and the National Union Catalog of Manuscript Collections." *American Archivist* 27 (July 1964): 401–9. This article also analyzes the weaknesses of NUCMC and lessons learned.

——. "Arrangement and Description: Some Historical Observations." *American Archivist* 41 (April 1978). See particularly pages 170–74 for a brief overview of library influences on archival description from 1904 to 1950, including development of the NUCMC descriptive rules.

Eliot, Margaret S., George M. McFarland, and Dan Lacy. *Preparation of Inventories of Manuscripts: A Circular of Instructions for the Use of the Historical Records Survey Projects*. Preliminary ed. Washington, DC: Federal Works Agency, WPA, Division of Professional and Service Projects, Research and Records Projects Subdivision, October 1940. Compare this edition with *Supplement 6* listed later this chapter. Most notable are the changes in the collection description instructions based on what was learned in the previous three years of surveying. They point out the difficulty of clearly describing a large collection with records from multiple individuals over many years and topics: "Hence a necessary step in describing a collection of any size is to break it down into groups of papers of similar origin (provenance), and content which can be described in specific terms. Each such relatively homogeneous group should be described separately." The instructions describe the identification of subgroups, the level between collection and series.

Henson, Steven L., William E. Landis, Kathleen D. Roe, Michael Rush, William Stockting, and Victoria Irons Walch. "Thirty Years On: SAA and Descriptive Standards." *American Archivist* 74 (2011 Supplement): 1–35. Accessed November 24, 2015, http://www2.archivists.org/sites/all/files/AAOSv074-Session706.pdf. Originally session 706 at the 2011 SAA annual conference, this article is a series of papers providing an overview of the first thirty years of the archival profession's participation in developing descriptive standards, largely by participants in the process.

Land, Robert. "The National Union Catalog of Manuscript Collections." *American Archivist* 17 (April 1954): 195–207. See this article for more specifics on the development of NUCMC and the descriptive rules. Land worked at the Library of Congress.

Library of Congress. *Departmental and Divisional Manuals No. 17, Manuscripts Division*. Washington, DC: Library of Congress, 1950. This forty-three-page manual is historically interesting. It gives a comprehensive overview of the Manuscripts Division, including its establishment, the names of all its division heads, division responsibilities, staff organization, job descriptions, and more. The sections on acquisition and processing, including explanation of the new Manuscript Group System and description of the new types of finding aids (pp. 24–25), are the most interesting.

Lytle, Richard H. "An Analysis of the Work of the National Information Systems Task Force." *American Archivist* 47 (Fall 1984): 357–65. This article provides an overview of the NISTF's work and lists the task force members.

Miller, Fredric M. *Arranging and Describing Archives and Manuscripts*. Archival Fundamentals Series. Chicago: Society of American Archivists, 1990. Page 24 has a visual chronological timeline of key events for the separate archives and manuscript traditions and their merger up to 1983.

"Report of the Working Group on Standards for Archival Description." *American Archivist* 52 (Fall 1989): 440–61. This article includes a detailed timeline of the development of standards for archival description up to 1989.

Schellenberg, T. R. *The Management of Archives*. New York: Columbia University Press, 1965, pp. 32–41. Schellenberg describes classification schemes and gives examples of their use by specific institutions.

Society of American Archivists' Committee on Finding Aids. *Inventories and Registers: A Handbook of Techniques and Examples*. Chicago: Society of American Archivists, 1976. This pivotal report, published before NISTIF was formed, shows how similar description in inventories and registers really was.

"Supplement 6 to the *Manual of the Historical Records Survey: The Preparation of Guides to Manuscripts*." WPA, Division of Women's and Professional Projects, September 10, 1937. This twenty-two-page supplement provides detailed instructions for the completion of the WPA form 21HR, "The Manuscript Depository Form," and WPA form 17HR, "The Manuscript Collection Form, Revised." Surprisingly, the information asked questions about access, conditions of access, dates, quantities, history of ownership, and how the source arrived at the repository and still resembles information included in finding aids today. It is interesting that by 1937 those managing the WPA surveys already had a good grasp on what was significant about records and manuscripts and that it has remained valid for so long. Also compare this with the 1940 version listed earlier by Margaret S. Eliot, George M. McFarland, and Dan Lacy. My conclusions after reading the instructions and studying the form's questions were different than Richard Berner's, especially "Arrangement and Description," pp. 171–72.

Taylor, Arlene G., and Daniel N. Joudrey. *The Organization of Information*. 3rd ed. Westport, CT: Libraries Unlimited, 2009. Chapter 3 provides an overview of the historical development of recorded information in western civilization, with an emphasis on libraries.

Virtue, Ethel B. "Principles of Classification for Archives." In *Annual Report of the American Historical Association for 1914, Fifteenth Report of the Public Archives Commission, Proceedings of the Sixth Annual Conference of Archivists*, pp. 373–84. Vol. 1. Washington, DC: Government Printing Office, 1916. Virtue was a distinguished manuscript curator at the Minnesota Historical Society. Here she presents the "Iowa Plan" (developed in 1906 as the first based on provenance) as adapted for Minnesota. Note, too, her use of the series already in 1916.

2

Performing Arrangement and Description

People create information as they go about their daily living, both in their professional work lives and their personal lives. Much of this information is recorded by a diverse range of methods, tools, and formats, including paper, photographs, videos, blogs, posts on social websites, word-processed documents, e-mail, electronic spreadsheets, and complex relational databases. Some of this information has minimal value: a grocery list, the e-mail setting a meeting time, or the funny cat video. Some of this information has enduring value because of its evidential, informational, intrinsic, or legal value. Archival appraisal distinguishes between information of enduring value and information with minimal value. Information with sufficient enduring value, or information required by law, regulatory bodies, records retention schedules, or other reasons is identified for permanent retention.

Terminology and Concepts

Archival information worth permanent retention has specific qualities. It grows organically out of the process of creating and receiving information during the course of the routine activities and functions of its creator.[1] When the creator is a government body; corporation; nonprofit service, charitable, civic, or religious organization, it tends to retain its own information, which is called *archives*, *records*, or *archival records*. When the creator is an individual or family, their information is collected by institutions, like academic special collections departments, historical societies, and libraries, and is called *manuscripts* or *manuscript collections*. The term *personal digital archives* is coming into use to refer to digital records still in the possession of their creator when he or she is an individual as opposed to an institution.

Individual items are part of a larger body of interrelated records. Relationships among institutional records are often more complex, like their organizational chart, while the relationships between items in manuscript collections tends to be simpler, often following a familial structure. Archival materials are generally unique or of very limited quantity and unpublished. Their uniqueness, organic creation in response to daily activities, and interrelatedness as part of a body of records distinguish archival records and manuscripts from published materials.

An archival record is "data or information that has been fixed on some medium; that has content, context and structure." It is "of a legal or official nature that may be used as evidence," proof, or accountability. It can exist physically as a document or electronically. Whether information is a record depends on the information content, not the carrier; that is, the manner, format, or medium by which it is recorded. Official correspondence can be recorded on parchment with a wax seal, handwritten on paper, or transmitted electronically via e-mail software. Context goes hand in hand with content. The context of a record's creation is important because it helps with the comprehension or interpretation of the information content

> If content is the "what" and structure the "how," context is everything else: the "who," "where," "when" and possibly even "why." Context identifies who created the record, how the record was used and stored and perhaps even why the record existed in the first place. Regardless of media, records gain their context by being kept as part of a larger, organic, unified body of records, not as single items separated from their documentary origins.[2]

The archival principles of provenance and original order are the foundation for arrangement and description. *Provenance* refers to the organization, individual, or family who created, received, or accumulated a body of records maintained or used during the course of that creator's activities and functions. A *record* is information that is recorded in any form or medium that is "created or received and maintained, by an organization or person in the transaction of business or conduct of affairs."[3] The principle of provenance requires that records be maintained according to their origin or provenance, meaning that the records of one creator should not be mingled with those of another. *Respect des fonds* is the term used internationally for the concept of provenance.[4]

The closely related principle of original order stipulates that archivists should maintain records in the original order in which they are received by the archives, under the assumption that this is the same order in which they were originally maintained and used by their creators. Institutional records are more likely to retain their original order than personal or family papers, which tend to be handled a lot between the time they are used by their creator and when they reach an archives. In the latter case, the archivist must closely examine the materials and often imposes a new arrangement. The concepts of provenance and original order both reflect the importance of context to informed interpretation of information found within a body of records. Provenance reflects who created the records and their relationship to other records creators. Preservation of the original order reveals the functions or activities of the records-creating individual or office, how those activities relate to each other, or how they might relate to another office or individual, thus providing context for the records.

Arrangement and description are interrelated halves of a whole. Neither is complete without the other. Arrangement precedes description. It is the process by which an archivist physically or intellectually organizes records based first on their provenance and second on their original order. Arrangement should be performed based on the original order and information content, regardless of the formats involved, but in practice, sometimes archivists have grouped materials by format.[5] For example, all the photos might be put in the same series based on their format, not their creator or function. While potentially desirable from a preservation perspective, it may obscure intellectual relationships and context. Description is the process of creating a finding aid or other access tools that describe the physical or intellectual arrangement of a body of records. The finding aid functions as a searchable surrogate for the body of records, providing access to them and protecting them by creating a record of the collection or record group and by minimizing the amount of handling they receive.[6]

In 1964, archivist Oliver Wendell Holmes wrote one of the clearest explanations of the hierarchical levels, hierarchical groups, or levels of control archivists use to arrange records, citing five: depository level, record group and subgroup level, series level, filing unit level, and document level.[7] Speaking primarily from his experience at the National Archives, Holmes says there is a need for divisions above the record group level to organize hundreds of agencies, each being a separate record group, into a smaller, more manageable number of major divisions for administrative purposes. While appropriate for larger archives, this depository level does not seem to be in use much today, or at least not in as visible a manner as in Holmes's era. Before the advent of the World Wide Web, larger, more notable institutions published repository guides to their holdings. It is understandable that, in such a guide, record groups or manuscript collections might be organized into larger divisions, especially for the federal government. Today, depending on size and staffing, some academic archives manage both the college or university archives and special collections.[8] The records of each of these could be considered divisions in Holmes's terminology.

The record group and subgroup levels are very important. Records are assigned to each of these levels based on provenance. Organizational structure can be quite complex. If the Office of the President is the record group, then the records of Presidents Gibbs, MacGyver, and Reagan would each constitute subgroups. The records are related because they were created by the same office, but they need to be separated because each individual president is a separate creator. Because Holmes discusses federal records, he doesn't mention manuscript collections, but they would clearly be the equivalent of the record group for purposes of arrangement and description. If a couple, George and Winifred Banks, donated their personal papers to an archives, then his records would constitute a separate subgroup from hers. While the subgroup can be further divided into sub-subgroups if needed, it is preferable to not make the arrangement structure any more complex than necessary. In the case of a simple body of records, there may be no subgroups.

When Schellenberg originally wrote about the subgroup in 1956, he described their creation as based on function, subject, or administrative hierarchy. Writing later, Holmes refined and limited the formation of subgroups to provenance, so that the subsequent series and file units would have parents, records creators, when they were assigned to a subgroup. By 1977, archival educator David B. Gracy II described the subgroup as being a separate level, subordinate to and just below the record group or collection level.[9]

In contrast to the record group or collection and subgroup levels, the final three levels—the series, filing unit, and document or item—are identified based on the filing structure of the records, their original order. A series is a group of records based on a "filing system or maintained as a unit because they relate to a particular subject," "result from the same function or activity, have a particular [physical] form, or have some other relationship resulting from their creation, accumulation or use." A series is composed of similar filing units arranged in a consistent pattern, possibly as simple as alphabetical, chronological, or numerical, or more complex. Modern practice allows for the use of subseries as needed for complex bodies of records. A filing unit or file is a "group of documents [or items] related by use or topic," typically stored in a folder or group of folders if the file is large. An item is the smallest individual unit or lowest level for arrangement and description purposes. It is complete in itself, distinguishable from a group, and can take any analog or digital form.[10] A photograph, a multipage letter, and a report of many pages would all be an item.

Records Acquisition

If an archives is part of the government or an organization, the majority of its records should come from the organization's own offices. Records will be transferred internally because the creator or owner of the records and the archives are the same entity rather than being donated by an external source or records creator requiring a deed of gift. A transfer form recording basic information about the transferring office or records creator, including contact information, dates, quantities and formats of the records, a brief description, and a record series, if applicable, should accompany the records. Sometimes offices create box lists with the folder headings for each box. Federal, state, and local governments; corporations; and nonprofit educational, service, and religious groups and charities are examples of organizations. In those organizations, with an effective records management program, only records for permanent retention should arrive at the archives, accompanied by documentation. In reality, sometimes records just show up with no documentation regarding the records creator or even who delivered them. This makes it challenging to determine who created the records, where they came from, what function or activity they relate to, dates, and other important information.

The records creator or a person who regularly works with a particular body of records knows a lot about them. Many do not realize how much they know that is of value to the archivist for understanding and interpreting a new accession. It is extremely valuable to have the opportunity to speak with the records creator or a knowledgeable user at the time of a new records transfer. Time permitting, the ability to conduct a brief examination of the materials while the records creator is present can trigger immediately obvious questions about unfamiliar records, which will be answered faster than if the archivist has to conduct research, assuming she even has the information that will answer her questions. As an archivist becomes familiar with the records the institution creates, the number of her questions will decline, unless there is something different about a new accrual or records arrive from a new office. In some cases, a preaccession survey or visit may be conducted, during which time the archivist has the opportunity to discuss the records and gather pertinent information.

For archives that collect other organizations' records or personal papers, a donor interview is even more important and may be a one-time opportunity. It may take place when the donor first contacts the archives to offer the records or simultaneous with the legal transfer of ownership and physical delivery of the records. The donor may not have created any of the records being given. If this is the case, he will have varying levels of familiarity with the records. Manuscript collections have a greater likelihood of including nonpermanent materials and having a disrupted or nonexistent internal order. These factors may require the archivist to conduct more research and yet may result in less information known about the records' context and creator in comparison with organizational records.

In the case of digital records, additional questions should be asked if they weren't discussed during negotiations about the donation. Pertinent questions include whether personally identifiable information (PII), like Social Security numbers, credit card numbers, and medical or financial records; passwords or PINs; or licensed or pirated software are likely to be present.

When new records arrive, they need a minimal physical review. Depending on the findings, actions may be required. If this hasn't happened yet, accessioning is another opportune time. First, identify any physical condition that is cause for concern, either for the records being reviewed or the clean records they will join in storage. The presence of insects and mold, which can spread, may require immediate action, depending on the severity of either. Ideally these would be identified at the loading dock and the records quarantined until treated. A few dead insects or a single water-damaged item can be handled differently than a widespread problem. Fragile items may require immediate reboxing. The presence of computer storage media, audiovisual, or obsolete formats should be noted for eventual separation, in part for their safer physical storage, but also due to their shorter lifespan. Digital records will need to be addressed sooner than paper records, but many audiovisual formats are also reaching format obsolescence. Their presence may affect the processing priority for the records.

The original containers in which records arrive may need replacement due to damage or size. Nonstandard sized boxes don't fit shelving, while half-empty boxes waste space. Oversized, three-dimensional, or framed items are likely to require specialized storage to avoid damage and to economize on storage space. Obviously inappropriate or nonarchival items and excessive amounts of duplicate copies can be removed. The purpose of this very cursory review is to ready the materials for shelving or storing wherever newly received materials are kept. Simultaneously, the review confirms that the new materials will not harm existing records already in the same storage location. If the new materials are not all stored in the same place, the locations of all the parts need to be noted somewhere for when they are eventually processed.

Accessioning

After records arrive at the archives, they need to be accessioned. Many archivists consider accessioning to be the beginning of archival control. It also helps establish preliminary intellectual control over the records. Information for the accession record may come from the deed of gift, a transfer form in the case of institutional records, examination of the materials themselves, conversations with the donor, personal knowledge, or other sources. Regardless of whether records are organizational or personal, the start of a new record group or collection or an addition to an existing one, the same information will be collected about each accession. It can be recorded as a paper copy of a word-processed form, an electronic spreadsheet or log, or in an archival information management system.

Typical information includes the name of the creator, donor, or transferring office, the date the materials arrived at the archives, span and bulk dates for the records, a generic title for the body of records (photographs, correspondence, subject files), the quantity of materials in each format, and a basic description thereof. The donor or transferring office may provide descriptive lists that can be attached to and referenced by the master accession record. If not and depending on the level of detail in the deed or gift, the archivist may choose to provide additional information to distinguish whether the materials arrived as part of this specific accession or another accession. If items in the accession have monetary or collectable value, the archivist may choose to describe them in sufficient detail to establish ownership in case of theft; for example, the specific number of its copy for a limited run of prints, the dimensions and media for unique art by an outstanding artist, or the presence of desirable autographs to name a few. Another option is to selectively photograph items. High-value items, pieces of art, damaged items, or oversized or framed pieces that may be stored separately from the rest of the records in the accession are potential candidates for photographing. The photos can be used to document ownership and condition on arrival or intellectually link parts of an accession that are physically stored separately. The accession number can form part of each photo's file name to link the number to the photographed item. The photos can be stored in an electronic folder serving as a donor or control file for the record group or collection to which the item will be assigned, attached to, or inserted in electronic accession records or printed and added to an electronic donor or control file, depending on the archives' practices. Other optional information might include a preliminary assignment to a record group or collection, information about intellectual property rights, or the initial storage location where the new accession will be kept until processing.

Each accession is assigned a unique accession number. Depending on other software and processes in use by the archives, the method of its formation will vary. DACS requires a reference code (unique identifier, see rule 2.1). The accession number may form part of the reference code. Decisions about which information to include in accession records may be affected by the method used to record the information, the level of intellectual control over materials between their receipt and processing, security practices, or whether accession records are made available to researchers until finding aids are completed, among other factors.

In addition to a record in the master accession log, work copies of an accession record have other uses. Donor or control files should be established for each donated collection. A control file may also be beneficial for institutional records by serving as a single location (per record group) to gather useful information for their management. Adding a copy of the accession form to the control file will help create a link between a deed of gift, the finding aid when written, and the records themselves. This can be done whether the control files are paper, digital, or a blend. If there are designated storage areas for newly arrived records, attaching a copy of the accession record to the box exterior can signal records ready for processing, link the accession number to the records, and provide minimal control over a body of records until processing.

Accession records are critical permanent records for reasons unrelated to description. They help document ownership, like deeds of gift, but may exist in the absence of a deed of gift or include more detailed information than the deed of gift. Accession records can be used for proof of ownership in the case of theft or damage. If accession records include monetary value, either by purchase or appraisal, an institution should restrict access to these records to avoid their use as a shopping list for theft. It may also choose to restrict access because it wants to keep donor names private. Due to their potential additional value for security and insurance purposes, accession records should have backup copies in a second location. This could be the donor or control file if it is on a different server than the first copy or if a separate paper donor or control file is maintained. Accession records should also be assessed for inclusion in protections developed during emergency planning. New acquisitions should be segregated in their own holding areas and accessioned as soon as possible to obtain the added layer of security provided by accession records.

Arrangement

Once accessioned, a new record group or manuscript collection is ready to process. Arrangement and description are the major archival functions performed during processing, although the archivist may observe, assess, and note other information about or in the materials. Possibilities include materials for potential exhibit, digitization, or preservation.

Start with background research. Review the donor or control file for information about both the records creator and the records themselves. Review the accession or transfer form(s) for the record group or manuscript collection. Look for names; dates; locations; related organizations or people; potential topics; and information about materials that are sensitive, restricted, of high value, or are in poor condition. Also be alert for information identifying copyrighted material and its copyright holder. Depending on the significance of the records creator, the research value of the materials, the processing priority, and staff time, further research may be necessary in current or historical biographical, historical, or news sources; specialized trade, business, or subject sources; maps; institutional organizational charts; employee lists; or resources to identify the technology used to record information found in the materials. This research provides context for the materials, helps the archivist determine the provenance of items in the materials to be processed, may identify more significant items and materials, or help with dating or identification.

Next, examine each container of materials in the record group or collection. Avoid the temptation to read every document or to start arranging items. The purpose of this step is to collect additional information from the records themselves in order to confirm whether there is a single collection, to confirm information found during the background research, and to write a processing plan. Do the materials confirm or supplement information about the identity of the records creator? Make notes about the record types; formats; bulk and span dates; extent; physical condition, if preservation or special housing is indicated; the presence of oversize or nonpermanent materials for removal; and the presence of confidential, sensitive, or personally identifiable information. Include the current box location and quantities for records that are called out. Are there other potential problems? Assess how (dis)organized the records are. Note the current and original order of the materials. Look for logical, large groupings of materials (these are likely to be series or subseries). Try to identify their arrangement and how consistently it is followed. Look for unexpected record gaps, evidence of missing items, as well as unexpected finds. Look for indexes or documents explaining the filing system. Check whether file folder headings are accurate and meaningful. When examining the information content, try to determine the type of information included: the subjects, scope, and research strengths. Look for organizational charts, lists of key officers for organizations, and a company history, including important dates in its development. For personal or family papers, look for biographical or genealogical details, important dates in their lives, and addresses where the person or family lived. In 1981, MIT's processing manual estimated that conducting this survey and writing a one- to two-page work plan for a medium-sized collection (ten to twelve record cartons) should not take more than one week.[11]

At this point, there should be sufficient information to write a processing plan or decide which arrangement to use for the record group or collection being processed. It should be possible to conclude whether the records constitute a single record group or collection or more than one. Bear in mind that family papers may include the records of a couple, siblings, several generations, or other family permutations. Five different people may have written about the same person, and it will still be a single collection—that of the recipient. Another type of collection may include materials created by multiple individuals that are collected by a single individual unrelated to any of the creators. This is an artificial collection. The collector "creates" the collection in the sense that he or she decides what will or will not be included in the collection but does not create any of the actual content. An autograph collection would be an example of an artificial collection. Note that some descriptive standards treat artificial collections differently than organic ones.[12] The existing arrangement, including type (alphabetic, chronological, geographic, etc.) and how comprehensively it was applied, was noted in the survey stage. If the original order is largely present and works reasonably well for locating materials, little additional arrangement will be needed other than to correct any misfiling.

The series is the workhorse when it comes to arrangement. As already mentioned, the series is a group of records based on a "filing system or maintained as a unit because they relate to a particular subject," "result from the same function or activity, have a particular [physical] form, or have some other relationship resulting from their creation, accumulation or use."[13] Next, go through your survey notes, identify the record series, and assign them to their records creator. Do this intellectually on paper or perhaps a spreadsheet for a more complex collection; don't move any files yet. For the person managing three offices, his office may be the record group level, with each office representing a subgroup, with the series for each individual office falling under the subgroup represented by that office. Although five correspondents have created letters, which is important from a copyright perspective, they all wrote the same recipient, so this is arranged as a single collection. Depending on the quantity of correspondence and whether there are any other records, "Correspondence" might be the series, while each author is a subseries. Additional records created by the recipient would be placed in other series. Or, each correspondent is a separate subgroup, with a single series under each for correspondence because there are no other records. In the case of records from multiple family members, treat each member as a separate subgroup; then within each subgroup, arrange their records into series and so on, depending on the complexity of the materials.

Personal or family papers are often at the other end of the spectrum, retaining little original order and requiring a new arrangement. Personal papers tend to have gaps in coverage, both time-wise and topically or by record type. Collections may have just correspondence, photos, or memorabilia; the records of a favorite activity or organization; or an artificial collection based on a hobby because that was all that was saved. Gaps or shallow coverage can be a weakness that decreases the collection's research value because it provides limited information. Collections with little intellectual unity among the materials may be difficult to arrange.

If a new arrangement is required, again, first assess the provenance to determine whether there is more than one collection. Given a sufficient quantity, records from an individual's employment or their own business might be separated from their personal papers. Having once determined there is a single collection, try to create series from the existing records. Organizing materials by record type (correspondence; legal, financial, or business papers; school records, etc.) should produce the same results as records resulting from the same function or activity. Creating series based on format (photographs, postcards, maps, objects) is the same as having a particular physical form. An artificial collection may be based on a particular subject or the result of the same activity, like collecting stamps.[14]

When it comes to arrangement, it should be understood that there is no single "correct" arrangement for a particular collection, rather that there are multiple choices, some of which are preferable to others. A new arrangement depends on the overall quantity of materials and their specific types, size, format, coverage, and gaps. Arrangement tries to present records that are more general before more specific (corporate headquarters records before local branch office records); broader before more detailed (records applying to the whole university before the records of a single department); more substantive records before less substantive records based on topical coverage, length of time covered, or other qualities; or a larger quantity of records before single items (many letters from the same correspondent before a single letter from another individual).

Avoid oversubdividing records. A given arrangement will depend on how much of an item, type, or series there is. The arrangement chosen for a small quantity of records will differ from a large quantity. A single folder may contain a small amount of correspondence, two or three financial or legal documents, and a single photo, all pertaining to the same family member. That arrangement would be preferable to separating each of those record types into separate folders of one or two items only.

Once all series have been identified or created and assigned to subgroups, if applicable, the next step is to arrange the series in sequence relative to each other within their subgroup or within the record group or collection. It has been pointed out that, while original order determines the sequence of the records within a series, it doesn't generally place one series before or after another. Still, some of the logic used to create series from scratch or guiding arrangement in general can be applied here. Work from broader, more general to more specific, more significant series ahead of lesser series; series that are more complete, substantive, or have a greater quantity of materials before less complete, substantive series or those that contain fewer records. Series relating to the same function or activity should probably be grouped together.

At this point, it should be fairly easy to finish arranging the remaining materials. Organizational records should be in generally good order within any given series and reveal their filing pattern. There may be missing files or filing errors that need correction. If items arrive unfoldered, they need to be assigned to a folder. Personal papers are less likely to be in as good an order. While item-level arrangement has been practiced in the past, this needs to be applied more sparingly. However, records of high research value, high risk of theft, or with personally identifiable or other restricted information may need work at the item level.

Review the arrangement once it has been worked out on paper. Does it observe archival principles, best practices, and any institution-specific requirements? Are there any leftover records unaccounted for? If so, the arrangement may need revision. These materials could also be missing files whose location can now be determined. Once a satisfactory arrangement is worked out on paper, it is ready for application to the actual materials.

During processing, a lot of tasks can potentially be performed. They aren't arrangement per se, but this would be an optimum time to perform them. Handling materials once to perform multiple tasks is much more efficient than making repeated passes to perform separate tasks. Screening for confidential information, identifying records at high risk for theft, noting preservation needs that won't be addressed during processing, noting obsolete or at-risk formats, and assessing records for digitization or exhibit use are all potential tasks that could be accomplished. Some of these activities simply require accurate notation for potential future action, while others may require revision of the processing plan to accommodate handling them. This will vary by institution. Processing is also an opportunity to confirm or further refine information gathered during background research or review of the materials to develop the processing plan.

"More Product, Less Process," Better Known as MPLP

Starting about the midtwentieth century, the quantity of records created exploded due to the introduction first of photocopiers and later desktop computers, which could instantly create large quantities of documents. As these increasingly larger collections arrived at archives, processing backlogs developed and grew. Writing in 2005, Mark A. Greene and Dennis Meissner observe in their thought-provoking article that, despite decades of growth in backlogs, archivists had not responded by making changes to how they processed records. While there are many tasks that can be done during processing, Greene and Meissner propose *adequate* arrangement, *minimal* preservation, and *sufficient* description; that is, only what must absolutely be done.[15] They felt it was time to do a "good enough" job and start aggressively addressing the growing backlog.

MPLP is a pragmatic, realistic approach to balancing limited resources for processing collections with the need to provide access to records. Writing in 1981, the authors of the Massachusetts Institute of Technology (MIT) processing manual direct staff to "remember the purpose of your work and never do more work on a collection than is necessary to make it usable. Extra work on one collection detracts from the work that can be done on others, and our aim is to make all holdings accessible."[16] It would seem that, nearly twenty-five years later, the profession had not widely applied this advice.

Actual application of MPLP could mean arrangement at the series or folder level only. If at the series level, it would mean neither rearrangement of folders within the series nor performance of any work on the contents of any folder, including weeding and preservation tasks.[17] Arrangement at the folder level would allow for rearrangement of the folders within a series but still no work on the contents of any folder. Either option might mean no refoldering into acid-free folders, unless folders are overfilled, missing, or too damaged, and retaining original folder labels unless they are missing or too ambiguous.[18]

MPLP urges archivists to not treat all record groups and collections equally but to assess them and determine how much time can be spent preparing them for use. All records do not have equal research value. Appraisal recognizes this. Some of the same factors used to appraise records can also be used to determine the degree to which they are processed. Those that have lower research value and are likely to receive less use should have less work done to them. An assessment tool for assigning a processing priority would provide a more objective, repository-wide comparison of all unprocessed records. The processing priority would guide the amount of time and work committed to a specific record group or collection, thus helping to answer questions about which level to process the records.

One factor that is difficult to measure but that affects processing time is the degree of disorder for a set of records. The 2001 version of the *Northeastern University Libraries, Archives, and Special Collections Processing Manual* attempts to describe order on a sliding scale, from disorder to more order, while generalizing across sets of records:

Processing Rate 1 (24–30 hours per cubic ft.): Used for collections that have little or no arrangement and order. Different kinds of materials are mixed together, correspondence is unsorted or stored in original envelopes, some papers and correspondents are unidentified, and extensive preservation work may be required.

Processing Rate 2 (14–20 hours per cubic ft.): Used for collections that have an average number of problems. Papers may have some order, and sections of the collection may be properly sorted, although significant portions will have to be arranged, and a good deal of interfiling work will have to be done. Most collections can be processed at this rate.

Processing Rate 3 (4–10 hours per cubic ft.): Used for collections that have no significant organizational problems. A minimum amount of interfiling and reorganization is needed. The major portion of staff time will be expended on the basic work required for all collections: reboxing, refoldering, listing, and describing the contents of the papers.[19]

Greene and Meissner add that Northeastern's manual recommended replacement of all folders but discouraged item-level arrangement or description, except for those very few meritorious collections or portions thereof. This level of work was reserved for records with "extremely high research value."[20]

A more recent metrics project at Harvard University's Countway Library ranks sets of archival records based on the estimated amount of time required to arrange them. The ranking scale includes a brief explanation of the arrangement needs.

Complexity, for us, is based on the amount of time needed to review and physically arrange a collection. A very large collection may receive a 2 because it requires only a small amount of physical rearrangement, and a very small collection may be a 4 or 5 if papers have been dumped into boxes and are a big mess. Rankings are assigned at the onset of processing, not at the conclusion of a project. If our original assessment is inaccurate, we record this information in our collection-level record. Here is our list:

1. No rearrangement necessary. Processed as is.

2. Some rearrangement required but of the "minor housekeeping" variety. (Some folders need to be moved to different boxes, etc.)

3. Rearrangement necessary to restore (perceived) original order, but series are identifiable/recognizable.

4. Rearrangement necessary, but series are hard to determine "up front," requiring periodic reevaluation of processing plan as records are handled.

5. Full archivist-imposed organization necessary. Records are not in any discernible order or groupings, requiring record-by-record handling and grouping. (We call this the "worst night-mare" category. We are processing one of these right now, basically five boxes of 1910–1940 paper records dumped from desk drawers.)[21]

In 2010 Christopher J. Prom, an academic archivist, analyzed processing backlogs and productivity. While agreeing backlogs are indeed a problem, he concludes, unlike Greene and Meissner, they were not statistically related to the practice of labor-intensive processing techniques. He does find a slight correlation to the use of complex descriptive technologies and processing backlogs. Prom's findings reveal that smaller archives have larger backlogs than large archives, which he attributes in part to less student help at smaller archives. Overall, backlogs are a result of many factors; expecting one solution to solve them is not reasonable.[22]

Preservation

Preservation tasks are frequently also performed as part of processing. This can include reboxing or rehousing in a manner appropriate to the size, shape, or format of the items in question and refoldering or flattening. It has often included removing records from inappropriate boxes, binders, albums, or plastic storage materials; removal of harmful fasteners, like rubber bands, string, clamps, paper clips, or staples; preservation photocopying; and sleeving photographs. MPLP challenges archivists to let go of some of these tasks for record groups or collections of lesser research value or lower processing priorities. Its authors cite Mary Lynn Ritzenthaler, author of both the 1993 *Preserving Archives and Manuscripts* manual and a 1990 NARA technical paper on preservation. Ritzenthaler's manual is part of SAA's Fundamentals Series released in the 1990s and used by many an archivist in graduate school and thereafter. Readers of Ritzenthaler's manual come away with the impression that they should be performing all the preservation actions described to the best of their ability and resources in order to be responsible caretakers of the materials in their holdings. Her technical paper, still followed at NARA, says, in Greene and Meissner's words, "holdings maintenance is not something that, in the real world, can or should be assumed to apply to all or even most collections in a repository." Original folders are replaced only when they are damaged and can't protect or support records or are absent, as is the case for loose papers. In 1982, Megan Desnoyers challenged the assumption that all original folders should be replaced, also citing the National Archives practice against automatic replacement. The 1981 MIT and 2001 Northeastern University processing manuals argue that preservation be selectively applied based on the "collection's research value and the degree of physical deterioration of the records" and applied to the level at which arrangement is performed.[23] Archivists need to be mindful of the research value of the collection they are processing and the relative degree of potential damage if no action is taken when they make decisions about which preservation tasks to perform. Once those decisions are made, resources like Ritzenthaler's provide sound information on how to perform those tasks. Greene and Meissner rightly point out that, while Ritzenthaler explained how to perform many preservation tasks, that does not mean that all those tasks should be performed indiscriminately for all collections. Greene and Meissner are not the first or only archivists to recommend differentiated application of the same tasks across collections or even within a single collection. As long as archives have limited resources, they must continue to assess collections when making management decisions about them.

Arrangement for Other Analog Formats

Everything that has been said to this point about how arrangement is performed is applicable to archival records regardless of format, whether documents, maps, photographs, audiocassettes, videotapes, or objects. Arrangement is based on the information content, not the format or carrier. Once records are arranged by content, if some of the information is recorded in a nondocument format or doesn't fit in a manuscript box, then it can be separated and stored elsewhere in a location appropriate to its size and format. When an item is removed from the location in which it is found, in order to preserve the context of the removed item, a separation sheet is physically filed in the original location of the item. The separation sheet briefly describes the item, then specifies its new location, which could be another series within the same collection or another physical location within the archives storage room. Additionally, wherever the item is moved, it needs to carry a description that links it back intellectually to the record group or collection, series, or file from which it was removed.

It is acceptable to form series based on physical form, such as photographs, audiocassettes, or film. Arrangement by format should be used when it makes sense, not as an easy way out of performing arrangement. From a preservation perspective, it is easier to care for specialty formats like these when they are limited to a few locations within an archival storage room. Trying to interfile some of these formats with paper documents can also cause damage to the paper items. Even when all items of a specific format are stored together, it is still possible to arrange them within their format. Photos in a manuscript collection may be arranged in a single series that is further divided intellectually into subseries. Or, all the photos taken by the university photographer or other university employee may be arranged into separate record groups or series for faculty, students, buildings, or athletics.

A Word about Photographs

Photographs may be arranged a number of ways, depending on their quantity, who created them, their purpose, whether they are part of a manuscript collection or a stand-alone collection, and other factors. Some photo collections are quite large, stand-alone collections; for example a newspaper photograph morgue; all the photos taken by the university photographer or a notable, named professional photographer or firm; or photos taken of the entire New York subway system for a lengthy period of time. Each example would be treated as a separate collection or record group. The photos would be arranged based on the images, although the newspaper morgue might be arranged by date if that was how it was kept by the newspaper. Chronological arrangement only for photos is not helpful for retrieval, unless some type of log was maintained indicating which subjects or events were shot day by day to serve as an index to locate images by subject or activity. Photos of the subway would be arranged by geographic location first, with known dates indicated. Depending on the clientele of the professional firm, the photos might be alphabetic by last name of the subject, if known. University photos can be organized by function: buildings, athletics, academic and classrooms, faculty, students, and so on. Although researchers typically request specific photos, meaning item level, it is not necessary to arrange them at the item level. Photos can be arranged collectively, grouping all photos of the same person, building, activity, and so on as appropriate for the photos being arranged. Even partially identified photos can still be collectively arranged: unidentified schoolchildren, undated photos of athletes playing soccer.

Description, Archival Description, Archival Control

Arrangement and description go hand in hand. Arrangement must be performed in order to write description. Description completes work begun during arrangement. Arrangement intellectually identifies groupings within a body of records and if necessary physically places records in a particular sequence.[24] Description captures a somewhat standardized set of information recording the physical or intellectual arrangement, context, and contents of that body of records.

When I refer to description or archival description, I mean the creation of finding aids or other tools based on archival best practices and standards, not bibliographic standards or software systems. The qualities of archival records are distinct from published library materials and require the use of archival descriptive practices or archival control to capture and convey these qualities, a task bibliographic description is incapable of meeting. The creator of archival materials is often unknown, particularly for personal or family records. Photographs are frequently missing dates or any identification. As unpublished materials, they lack publication information. The biggest difference is that archival records share hierarchal relationships unlike books, and their description and standards must express these relationships.

Archivist William E. Landis prefers the term *archival control* to *description* and points out that it "focuses on resources accumulating organically from the activities of people, families and organizations. Archival control has two purposes: First it is an internal tool used by the archives staff to manage collections."[25] It provides intellectual control first through accession or transfer forms in the preprocessed stage, later by the completed finding aid. It identifies what the institution owns (insurance coverage, security in case of theft), describes quantities and physical storage location(s) (space management), and acts as a surrogate (aiding preservation). Second, it is used by researchers to determine whether a particular record group or collection will be useful for their research. The most common descriptive tool is the finding aid.

The information content of a finding aid, how the information is organized and formed, and its method of presentation has evolved greatly in the last twenty to thirty years. The mid-1970s to the mid-1980s saw increased alignment of the information content included in finding aids produced by both institutional archives and manuscript repositories and how the information content was structured with the start of descriptive standards. The period of 1994 to 2004 focused on using the web to deliver finding aids, especially using the EAD format. The release of DACS in 2004 influenced another round of changes in information fields to include in finding aids and how to standardize the information within those fields. Web delivery of finding aids has resulted in unmediated, self-serve access by researchers. The dual functionality of finding aids combined with the reduced or eliminated presence of the archivist to explain them to researchers has caused archivists to reassess finding aids, particularly which information is presented, in which sequence and where in the description, and with which vocabulary and visual layout. Elizabeth Yakel, Wendy Duff, and other archivists have conducted or encouraged user studies to determine how well our finding aids are communicating information to our researchers and how they might be improved.[26]

As finding aid content has been changing, so, too, has its manner of presentation to researchers. Finding aids have evolved from typed or word-processed documents to searchable portable document format (PDF) documents or EAD-encoded finding aids presented on websites; to institutional repositories using DSpace or Fedora; and archival information management software like ArchivesSpace, Cuadra STAR/Archives, Eloquent, ICA-AtoM, and others that present searchable inventories in a single unified portal or search.[27] For those institutions able to invest in such tools, the use of archival information management software to manage most facets of work on collections and information gathered about them should reduce the degree of reliance on finding aids for this purpose. It will be interesting to see whether the use of such systems results in a reduction of information in finding aids oriented to the archival staff for collection management purposes.

Once a new record group or collection has been physically or intellectually arranged, it is time to finalize the finding aid in order to provide information about the record group's or collection's content, as well as contextual information to aid interpretation of the records. Archival description describes related groups of records collectively, as a single folder, series, subgroup, or record group or collection rather than as individual documents. Collective description shows where individual units fit intellectually, thus providing context to aid their interpretation.

The person who arranges a record group or collection should also write the finding aid, although it may be possible to delegate the container list to someone else. Fields in the finding aid are not necessarily written in the order in which they appear. The processor may take notes for complex collections while still arranging and can start to complete some descriptive fields. A finding aid is meant to be a factual document that conveys information about a group of records, their creator, and the circumstances of their creation. "The language and writing should be neutral, not an expression of the processor's personal opinions."[28] The researcher should form his own opinion on the basis of his own research, not the processor's interpretation. The finding aid should be concise, informative, and accurate; include pertinent information; and provide an overview rather than focus on one event or period of time to the neglect of the rest of the records. Writing should be clear, free of technical jargon, and explain any acronyms.[29]

The goal of a well-written finding aid is to assist the researcher by narrowing his search and saving him time in identifying the most pertinent records for his research. The finding aid is not meant to be a book describing the entire record group or collection in great depth or to repeat large sections of biographical information readily available elsewhere or about time periods not addressed by the records at hand. Just as the narrative should be to the point, so, too, should the visual presentation help the researcher quickly "grasp the essence of the collection at a glance."[30] The use of headings, white space, and font types and sizes all affect the readability of archival description, especially if presented on a web page. The many types of software used to present finding aids (for word processing, web, archival information management systems, and institutional repositories or to create EAD finding aids) all put constraints on these presentation features. However, when possible, be mindful of their role, and consider consulting resources on good web design or graphic design for best practices.

Components of a Finding Aid

Textbox 2.1. Finding Aid Template
[Collection or Record Group Title]

MS-[#] or RG-[#]

Abstract
This section is for the abstract.

Summary Information
Creators:

Span Dates:

Bulk Dates:

Extent:

Languages:

Repository Location:

Access Points
Subjects:

Names:

Places:

Formats:

Functions:

Occupations:

Related Materials
Separated Materials:

Related Archival Materials:

Existence and Location of Originals:

Existence and Location of Copies:

Publication Note:

Administrative/Biographical History

This section is for the administrative or biographical history.

Scope and Content

This section is for the scope and content.

System of Arrangement

This section is for the system of arrangement.

Container Listing

Description	Date	Box	Folder
Series 1:			
Indent two spaces if folder title spills onto second line			
Subseries 1:			
Leave blank			
Series II: leave one blank space above to distinguish series			

Conditions Governing Access and Use

Conditions Governing Access:

Physical Access:

Technical Access:

Conditions Governing Reproduction and Use:

Preferred Citation:

Acquisition and Appraisal

Immediate Source of Acquisition:

Custodial History:

Notes

Processing Information: Processed by [Name], [Date]

Alphanumeric Designations:

Variant Title Information:

Instructions for using template:

- If not using fields indicated as optional in the finding aid instructions, delete those fields from the finding aid. If creators are unknown, enter "unknown." For other unknown fields, delete the field.

- Brackets indicate information that will change for each collection or record group. Complete the information that is required, and remove the brackets.

- Enter metadata next to the field name. For "Abstract," "Administrative/Biographical History," "Scope and Content," and "System of Arrangement," enter it below the appropriate header.

- Use Arial, 12-point font and normal margins (one inch on all sides).

- If text is a complete sentence, use a period. If it is incomplete, don't use a period.

- Extent: linear feet includes all boxes, regardless of whether they sit on top of each other on a shelf or not.

Table 2.1. Finding Aid Application Guide

Special Collections and University Archives (SC&UA) Finding Aid Element	SC&UA Use	DACS Element	DACS Rule	Requirement
Header	Enter: "Special Collections and University Archives, W. Frank Steely Library, Northern Kentucky University"	N/A	N/A	SC&UA locally required
Record Group or Collection Title	The first letter for each noun is capitalized in the title. Title = name of creator(s) or collector(s) + a term indicating the nature of materials being described + optional topical segment for collections documenting a very specific topical concept.	Title	DACS 2.3	DACS required
Record Group or Collection Number	MS-[#] or RG-[#]. This number is assigned during accessioning and in some cases in processing. Special collections numbers can be found in K:\Special Collections\Inventories _Spec_Coll\Processing Information\manuscript_collection_numbers.	Reference Code	DACS 2.1.3	DACS required
Abstract	Use scope and content and administrative/ biographical history information if available to construct abstract. The abstract is important for resource discovery.	N/A	N/A	SC&UA locally required

(continued)

Special Collections and University Archives (SC&UA) Finding Aid Element	SC&UA Use	DACS Element	DACS Rule	Requirement
Summary Information				
Creators	If creator is unknown, SC&UA requires that "unknown" be entered in this field. If there are significant creators other than the main one, include them in the administrative/biographical history if they have a role in the provenance of the collection.	Name of Creator(s)	DACS 2.6	DACS required if known
Span Dates	Dates of creation. Supply an inclusive date range comprising the date of creation for the earliest and latest materials in the collection, separated by a hyphen.	Date	DACS 2.4	DACS required
Bulk Dates	Dates of majority of material. Use only when a majority of the materials were created between these dates but a few outliers of more than twenty years exist outside of the span dates.	Date	DACS 2.4	Optional; use as needed
Extent	Record physical quantities in linear feet or cubic feet. If the collection includes digital content, express digital extent (15 megabytes) separately.	Extent	DACS 2.5	DACS required
Languages	"The materials are in [English]."	Languages and Scripts of Material	DACS 4.5	DACS required
Repository Location	Enter: "Eva G. Farris Special Collections and Schlachter University Archives, W. Frank Steely Library, Northern Kentucky University, Highland Heights, Kentucky"	Name and Location of Repository	DACS 2.2	DACS required
Access Points	*Goal is 5-10 terms per record group or collection.*			
Subjects	Use LCSH, AAT, other controlled vocabulary as necessary.	Subjects	DACS xxii–xxiv, 9	SC&UA locally required
Names	Use LCNAF, local authority records. Includes names of persons, organizations, and corporate bodies.	Names	DACS xxii–xxiv, 9	SC&UA locally required
Places	Use LCSH, TGN, local authority records.	Places	DACS xxii–xxiv, 9	Optional; use as needed
Formats	Use TGM, AAT, other controlled vocabulary as needed. Generally skip *paper* and *photograph*.	Documentary Form	DACS xxii–xxiv, 9	Optional; use as needed

(continued)

Special Collections and University Archives (SC&UA) Finding Aid Element	SC&UA Use	DACS Element	DACS Rule	Requirement
Functions	Use LCSH, AAT, other controlled vocabulary as necessary.	Functions	DACS xxii–xxiv, 9	Optional; use as needed
Occupations	Use LCSH, AAT, U.S. Department of Labor's *Dictionary of Occupational Titles*, other controlled vocabulary as necessary.	Occupations	DACS xxii–xxiv, 9	Optional; use as needed
Related Materials				
Separated Materials	Use this field to note the existence and separation of book collections or other separated materials.	N/A	N/A	Optional; use as needed
Related Archival Materials	Include if there are related materials in subject folders, other SC&UA collections, or collections at other institutions closely tied to the one held by SC&UA. Example language: (1) "For related secondary material, see subject folder '_____.'" (2) "For directly and significantly related collections, use the collection citation 'MS-[#] _____.'"(3) "For records at other repositories, use 'Other records directly pertaining to _____: [citation].'"	Related Archival Materials	DACS 6.3	Optional; use as needed
Existence and Location of Originals	Enter: "Originals of _____ held by [name of institution]." Include readily available information for locating collection materials.	Existence and Location of Originals	DACS 6.1	Optional; use as needed
Existence and Location of Copies	Enter: "Copies of [name of materials] are held at _____." Can include information about nature of copies (e.g., microfilm, access copies). Include readily available information for locating collection materials.	Existence and Location of Copies	DACS 6.2	Optional; use as needed
Publication Note	Cite any publications about or based on the use of the materials being described.	Publication Note	DACS 6.4	Optional; use as needed
Administrative/ Biographical History	The purpose of the note is to provide the researcher with a ready reference to the subject's activities so that information in the rest of the finding aid will have greater meaning. Emphasis should be on that portion of the subject's career or life to which the bulk of the collection relates.	Administrative/ Biographical History	DACS 2.7	SC&UA locally required

(continued)

Special Collections and University Archives (SC&UA) Finding Aid Element	SC&UA Use	DACS Element	DACS Rule	Requirement
Scope and Content	Can be brief or full, depending on which level the collection is being processed at or to. In most instances, describe collection at series level, noting the overall type and function of the contents, as well as dates and creators. Use DACS title rules to form series titles. See DACS rules 2.3.18–2.3.22. Use the "Scope and Content" to explain significant chronological gaps in the materials. Bold series headings and italicize subseries headings.	Scope and Content	DACS 3.1	DACS required
System of Arrangement	The need for using the "System of Arrangement" element is based on the complexity of the collection but not the length of the container list. Describe arrangement, like "Collection (or series) is arranged chronologically."	System of Arrangement	DACS 3.2	Optional; use as needed
Container Listing	Table settings for Microsoft Word: ½-point solid line, light gray (second one down on the far-left side). Color settings all at 217. All table components should be left-justified. For locations in the container list, use "O/S Box #," "Map Drawer #," "Art Rack Location #," "See staff," "Row 103."	N/A		SC&UA locally required
Conditions Governing Access and Use				
Conditions Governing Access	Enter one of these options as applicable: (1) "This collection is open for research access." (2) "This collection is open for research access, with the exception of [_____]. These have restricted access and are unavailable to any researcher." (3) This collection is open for research access, with the exception of one folder due to FERPA restrictions."	Conditions Governing Access	DACS 4.1	DACS required
Physical Access	This field provides information about access restrictions due to any physical characteristics or storage locations that limit access to the materials being described. Such restrictions include location, physical condition of the material that limits use, and requirement to use copies instead of originals for preservation reasons. Example language: (1) "For fragile images, researchers will be asked to view digital copies of originals. Department personnel will authorize use of originals on a case-by-case basis." (2) "Some audiotapes may require duplication and migration prior to patron access."	Physical Access	DACS 4.2	Optional; use as needed

(continued)

Special Collections and University Archives (SC&UA) Finding Aid Element	SC&UA Use	DACS Element	DACS Rule	Requirement
Technical Access		Technical Access	DACS 4.3	Optional; use as needed
Conditions Governing Reproduction and Use	Enter: "The copyright law of the United States (Title 17, U.S. Code) governs the reproduction of copyrighted material. The user assumes full responsibility and any attendant liability for the fair use of materials requested in total compliance with the copyright law of the United States (Title 17, U.S. Code) that may arise through the use of any requested materials."	N/A	DACS 4.4	SC&UA locally required
Preferred Citation	Enter: "[Box #, Folder #,], MS-# or RG #, Name of Collection, Eva G. Farris Special Collections [or Schlachter University Archives], W. Frank Steely Library, Northern Kentucky University"	Citation	DACS 7.1.5	SC&UA locally required
Acquisition and Appraisal				
Immediate Source of Acquisition	Enter one of these three options to indicate method, source, date, and accession numbers: (1) "Gift from [Name], [Date] (Accession Number)" (2) "Transfer from [Name], [Date] (Accession Number)" (3) "Purchase by Steely Library, [Date] (Accession Number)"	Immediate Source of Acquisition	DACS 5.2.5	SC&UA locally required
Custodial History		Custodial History	DACS 5.1	Optional; use as needed
Notes				
Processing Information	Enter: "Processed by [Name], [Date]." If reprocessing, add name and date below the initial processing information to capture revision history. SC&UA uses this field to indicate both processing and finding aid creation.	Archivist and Date	DACS 8.1.5	SC&UA locally required
Alphanumeric Designations		Alphanumeric Designations	DACS 7.1.6	Optional; use as needed
Variant Title Information	Use if collection material has been published under a significantly different name (e.g., Mary North Collection instead of the NKAAHTF Records)	Variant Title Information	DACS 7.1.7	Optional; use as needed

Developed by Lois Hamill, Anne Ryckbost, and Vicki Cooper

Table 2.1 explains how to complete the sample finding aid shown in textbox 2.1 based on department decisions about our overall descriptive program. Boilerplate language is included for some fields. The finding aid template in textbox 2.1 was recently revised to what is shown in order to make it DACS-compliant; that is, it includes all the required DACS fields. It also includes additional DACS value-added fields that correspond with fields the archives had been using for the last five years and wanted to continue using. The names chosen for some finding aid field names do not match the DACS field names; however, they are correlated in table 2.1. The department selected field names it thought would be readily understood by researchers. The decision was also made to sequence the fields in an order different from the one DACS uses. Remembering that some finding aid fields are more oriented to the archives staff and internal management functions, we deliberately moved some of those fields to the bottom of the description. Fields oriented to the researchers' use are put first in the sequence we think will help them most rapidly determine whether this collection or record group might help them answer their research questions. We were also influenced by the fact that sections of finding aids can be collapsed and expanded depending on the technology used to display them and that some systems show a short version in the opening screen, hence the choice to place the abstract first. The template and application guide shown illustrate one version of how to write a DACS-compliant finding aid. They represent considered decisions about our descriptive program, are consistent with our descriptive approach for our DSpace digital repository, and are intended to prepare us for eventual use of EAD. The plan is to transition to ArchivesSpace in the next several years to deliver our finding aids. As that transition is made, we will monitor the presentation among other factors to determine whether further revisions are needed.

The DACS manual explains the function of each element or field, includes guidance on formation of the field contents, and provides examples. DACS principle 7 allows for description at the collection level or multilevel description matching the levels identified or created during arrangement. Depending on the method the archives uses to deliver its finding aids, it may find that web browsers or software searches take researchers directly to series, folder, or item arrangement levels, bypassing a collection- or record-level description.[31] Some archivists recommend placing series description, for example, at the beginning of the container list or description of records for that series as a way to connect contextual information to the specific files it describes.

Individual lines within a container list include a description of a portion of the records and their location. Many finding aids emphasize the physical folder location and list it first in each line. Because it is the information content of the folder or other storage medium that interests researchers, it makes more sense to place the information description first on each line, followed by the location. This places the emphasis on the intellectual content of the records, not their location. Intellectually related records recorded on CD, DVD, audio- or videocassette, or other format or stored in flat files, oversized boxes, on server space, or other storage mediums or locations can more easily be integrated with paper-based documents when the description focuses on the information content over the location.

Textbox 2.2. Describing Diverse Formats in a Finding Aid

Description	Date	Box
Annual Reports	1972–2000	1-4
	2001–present	CD 1-5
	Or	K/archives/findingaids/presidents/sterling/annual_reports
	Or	https://dspace.nku.edu/handle/11216/58
Speeches	1971–2003	Box 5, also audio cassette 7
Correspondence	1970–1998	Boxes 6-10

See "Additional Reading and Resources" at the end of this chapter for some examples of better finding aids.

Standards

SAA's Standards Committee defines *standards* as an "industry agreement that establishes qualities or practices that make possible sharing of information, development of common vocabularies and practices, and more effective interaction" among a range of professionals who work with archival records.[32] There are three types or categories of descriptive standards: data structure, data content, and data value. Imagine a storage system of cubbyholes. Data structure standards define each cubbyhole, the data elements or fields in which information is organized. Current archival description data structure standards include EAD and EAC-CPF. Archivists also use externally developed data structure standards, meaning they were developed by nonarchivists. (Qualified) Dublin Core is one example. Data content standards provide rules on how to form the information in the cubbyhole. They may address punctuation, capitalization, how to form dates or quantities, and whether information is required or optional.[33] Current archival description data content standards include ISAD(G), DACS, ISAAR(CPF), International Standard for Describing Functions, and International Standard for Describing Institutions with Archival Holdings. Data value standards are embodied in regulated lists of terms, names, or codes called controlled vocabulary or thesauri. Currently there are no formally accepted de jure archival description data value standards, but the *Thesaurus for Use in College and University Archives* was developed by archivists. There are bibliographic-controlled vocabularies as well as specialized thesauri that are data value standards that are acceptable for use with archival descriptive data structure and data content standards. These include the Library of Congress Name Authority File, Library of Congress Subject Headings, Union List of Artists' Names, Art and Architecture Thesaurus, Thesaurus for Graphic Materials, and Getty Thesaurus for Geographic Names, among others.

The Library of Congress Name Authority File lists names of people and organizations that have been formed according to bibliographic standards, but it only includes names. Archivists are interested in additional contextual information, such as the role played by the person or organization relative to the records being described or their relationship to other people or organizations. Part 2 of the second edition of DACS, released in 2013, explains how to develop an archival name authority record, how to form a name, and the requisite documentation about the development of the record. EAC-CPF, released in 2011, allows for the international exchange of name authority files.[34] When it was created, it was developed for authority records based on the ISAAR(CPF). Because DACS's guidance on name authority record development is based on the *International Standard for Archival Authority Records—Corporate Bodies, Persons, Families*, DACS authority file records should be compatible with the EAC-CPF exchange standard.

"Metadata is structured information that describes, explains, locates, or otherwise makes it easier to retrieve, use, or manage an information resource." "Metadata describing digital content is often structured (e.g., with tagging or markup) and it may be embedded . . . within a single file, incorporated within the 'packaging' that is associated with a group of files." Types of metadata include descriptive, structural, technical, and administrative. Descriptive metadata describes a resource for discovery and identification purposes. Title, creator, and date are sample fields or elements. Structural metadata documents or records how elements are assembled, such as pages that form a chapter or the necessary files to create a web page.[35] Technical metadata about digital files includes file characteristics, like file format, size, and software that it was created with, as well details about the file content, like dimensions, duration, or method by which it was recorded. Technical metadata is often machine-generated and is very important for file preservation. Administrative metadata aids management of a resource and could include when and how the file was created, file type, and other technical information. Depending on the source consulted, "Rights Management" and "Preservation" metadata are either subsets of "Administrative" metadata or constitute separate categories. The former addresses intellectual property rights, while the latter includes elements crucial to long-term preservation of the digital resource. Some metadata schema are also standards. Preservation Metadata Implementation Strategies (PREMIS) is an example of an international preservation metadata standard. OCLC and RLG convened the Working Group on Preservation Metadata, which developed the PREMIS data dictionary.[36]

Benefits of Using Standards

Standards are a commonly agreed-upon practice, a convention. When widely adopted, a standard is well known and associated with a specific, predictable behavior that people come to depend on. Even before one can read the letters on a solid red octagon on a post at the corner of an intersection, drivers of motorized vehicles know they are approaching a stop sign, which requires them to come to a full stop and check for traffic before proceeding through the intersection. Standards make it easier to learn how to operate equipment or perform tasks and reduce the learning curve the next time a person encounters a similar example of a red octagonal sign, a piece of equipment, or a task performed according to a standard. Once a researcher familiarizes herself with a finding aid prepared using descriptive standards, she has the ability to predict the kind of information she will find in the next finding aid, where it is likely to be located, and how it might be organized. This improves her ability to locate the information she seeks with less effort.

Archival descriptive standards are applied independent of any specific software used to display finding aids or automate their creation. The use of standards increases the interoperability of networks, computers, software systems, and information or data. The ability to exchange information between systems and institutions enables the development of larger, interinstitutional information-sharing networks. The *National Union Catalog of Manuscript Collections*, Digital Public Library of America, Online Archive of California, OhioLINK, and Pass the Word oral history portal are examples of shared networks created through the use of standards. One purpose of description is to provide wider access to collections. The use of standards makes it possible to share finding aids across institutions, greatly improving their discoverability.

Access

Once a finding aid has been written, how is it used to help researchers discover a record group or collection and provide access to the records or information content? In his 2010 article, archivist Christopher J. Prom focuses on measuring the impact of processing tasks on backlogs. While he finds a "mild" correlation between the "application of complex descriptive technologies" and backlogs, there are some other interesting findings. Some college and university archives use a patchwork system of three or four software tools to create description, while some deliver the same information in multiple formats. While it sounds like a good idea to deliver collection description through multiple venues to increase the likelihood of being found by researchers, Prom finds that users rarely have a single interface to search for all description produced by an individual archives.[37] The inability to provide a single search portal for all collection description is a worse offense against access than having only one descriptive tool or not using EAD. Providing a minimum baseline description for as many collections as possible through a single search tool should be the highest priority for any description program. This does not mean that decisions made about description should prevent the addition of more advanced descriptive practices as part of future expansion. To the contrary, decisions should be made that will enable integration and compatibility with desired additional practices rather than setting up roadblocks. For example, organizing certain types of information in a spreadsheet is more advantageous than using word-processing software because the spreadsheet produces comma-separated values. Comma-separated values are relatively easy to import into another software, making the information more portable, reusable, and flexible and staff time more efficient.

Web-delivered finding aids have advantages. Word-processing software is readily available and easy to use. Documents can be converted to PDF to prevent changes, maintain searchability and a particular visual appearance, and increase portability. They provide more information than online card catalog records in a format more readily understood than MARC fields and are word-searchable to locate desired information. This is affordable and technologically simple. Standards can still be used for the formation of information in the finding aid. Such finding aids can be made available in a single web location. The same finding aid can be printed and made available in the archives research room with no modifications required. This may not sound flashy, but it has a lot of positive qualities. There are several methods at least for delivering such a word-processed finding aid via the World Wide Web. The first is to use web software to provide access from a web page where it is hopefully readily discovered by Google or other web crawlers. Web software introduces the requirement for varying levels of technical skill and expense. Depending on one's employer, web software also introduces other disadvantages. Design, presentation, and search options are controlled by the web software, which is frequently chosen at the institutional level and may change every three to five years, requiring regular migration. The software itself or the institution's Information Technology or Marketing Departments may regulate customization, or this may be limited by the software language skills of the archivist or systems librarian and his availability. Customization can create problems when migrating to the next institutional choice for web software.

Finding aids can also be delivered through institutional repositories (IR). IRs require additional technical skill and descriptive work. The IR software also imposes restrictions on visual presentation, but it provides the ability to search all finding aids in a single pass. Web crawlers are still able to crawl IRs, providing added discoverability. Some integrated library systems can treat an IR like commercial electronic databases and search it simultaneously with the library's print and digital database collections, thus integrating all the contents of the IR with the primary library catalog. In the case of a hosted version of an IR, like DSpace by DuraSpace or Bepress's Digital Commons, options and customization are limited by the vendor, software, and money.

Larger institutions that can afford programmers are able to develop custom combinations of (open source) software that give them greater flexibility in the design and presentation of their IR or finding aids, but many can't afford this option. Larger institutions, with their greater availability of technical or programming support, are more able to automate finding aid production, such as the EAD format, than smaller institutions. Other options include the use of archival information management software, like ArchivesSpace, CuadraStar/Archives, Eloquent, and ICA-AtoM to provide web access to finding aids through a single portal.

Changing from information delivery through print finding aids in the research room to the web has changed users' expectations. Because they encounter the finding aid on the web, they seem to expect it to conform to practices used by commercial retail, news, or entertainment sites with short chunks of information, unmediated use by the consumer, even the ability to interact with or comment on archival materials. While archives may have selected the web for potentially greater ease of delivery, greater discoverability, a simplified system in terms of technology and software requirements, or possibly bypassing library cataloging and MARC, users have interpreted finding aids in the context of other information presented on the web.

While archivists work to identify the ideal finding aid design, not all archives are operating on the same playing field. Some are struggling with processing backlogs, limited technology, software, personnel, personnel with the necessary technology skills, or time. Producing a good enough finding aid that includes the pertinent information and uses DACS fields with details to the series or folder level in a word-searchable PDF file may be about all that is manageable. It is better to provide some description for all collections than several advanced finding aids. Yes, it is important to consider our users and possibly reformat our finding aids to take advantage of the technology delivering them, but it should be understood that what is discussed in journal articles may be an ideal not achievable in the real world all the time by all archives.

Program Considerations

When this book presents specific guidance on work at the folder or item level it is done with the intent of instructing how to perform this work if it is needed, or to explain a concept. It should not be interpreted to mean that the work is required or appropriate in all cases. As has already been said, there is a range of tasks that can be done during processing, from least to most time-consuming for arrangement, preservation, and description. Significant processing backlogs exist for analog records, and digital records will only compound the problem. Archivists must make intentional decisions to address them based on priorities and the specific resources available within their institutions. There has been a trend in archival literature, workshops, and conference presentations of increasing specialization, technical information, and detail on topics like EAD, DACS, how to describe or preserve audio and video formats, digital records arrangement and description, workflow, and forensics. This trend includes many archival topics outside the scope of this book. The reader or participant is given the impression she needs to apply or perform all that is discussed on specialty after specialty. The implied expectation that everyone will do so if they are a competent archivist is exhausting. Archivists in smaller archives especially need to know enough about many aspects of archival work. While it is helpful to know a fuller range of what can be done for a particular function, understanding that it is acceptable to intentionally perform a smaller percentage of that range of tasks due to resources or priorities is beneficial.

Assessment to Prioritize Processing

Either at the time of accessioning or before the start of processing, an assessment to determine a processing priority for the materials provides greater consistency to managerial decisions. It is also useful when arguing for funding or other resources. Ideally a formal assessment tool is used to assign a processing priority rating to a set of records, comparing them with all the records waiting to be processed. Such factors as research value, significance of the records (national, regional, state, local), their completeness, breadth of scope, the number of topics or audiences served by the records, and degree of order considered during appraisal also help determine their processing priority. Preservation criteria, such as physical condition or format obsolescence, and the complexity of processing should also be considered. Some records are not appropriate for the novice archivist or may require specialized expertise and limit the personnel able to work on them. Access or use restrictions and copyright status may also be pertinent because they affect how records are delivered to researchers. For an institution that only wants to deliver oral histories via the web, access barriers preventing that are important.

A simple assessment tool consists of an institution-specific list of factors like those in this chapter. Each factor is assigned a high, medium, and low point value that reflects how strongly a specific set of records meets that factor. The points assigned to the ratings for each factor may be the same; for example, 3, 2, and 1, respectively. Or factors that are considered more important can be weighted. Their ratings are given more points; 9, 6, and 3, for example. All factors of equal weight should use the same values for their high, medium, and low ratings. As collections arrive, they are assessed and assigned a cumulative score that is the total of their ranking points for all factors. Collections having scores within point range A are assigned processing priority 1; point range B, processing priority 2; and so on. It stands to reason that priority 1 records would have more time spent on processing them than priority 3. The processing rating could be used to determine the level to which all or part of a record group or collection is arranged and described and preservation tasks are done, including folder replacement.

Processing Plans

A written processing plan that gathers standardized information and answers a standard set of questions about the proposed processing for a specific record group or collection is another useful management tool. The plan describes the existing and proposed arrangement and description, assesses preservation needs, records proposed remediation, and estimates the time and experience level needed to complete the proposal. One of its strengths is a running record of decisions made both during the planning phase and while processing. It allows for adjustments based on new information gained during execution. Once some of the processing decisions are made and recorded, tasks can be broken up according to skill level or specialized knowledge. Processing decisions are made on the record group or collection level by a qualified archivist, rather than piecemeal task by task. If the work is interrupted or there are personnel changes, the processing plan provides consistency for the work on that collection. Series do not have to be processed sequentially and can even be assigned to different people. The written documentation becomes a reference tool the next time a similar situation arises in another set of records.

A companion processing checklist can specify the processing tasks an institution considers mandatory or optional, sequence their workflow, and ensure consistent application. For example, all items over a certain dollar value are photographed and stored in a more secure location.

Notes

1. Richard Pearce-Moses, *A Glossary of Archival and Records Terminology* (Chicago: Society of American Archivists, 2005), s.v. "archives," accessed January 6, 2016, http://www2.archivists.org/search/saasearch_glossary/archives.

2. Pearce-Moses, *Glossary*, s.v. "record," accessed May 8, 2016, http://www2.archivists.org/glossary/terms/r/record#.Vy91XnoYFHo; Laura A. Millar, *Archives: Principles and Practice* (London: Facet, 2010), 7–8. Millar's book won an SAA prize in 2011.

3. International Council on Archives, *ISAD(G): General International Standard Archival Description*, 2nd ed. (Ottawa: International Council on Archives, 1999), 11, http://www.ica.org/en/isadg-general-international-standard-archival-description-second-edition. What I wrote is not identical to ISAD(G), DACS, Pearce-Moses's glossary definition, or the definition in Lewis J. Bellardo and Lynn Lady Bellardo, comps., *A Glossary for Archivists, Manuscript Curators, and Records Managers* (Chicago: Society of American Archivists, 1994), because there are slight, nuanced differences between them, but I did use these for reference when I wrote this because I want to keep pretty close to what is nearly but not officially a standard.

4. Provenance was the American interpretation of the French phrase *respect des fonds*. In 1941, the National Archives defined *record group*, which, although based on the *fonds*, was somewhat different [Donald R. McCoy, *The National Archives: America's Ministry of Documents, 1934–1968* (Chapel Hill: University of North Carolina Press, 1978), 106–7]. Although American archivists said they practiced provenance, as shown in chapter 1, there wasn't uniform consensus of its interpretation and application. Provenance is based partly on the definition of *record group*, the same as *respect des fonds* is based on the definition of *fonds*. Frank Evans, Donald Harrison, and Edwin Thompson, "A Basic Glossary for Archivists, Manuscript Curators, and Records Managers," *American Archivist* 37 (July 1974): 427, defines *provenance* and *respect des fonds* as conceptually the same; *original order* is a "corollary, frequently designated as a separate principle." Lewis J. Bellardo and Lynn Lady Bellardo, comps., *A Glossary for Archivists, Manuscript Curators, and Records Managers* (Chicago: Society of American Archivists, 1994), 27, is similar; *original order* is defined separately on p. 30. Kathleen D. Roe, *Arranging and Describing Archives and Manuscripts*. Archival Fundamentals Series II (Chicago: Society of American Archivists, 2005), 15, also treats original order as a separate principle. Anne J. Gilliland-Swetland, *Enduring Paradigm, New Opportunities: The Value of the Archival Perspective in the Digital Environment* (Washington, DC: Council on Library and Information Resources, 2000), 12, also treats provenance and *respect des fonds* as equivalents but describes provenance as having two directives: Don't mingle records of different origins, and respect original order. DACS, p. xvi, principle 2, seems to suggest that provenance and original order are subsets of *respect des fonds*. Historically, *respect des fonds* was developed by the French in 1841, while *Strukturprinzip* was developed by the Prussians about forty years later. *Strukturprinzip* reflected a registry system that was practiced in Prussia, Holland, and Great Britain but not the United States and came to the United States from the Dutch, who learned it from the Prussians. DACS was the product of the joint Canadian–American CUSTARD Project. Canadian description differs "genetically" from American description. *Rules for Archival Description* (Ottawa: Bureau of Canadian Archivists, Canadian Committee on Archival Description, 2008), pp. xxiii–xxiv, in the "Statement of Principles" says,

Respect des fonds is the basis of archival arrangement and description. The archival principle of *respect des fonds* states that the records created, accumulated, and/or maintained and used by an individual or corporate body must be kept together in their original order, if it exists or has been maintained, and not be mixed or combined with the records of another individual or corporate body. This principle is composed of two parts—provenance and original order. The principle of provenance means that the records created, accumulated and/or maintained by an individual or organization must be represented together, distinguishable from the records of any other creator. The principle of original order means that the order of the records established by the creator should be maintained by physical and/or intellectual means whenever possible to preserve existing relationships between records and the evidential value inherent in this order.

ISAD(G), pp. 10–11, in defining *provenance* and *fonds*, does not define either as including original order.

Charles Dollar says,

Most North American Archivists tend to equate provenance with the records creator and its organizational structure, while most European archivists tend to equate provenance with the competence that creates the records. In Europe, provenance is generally reinforced by hierarchical and subject-oriented filing plans that reflect the tasks or functions that an organization undertakes. [*Archival Theory and Information Technologies: The Impact of Information Technologies on Archival Principles and Methods*, edited by Oddo Bucci (Macerata, Italy: University of Macerata, 1992), 49]

It is my opinion that provenance and *respect des fonds* are essentially the same and that the principle of original order, although important and related, is not a subset of either provenance or *respect des fonds*.

5. If the practice of creating series based on format for analog records is extended to digital records, then this separates records that are intellectually related, damaging their contextual information. Gilliland-Swetland, *Enduring Paradigms*, 14, argues against this practice for digital records.

6. Pearce-Moses, *Glossary*, s.v. "description," accessed April 12, 2016, http://www2.archivists.org/glossary/terms/d/description#.Vw11IXoYFHo.

7. Oliver W. Holmes, "Archival Arrangement: Five Different Operations at Five Different Levels," *American Archivist* 27 (January 1964): 21–41.

8. According to "2015 SAA Employment Survey," *Society of American Archivists*, 2015, accessed January 11, 2016, 4, http://files.archivists.org/membership/surveys/employment2015/SAA-EmploymentSurvey2015-summary_0615.pdf, of approximately 3,500 archivists, the number-one employer was academic archives, with 41 percent. The second-largest employer was the government, with 23 percent.

9. Richard C. Berner, *Archival Theory and Practice in the United States: A Historical Analysis* (Seattle: University of Washington Press, 1983), 60; David B. Gracy II, *Archives and Manuscripts: Arrangement and Description*, Basic Manual Series (Chicago: Society of American Archivists, 1977), 6. Gracy allows for subgroups by function but not topic. Thirteen years later, Fredric M. Miller, *Arranging and Describing Archives and Manuscripts*, Archival Fundamentals Series (Chicago: Society of American Archivists, 1990), 58, narrows the definition to subordinate administrative bodies or groups of series related by common activity or use.

10. Steven L. Hensen, comp., *Archives, Personal Papers, and Manuscripts* (Chicago: Society of American Archivists, 1989), 8; Roe, *Arranging and Describing*, 61; Holmes, "Archival Arrangement," 30; Pearce-Moses, *Glossary*, s.v. "file," accessed January 12, 2016, http://www2.archivists.org/glossary/terms/f/file; Pearce-Moses, *Glossary*, s.v. "item," accessed January 12, 2016, http://www2.archivists.org/glossary/terms/i/item.

11. Karen T. Lynch and Helen W. Slotkin, *Processing Manual for the Institute Archives and Special Collections, MIT Libraries* (Cambridge: Massachusetts Institute of Technology, 1981), 14.

12. ISAD(G) treats artificial collections differently than organically created ones.

13. Hensen, *Archives, Personal Papers*, 8; Roe, *Arranging and Describing*, 61.

14. Roe, *Arranging and Describing*, 61; Hensen, *Archives, Personal Papers*, 8.

15. Mark A. Greene and Dennis Meissner, "More Product, Less Process: Revamping Traditional Archival Processing," *American Archivist* 68 (Fall 2005): 212-13.

16. Lynch and Slotkin, *Processing Manual*, 6.

17. Greene and Meissner, "More Product," 215, consider weeding to be a form of appraisal and argue that appraisal should be executed as a phase separate from arrangement and only to the record level to which the record group or collection will be processed. Lynch and Slotkin, *Processing Manual*, 47, link the level of preservation work to the level of arrangement.

18. See Megan Floyd Desnoyers, "When Is a Collection Processed?" 14, accessed February 28, 2016, http://www.jstor.org/stable/41101552, *Midwestern Archivist* 7 (1982): 14, regarding not refoldering and overfilled folders. See Greene and Meissner, "More Product," 220, for damaged folders.

19. Greene and Meissner, "More Product," 227n69.

20. Greene and Meissner, "More Product," 227n69.

21. Emily Gustainis, "Center for the History of Medicine Metrics Project Documentation," *Harvard Medical School Wiki*, last modified October 23, 2012, https://wiki.med.harvard.edu/Countway/ArchivalCollaboratives/CHoMMetricsDocumentation.

22. Christopher J. Prom, "Optimum Access? Processing in College and University Archives," *American Archivist* 73 (Spring/Summer 2010): 146, 154, 168. Smaller archives, defined as less than 4,000 cubic feet, have larger backlogs than large archives, over 20,000 cubic feet (Prom, "Optimum Access?" 169).

23. Mary Lynn Ritzenthaler, *Preservation of Archival Records: Holdings Maintenance at the National Archives*, Technical Information Paper, No. 6 (Washington, DC: National Archives and Records Administration, 1990); Greene and Meissner, "More Product," 220; Desnoyers, "When Is a Collection Processed?" 14; Lynch and Slotkin, *Processing Manual*, 47; Greene and Meissner, "More Product," 219.

24. Pearce-Moses, *Glossary*, s.v. "Describing Archives: A Content Standard," accessed April 14, 2016, http://www2.archivists.org/glossary/terms/d/describing-archives-a-content-standard#.V0TV-eQYFHo.

25. William E. Landis, "Overcoming the Bibliographic Conundrum in Archival Description," *American Archivist* 74 (Supplement 2011): 12-13; Luciana Duranti, "Origin and Development of the Concept of Archival Description," *Archivaria* 35 (Spring 1993): 47-54.

26. Wendy Duff and Penka Stoyanova, "Transforming the Crazy Quilt: Archival Displays from a User's Point of View," *Archivaria* 45 (Spring 1998): 44-79; Elizabeth Yakel, "Encoded Archival Description: Are Finding Aids Boundary Spanners or Barriers for Users?" *Journal of Archival Organization* 2 (2004): 63-77; Christopher J. Prom, "User Interactions with Electronic Finding Aids in a Controlled Setting," *American Archivist* 67

(Fall/Winter 2004): 234–68; Cory Nimer, "What Do You Mean It Doesn't Make Sense? Redesigning Finding Aids from the User's Perspective," *Journal of Archival Organization* 6 (2008): 216–32; J. Gordon Daines III, "Re-Imagining Archival Display: Creating User-Friendly Finding Aids," *Journal of Archival Organization* 9 (2011): 4–31.

27. Lisa Spiro, *Archival Management Software* (Washington, DC: Council on Library and Information Resources, 2009). This report compares archival management software and raises questions to consider when selecting a system. See especially appendixes 2 and 3 for brief and full comparisons of system features.

28. Lois D. Hamill, *Archives for the Lay Person: A Guide to Managing Cultural Collections* (Lanham, MD: AltaMira Press, 2013), 39; Gregory S. Hunter, *Developing and Maintaining Practical Archives: A How-to-Do-It Manual* (New York: Neal-Schuman, 2003), 152.

29. Hunter, *Developing and Maintaining*, 153.

30. Hamill, *Archives*, 40; Hunter, *Developing and Maintaining*, 153.

31. Christopher J. Prom, "Using Web Analytics to Improve Online Access to Archival Resources," *American Archivist* 74 (Spring/Summer 2011): 172, discusses this search engine behavior. His study documents that Google took 47.8 percent of their users directly to a series-level description. Only 11.9 percent of users started at the archives' homepage, of which the majority were suspected to be staff. The location of subject search terms seems to have influenced Google's behavior.

32. "Standards Development and Review," Society of American Archivists, January 2012, accessed May 8, 2016, http://www2.archivists.org/governance/handbook/section7/groups/Standards/Development -and-Review#.Vy-dhXoYFHo.

33. "Report of the Working Group on Standards for Archival Description," *American Archivist* 52 (Fall 1989): 454.

34. "Encoded Archival Context—Corporate Bodies, Persons, and Families (EAC-CPF) Tag Library," *Technical Subcommittee for Encoded Archival Context of the Society of American Archivists and Staatsbibliothek zu Berlin*, 2014, accessed May 15, 2016, http://eac.staatsbibliothek-berlin.de/fileadmin/user_upload/schema/ cpfTagLibrary.html.

35. National Information Standards Organization, *Understanding Metadata* (Bethesda, MD: NISO Press, 2004), 1, accessed May 12, 2016, http://www.niso.org/publications/press/UnderstandingMetadata.pdf; Federal Agencies Digitization Guidelines Initiative, *Glossary*, 2015, s.v. "metadata," accessed December 11, 2016, http://www.digitizationguidelines.gov/results.php?gltext=technical+metadata&x=0&y=0; National Information Standards Organization, *Understanding Metadata*, 1.

36. Shawn Averkamp, "Overview of Metadata for Archivists," Society of American Archivists Digital Archives Specialist webinar, June 19, 2015, 90, slide 14, and verbal instruction; National Information Standards Organization, *Understanding Metadata*, 1; "PREMIS Preservation Metadata Maintenance Activity," *Library of Congress*, January 15, 2016, accessed May 12, 2016, http://www.loc.gov/standards/ premis; OCLC/RLG Working Group on Preservation Metadata, *Preservation Metadata and the OAIS Information Model: A Metadata Framework to Support the Preservation of Digital Objects* (Dublin, OH: OCLC/ RLG Working Group on Preservation Metadata, 2002), 1, accessed May 12, 2016, http://www.oclc .org/content/dam/research/activities/pmwg/pm_framework.pdf; National Information Standards Organization, *Understanding Metadata*, 1.

37. Prom, "Optimum Access?" 146–74, 165–66.

Additional Reading and Resources

AIMS Work Group. *AIMS Born-Digital Collections: An Inter-Institutional Model for Stewardship.* 2012. Accessed June 26, 2016. http://dcs.library.virginia.edu/aims/white-paper. Appendix E includes four processing plans for digital records.

"Arrangement and Description." *Society of American Archivists.* Accessed May 25, 2016. http://www2.archivists.org/category/standards-topic/arrangement-and-description#.VzE22eQYFHo. This is SAA's standards website.

"Call for Participation: DLF Assessment Interest Group's 'Day of [Digitization Cost] Data.'" *Digital Library Federation.* April 20, 2016. Accessed April 7, 2017. https://www.diglib.org/archives/11721. This blog post mentions the cost calculator at http://statelibrarync.org/plstats/digitization_calculator.php.

"Collection Guides (Finding Aids) Usability Study of Novice Users (2010) User Studies." *North Carolina State University Libraries.* Last revised April 2010. http://www.lib.ncsu.edu/userstudies/studies/2010collectionguidesnovice. This study includes links to resources used to conduct the study, as well as its findings.

Conway, Martha O'Hara, and Merrilee Proffitt. "Taking Stock and Making Hay: Archival Collections Assessment." Dublin, OH: OCLC Research, 2011. Accessed February 24, 2016. http://www.oclc.org/content/dam/research/publications/library/2011/2011-07.pdf. This excellent OCLC report discusses collection assessment for a variety of purposes including prioritizing processing. It includes specific guidance on how to conduct an assessment, with examples. Appendix C includes detailed descriptions for each rating (1–5) to assess the housing, intellectual access, and research value of each collection. Appendix B is called out separately later in this list (see "Special Collections Library Unprocessed Collections Survey Project").

Desnoyers, Megan Floyd. "When Is a Collection Processed?" *Midwestern Archivist* 7 (1982): 5–23. A very practical article on four key tasks for processing a collection, with a range of tasks on a continuum of least to most labor-intensive for each. This is dated for the description choices and minimum record. The specific information for which records must be screened has increased, but the methodology is sound. Meissner and Greene cite this as an early precursor to their MPLP methodology.

Duranti, Luciana. "Origin and Development of the Concept of Archival Description." *Archivaria* 35 (Spring 1993): 37–54. This article reviews definitions of *description*, provides a history of its evolution from 1500 BC, and briefly contrasts surrogates and representations.

Hunter, Gregory S. *Developing and Maintaining Practical Archives: A How-to-Do-It Manual.* 2nd ed. How-to-Do-It Manuals for Librarians, no. 122. New York: Neal-Schuman, 2003. See chapters 5 and 6 on arrangement and description.

"International Standards." *International Council on Archives.* Accessed May 25, 2016. http://www.ica.org/en/public-resources/standards. This web page lists all the ICA standards.

Krug, Steve. *Don't Make Me Think: A Common Sense Approach to Web Usability.* 2nd ed. Berkeley, CA: New Riders, 2006. This book presents good, basic web design precepts that are worth considering when designing finding aids for the web. It is a quick read and entertaining.

"A Processing Manual for the Special Collections Technical Services Department at the University of North Carolina at Chapel Hill." *Special Collections Technical Services Department of the Louis Round Wilson Special Collections Library*. Accessed May 10, 2017. http://library.unc.edu/wp-content/uploads/2017/05/UNC-CH-Library-Archival-Processing-Manual.pdf. Section 3 discusses arrangement, while section 4 addresses description. Section 4 also details how UNC applies DACS field by field.

Quigley, Sarah. "Managing the Southern Christian Leadership Conference Records Processing Project: Team Processing, Work Plans and Action Plans." *Council on Library Information Resources*. 2010. Accessed May 23, 2016. http://www.clir.org/hiddencollections/meetings/symposium/powerpoints/Emory.ppt/view. This PowerPoint presentation shows a collection analysis that is used to develop the proposed arrangement. A series analysis determines the arrangement, description, and preservation work for the series. It also records calculations for the estimated time to process and decisions made once work begins. An action plan plots out each series against a calendar schedule, blocking off the estimated time to process. Processing plans can be a very useful planning tool that makes it possible to break a collection into sections and divide work.

Schaefer, Sibyl, and Janet M. Bunde. "Module 1: Standards for Archival Description." In *Archival Arrangement and Description*. Trends in Archives Practice series. Chicago: Society of American Archivists, 2013.

Society of American Archivists. *Describing Archives: A Content Standard*. 2nd ed. Chicago: Society of American Archivists, 2013. This archival descriptive standard should be used to complete fields in finding aids. It tells which fields are mandatory and which information to include in each field and provides examples.

"Special Collections Library Unprocessed Collections Survey Project." *University of Michigan*. Accessed February 24, 2016. http://www.oclc.org/content/dam/research/activities/backlog tools/michiganmanual.pdf. Appendix B referenced earlier (see Conway and Proffitt) details a specific survey methodology and how to organize the collected data and defines the terms recorded in each field. It includes a rating system with specific descriptions for qualities used to prioritize collection processing, including arrangement, description, and the physical condition of the housing.

Van Ness, Carl. "Much Ado about Paper Clips: 'More Produce, Less Process' and the Modern Manuscript Repository." *American Archivist* 73 (Spring/Summer 2010): 129–45. Van Ness critically examines both the research methodology and conclusions of Mark Greene and Dennis Meissner in their 2005 article "More Product, Less Process: Revamping Traditional Archival Processing." Van Ness finds both to be flawed, offering a counteropinion.

Finding Aid Examples

"American Legion, Department of Michigan records: 1919–1999." *Bentley Historical Library, University of Michigan*. Accessed April 23, 2016. http://quod.lib.umich.edu/b/bhlead/umich-bhl-85590?rgn=Entire+Finding+Aid;size=25;sort=occur;start=1;subview=standard;type=boolean;view=reslist;q1=American+Legion;op2=and;q2=1919;op3=and;q3=Dept. This finding aid has a clean layout, with good, consistent navigation on the left. The researcher is able to view one chunk of information at a time. Information is organized intellectually regardless of physical storage location; for example, see "Scrapbooks/Photograph Albums 1898–1970." I would prefer the column with content be on the left, but this is a well-done finding aid.

"C. Horace Hamilton Papers, 1920s–1970s." *The Southern Historical Collection at the Louis Round Wilson Special Collections Library, UNC University Libraries.* Last modified June 2011. http://www2.lib.unc.edu/mss/inv/h/Hamilton,C.Horace.html. This finding aid uses navigation on the top and left to give the researcher lots of control over the research path. Sections also expand and contract to control the amount of information viewable. Brief explanatory notes are sprinkled throughout, such as an explanation of what a finding aid is or the fact that subject heading terms do not easily connect to a specific folder in the collection. I do find the container list challenging. I would want to copy and paste the list into a Word document and re-sort it to get some idea of what I was looking at and which files were more similar to each other. The note explains that basically this is the original order in which the files were received. Perhaps researchers are happy just to have this finding aid and are willing to do the extra work themselves to determine the nature of the materials. There is a lot of undifferentiated correspondence, yet someone took the time to note that certain names were those of old girlfriends and which institution they attended.

"Ellen Henrietta Swallow Richards Papers, 1882–1910." *Five College Archives and Manuscript Collections.* Accessed March 28, 2016. http://asteria.fivecolleges.edu/findaids/sophiasmith/mnsss59_main.html. This finding aid also has a nice, clean presentation, with the ability to view only the information the researcher chooses. A short version is presented initially, but the whole finding aid is also available. The container list information is nicely presented, with the focus on the intellectual content, not its physical location.

3

Introduction to Digital Records

Anyone who reads appendix A is likely to identify at least one or two technological changes in the evolution of computer systems and the digital records they created that they remember personally, whether it was using flash drives to carry homework between computers or the transition from typing to word processing. You are also likely to encounter computer equipment, external storage devices, or computer files created or affected by the technology highlighted in this appendix as you work in present-day archives.

Obviously, the methods used to create records or capture information people consider important has evolved through the centuries; so, too, have the methods used to organize information, both as it is or is not managed during active use and once they reach the archives. The archival profession began in the United States in the early twentieth century. It developed and codified archival theory for paper records, addressed photographs and moving-image film, and progressed into recorded sound and video formats as technology and the profession evolved and advanced. The information requested by researchers and needed for preservation purposes for recorded sound and moving-image formats became more specialized. In some cases, standards development provided fields for recording some of this more detailed information, which improved the ability of archival description to more specifically describe examples of these formats. Over the course of the twentieth century, analog formats developed that were increasingly machine dependent and technical. The profession responded by revising existing techniques or developing new practices to manage evolving or new formats for the records in their care.

Core archival principles have remained valid for more than a century. The definition of a record has not changed simply because it is digital. It needs to have content, context, and structure and typically serves to provide accountability or aid human memory.[1] Archivists arrange and describe records based on their information content and creator, not the method used to record or store the information. In many ways, digital records are simply a new variant on the recording method, one that has made the record fully machine dependent as well as software dependent for interpretation.

Like the photocopier in the 1960s,[2] the development of personal computers created an explosion in the quantity of and ease with which digital files can be created. The quantity of records to be handled has increased exponentially. However, not everything that is created is worth permanent retention. Increased volume coupled with machine and software dependency to view files requires new techniques to perform the same archival functions of appraisal, arrangement, and description. Core archival principles are still valid for digital records, but they require new steps to be added to old processes, reworking workflows, and new specialized knowledge and tools to adjust to this format. The need for new techniques to accomplish archival functions, including arrangement and description, does not mean that the principles developed for analog records no longer apply.

Change caused by technology is not the only factor affecting records. Behavioral changes by records creators, users, and managers have also affected the quality and organization of analog and digital records transferred to the archives. In the earlier part of the twentieth century, businesses and government imposed standardized organizational systems on records, resulting in greater consistency in how records were filed. As recently as ten to forty years ago, the U.S. Air Force mandated how records were filed, so that the same forms were located in the same sequence in file cabinets from one military base to another. Now everyone has their own idiosyncratic system for file organization and naming. Lack of (accurate) dating is a chronic problem. Records created and managed by two successive holders of the same position in the same office reflect inconsistent practices and disorder.

Organizational employees who fail to actively practice records management cause compounded problems when the records are digital. Their bad records practices are amplified because the records are no longer confined to a filing cabinet or storage room. They create multiple copies and versions stored across multiple devices. Thanks to the ease of web publishing, unbeknownst to the archivist, they post records to the web. They imagine the archivist has time to routinely troll the organization's website, identify permanent records, and perform records management for the employee by transferring a copy.[3] Many times the web version is also in a less desirable format.

Analog records will continue to be present in archives and need to be managed along with the newer digital records. Some archivists may specialize in digital records only, just as there have been specialists for some analog formats. Those who wish to advance in the profession will need some understanding of both formats.

Hybrid repository holdings require integration of description for all types of materials. Open record groups and collections that include both analog and digital records require thought as to how to integrate both formats in the finding aids and descriptive or access software systems. Staff and researchers need to be able to locate the earlier analog counterparts of records from the same series that are now born digital. How will that be accomplished?

Employee failure to make timely transfers to the archives contributes to the agedness of both file formats and storage devices. Technology keeps shortening the time between new iterations and the window for preserving digital records before their information can no longer be unlocked. Because the lifespan of digital files is short by comparison with analog formats, it requires intervention much sooner to preserve them. The shortened lifespan also requires that more work be done on digital records sooner after reaching the archives than for analog materials. All these factors affect the workflow and timing of tasks that would have been done during processing, primarily moving them up earlier in the work sequence.

Not all organizations have equal resources, including equipment, technology, employee skills, knowledge, and training. This was true before the inception of digital records and remains true. The quantity of digital records and the ratio between digital and analog formats vary from one archives to another. Some archives are better able to manage digital records. They update all archival functions to accommodate them, integrate digital and analog records, and develop a comprehensive program. Other archives take a more hit-or-miss approach or may not be able to process as large a quantity of digital records because the work is labor-intensive.

Archivists believe in preserving records of enduring value for the benefit of future generations. Ethical archivists have argued against accepting records that they are unable to care for, meaning we are expected to care for the records we do accept. Archivists aspire to ensure the authenticity and continuing usability of records in their care.[4] These professional beliefs mean that archivists should not just collect digital records; they are also making a commitment to their long-term preservation. The challenge will be to persuade resource allocators to take this commitment seriously.

Textbox 3.1. Processing Tasks for Analog Records[5]

1. Accession
   1.a. Take physical and administrative control of the materials.
   1.b. Review the content and condition of the materials.
   1.c. Create control files.
   1.d. Determine the processing priority. [arrangement and description phases; still re-move files from original media or source before stopping work and shelve for later processing]

2. Gather contextual information
   2.a. Conduct background research on the individual or organization.
   2.b. List the events or activities reflected in the records.
   2.c. Identify record-keeping practices revealed by the records or manuscripts.
   2.d. Identify the functions that led to the creation of the records or manuscripts.

3. Conservation assessment
   3.a. Identify conservation problems.
   3.b. Segregate problem materials.
   3.c. Plan for mitigation of problem materials.

4. Decide intellectual arrangement
   4.a. Determine whether there is an original order.
   4.b. Identify relationships between the groups of materials within the record group or collection.

5. Arrange records, physically if necessary
   5.a. Rehouse.
   5.b. Arrange into subgroups, series, and subseries.
   5.c. Identify preservation needs.
   5.d. Identify formats found in the records or manuscripts.
   5.e. Note information content of the records or manuscripts.

6. Describe the records
   6.a. Determine the appropriate level of description for the materials.
   6.b. Gather information necessary to identify the materials.
   6.c. Describe the materials and their arrangement.
   6.d. Describe the access and use conditions.
   6.e. Identify and collect administrative information about the materials.
   6.f. Gather information about related materials.
   6.g. Identify and collect other useful information.
   6.h. Create access points.

7. Create access tools
   7.a. Identify the types of access tools to create.
   7.b. Create them.

Textbox 3.2. Processing Tasks for Digital Records[6]

2. Gather contextual information
    2.a. Conduct background research on the individual or organization.
    2.b. List the events or activities reflected in the records.
    2.c. Identify record-keeping practices revealed by the records or manuscripts.
    2.d. Identify the functions that led to the creation of the records or manuscripts.

1. Accession
    1.c. Create control files.
    1.a. Take physical and administrative control of the materials.
    1.b. Review the content and condition of the materials.

    3. Conservation assessment
        3.a. Identify conservation problems.
        3.b. Segregate problem materials.
        3.c. Plan for mitigation of problem materials.

    5.a. Rehouse. Reexamine this activity for digital records.
    5.d. Identify formats found in the records.
    5.e. Note information content of the records or manuscripts.
    6.b. Gather information necessary to identify the materials.
    6.e. Identify and collect administrative information about the materials.
    1.d. Determine the processing priority.

4. Decide intellectual arrangement
    4.a. Determine whether there is an original order.
    4.b. Identify relationships between the groups of materials within the record group or collection.

5. Arrange records, physically if necessary
    5.b. Arrange into subgroups, series, and subseries.

6. Describe the records
    6.a. Determine the appropriate level of description for the materials.
    6.c. Describe the materials and their arrangement.
    6.d. Describe the access and use conditions.
    6.f. Gather information about related materials.
    6.g. Identify and collect other useful information.
    6.h. Create access points.

7. Create access tools
    7.a. Identify the types of access tools to create.
    7.b. Create them.
    New. Load records or metadata into the tools.

Changes in Workflow

Although archivists share common principles, standards, and even software systems now, there will always be institutional variations in the tasks performed, their methodology, and sequence. With that given, textbox 3.1 presents one example of a processing workflow for analog records. Textbox 3.2 presents the same activities, with some new additions in a reconfigured sequence based on the distinctive qualities and needs of digital records. The digital model proposes conducting background research first, then accessioning. It also greatly expands the accessioning step to include the preservation assessment and moves up the components of arrangement and description before concluding by prioritizing the processing priority. All of step 3 of the analog model has been absorbed into digital accessioning, to be followed by intellectual arrangement, physical arrangement, description, and creation of access tools in the same sequence as before. Nearly all of the physical arrangement tasks were also absorbed into digital accessioning, while description was only slightly modified.

This new workflow recognizes the shorter lifespan of digital records and responds to it. The preservation assessment examines the condition of the records to determine whether there are correctable problems that could damage or shorten the life of the records being studied or even be transmitted to other records and harm them. The intent is the same, but the execution for digital records is different. Textboxes 3.1 and 3.2 illustrate one possible workflow comparison between analog and digital records. Later chapters address the relevant sections appropriate to each chapter.

Program Considerations

Archives may accept digital files or CDs and DVDs, but if they intend to provide access for longer than the lifespan of that CD or DVD, they need to do more than just accept the disks. It will require intentional, planned efforts to acquire records without altering them; to gather and create the right metadata to access, correctly interpret and provide context for the files; and to develop separate environments to preserve master files while delivering access copies. Preservation masters will require continuous monitoring to prevent degradation, to identify formats that will become obsolete before they do so they can be refreshed or reformatted, and to provide appropriate backup for the preservation masters. Additionally, appropriate metadata for the files must be preserved along with the files, and both parts must be clearly linked to each other. These steps ensure continuous access, accurate interpretation, and authenticity for digital records.

This book focuses on performing archival functions once digital records arrive at the archives. It does not address how they are obtained or whether such work can be supported by an institution. The most likely source of records is the institution itself. Effective programs for managing digital records require a comprehensive approach rather than a piecemeal effort. It requires administrative support, especially when addressing acquisition, management, and long-term preservation of an institution's own permanent digital records. "Successful programs have a good working relationship and buy-in from Information Technology/Systems Departments." Digital records programs are expensive for both personnel and technology needs. "Successful archivists/records managers have made strategic alliances with key players outside of the library."[7]

Notes

1. Mark J. Myers, "Electronic Records: The Next Step," Society of American Archivists Digital Archives Specialist webinar, April 13, 2015, 90; Richard Pearce-Moses, *A Glossary of Archival and Records Terminology* (Chicago: Society of American Archivists, 2005), s.v. "record," accessed June 8, 2016, http://www2.archivists.org/glossary/terms/r/record.

2. "Xerography," *Wikipedia*, last modified August 4, 2016, https://en.wikipedia.org/wiki/Xerography.

3. Thanks to Meg Miner for calling some of these problematic behaviors to my attention.

4. "SAA Core Values Statement and Code of Ethics," *Society of American Archivists*, last updated September 23, 2016, accessed June 11, 2016, http://www2.archivists.org/statements/saa-core-values-statement-and-code-of-ethics#.V1yFs6IYFHo.

5. J. Gordon Daines III, "Module 2: Processing Digital Records and Manuscripts," in *Archival Arrangement and Description*, edited and introduced by Christopher J. Prom and Thomas J. Frusciano, Trends in Archives Practice series (Chicago: Society of American Archivists, 2013), 100–110; Kathleen D. Roe, *Arranging and Describing Archives and Manuscripts*, Archival Fundamentals Series II (Chicago: Society of American Archivists, 2005), 46. Select material used courtesy of J. Gordon Daines III and the Society of American Archivists.

6. Daines, "Module 2," 100–110; Roe, *Arranging and Describing*, 46. Select material used courtesy of J. Gordon Daines III and the Society of American Archivists.

7. Lisl Zach and Marcia Peri, "Desperately Seeking Solutions: College and University E-Records Management (ERM) Programs" (presentation, Mid-Atlantic Regional Archives Conference, Morristown, NJ, October 27, 2006).

Additional Reading/Resources

AIMS Work Group. *AIMS Born-Digital Collections: An Inter-Institutional Model for Stewardship*. 2012. Accessed August 27, 2016. http://dcs.library.virginia.edu/files/2013/02/AIMS_final.pdf. Pages 120–23 present Stanford University's workflow for all stages of work on digital records.

Computer History Museum. *Timeline of Computer History*. 2017. Accessed May 30, 2016. http://www.computerhistory.org/timeline/computers. This website details many of the specific technology changes in computer history, from the machines to storage devices, software, languages, networking, the web, and more. This may be useful for dating older digital records or equipment.

Cornell University Library. *Digital Preservation Management: Implementing Short-Term Strategies to Long-Term Problems*. 2007. Accessed Aug 14, 2016. http://www.dpworkshop.org/dpm-eng/eng_index.html. This is a self-paced course on a broad range of digital preservation topics. Originally developed by Cornell University, since 2012, the site has been managed by MIT. A weeklong workshop was developed to accompany the web course and was still offered in 2016 (http://www.dpworkshop.org/workshops/fiveday.html).

Goldman, Ben. "Bridging the Gap: Taking Practical Steps toward Managing Born-Digital Collections in Manuscript Repositories." *RBM: A Journal of Rare Books, Manuscripts and Cultural Heritage* 1 (2011): 11–24. This article argues that custodians of digital records must take action or lose digital content. At least inventory all digital holdings to know the range of what is there; then transfer files from external or older media before the digital content ceases to exist.

POWRR: Preserving (Digital) Objects with Restricted Resources. 2012. Accessed December 27, 2016. http://digitalpowrr.niu.edu/survived-powrr-wkshp. Although the Digital POWRR Project focuses on digital preservation, it also analyzes software mentioned in this book to perform processing tasks for digital files. The website provides other helpful resources, while the project's final white paper expresses a practical and realistic philosophy.

Prom, Christopher J. *Practical E-Records.* 2011. Accessed August 14, 2016. http://e-records .chrisprom.com/about/about-this-blog. This well-written blog by a well-regarded archivist provides practical advice about digital records. Use the site navigation at the top to go to the "Recommendations" page suggesting how to begin work on digital records, resources, and bibliographies. Of particular interest is the post "Selected Email Preservation Resources."

Society of American Archivists. "Digital Archives Specialist (DAS) Curriculum and Certificate Program." 2017. Accessed August 14, 2016. http://www2.archivists.org/prof-education/das# .V7Cfr6IYFHo. This program provides instruction on a range of topics related to managing digital records. Any combination of courses or webinars may be taken, whether a person intends to pursue the DAS certificate or not. A group of people can watch a webinar together and split the cost, or it is possible to obtain a site license enabling multiple individuals to watch at separate times individually within a set time. In both cases, the fee only covers the cost of one exam. Additional individuals desiring to also take the exam would have to pay an additional fee.

Zach, Lisl, and Marcia Frank Peri. "Practices for College and University Electronic Records Management (ERM) Programs: Then and Now." *American Archivist* 73 (May 2010): 105–28. The authors of this article researched digital records programs at colleges and universities and identified qualities of some of the more successful ones. They also document how much progress has been made with digital records from 2000 to 2009.

4

Appraising Digital Records

Appraisal precedes arrangement and description and therefore is slightly outside the scope of this book, but because it should be performed differently for digital records than for analog records, the information that may be available to the archivist when she begins the arrangement and description phase won't be the same as before.

Records will continue to come from one of two sources. They will either be created internally by business, government, academic, or organizational offices or externally. External sources can be someone else's business, government, academic, or organizational office or a person or family group. Whether the creator is part of an organization or an individual or family makes a significant difference in how the digital records were previously managed, their potential file formats, and the method of their acquisition.

Most organizations have someone performing information technology functions, which might include updating software versions, scanning for viruses and malware, and backing up files. The larger the organization, the more intentional and active this technology management will be. Private individuals range the spectrum from also actively engaging with technology to using basic software in older versions.

Federal and state government units, including many state (public) universities and colleges, are required to participate in a records management program. Businesses and private academic institutions may choose to develop a custom records retention schedule that would apply only to their organization. Records retention schedules provide a structure for appraisal and acquisition of institutional records.

Archivists have developed a number of appraisal theories in an effort to provide consistency, handle the volume of modern records, and optimize limited resources. Theodore R. Schellenberg started with questions of evidential and informational value. Frank Boles and Julia Marks Young developed the "Black Box" concept that measured the value of information against the cost to keep it. Helen Samuels and Larry J. Hackman proposed a documentation strategy to share responsibility across institutions for adequately documenting an "issue, activity, function or subject." Others have recommended functional analysis to identify records that document the functions of the office or organization in question.[1] All of these are valid appraisal methods applied to analog materials and are an equally appropriate starting point for digital records. Archivists are first and foremost preserving information, so evaluating the information content is the first step. Because there is a second step of appraisal of digital records, in order to contrast the two, the first step has also been called macroappraisal.[2]

In working with analog records, especially paper records, the distinction is made between the original and copies. The original document may also be considered the record copy or the single copy designated as the official copy for legal, reference, and preservation purposes.[3] The distinction between original and copy makes sense for analog formats because copies are of lesser quality than the original; visual and other qualities degrade. The distinction between the official or record copy and other copies is significant largely for legal reasons. The record copy of meeting minutes is the version voted on and accepted as an accurate account of the meeting. Draft versions are not substitutes. Record copies may bear signatures or other markings also distinguishing them from similar copies or versions. The record copy is also frequently associated with the person or office that created it, while informational copies often appear in other offices for reference purposes.

In the case of digital records, there is no difference in quality in the 1s and 0s that comprise an original digital file and duplicates; that is the beauty of digital files. So the concept of original and copy may become moot for digital files, except for the fact that one copy needs to be designated as the copy to be preserved. The relationship between original and record copy is invalid for digital files; however, the distinction of a record copy remains valid. Digital record copies may carry electronic signatures or other distinctive indicators or may be converted to PDF. They are definitely the version that is selected for preservation.

Appraisal in General

The purpose of appraisal is to identify those records with sufficient (nonmonetary) value that an archives wants to acquire them. The starting point for appraisal should be a written collection policy that is based on the archives' mission and audience, which in some cases rests on the mission of a parent organization. The collection policy for many state archives and state universities and colleges is partly determined by public records legislation specifying records that must be kept according to a records retention schedule. Other laws may also specify records to be kept. A collection policy may also delineate qualities of digital files that make them acceptable or unacceptable for acquisition, such as file format.

When materials are offered to an archives, the designated archivist gathers information about the materials, determines whether they are within the scope of the collection policy, assesses their research value and other pertinent factors, considers the archives ability (including cost, technical skill, storage space, ability to process) to preserve the records, and makes a decision. It is probable that, at some point in the process, the archivist will need to open files to analyze them. Before doing so, she should make a disk image or a preservation copy of the files in a manner that will not alter file dates or other information. The preservation copy will be left untouched. If appropriate, virus and malware checks should be run on the copy to be opened and analyzed (more on this later). Some archives may require written documentation of the decision. Decision-making authority may be vested in one individual or shared. Use of a systematic process and a collection policy promotes consistency in appraisal decisions. Considering the volume of modern records created, a suggested figure is to retain no more than 5 percent of the total volume.[4] It is impossible to preserve everything. The goal of appraisal is to be selective, not inclusive. What is the importance and quality of the records being appraised? Are they worthy of continued preservation? Appraisal should prioritize the most significant records for acquisition and preservation. This may be for your archives or institution, the community, or the region.[5]

In its appraisal policy brochure, the National Archives and Records Administration asks some good general appraisal questions:

How significant are the records for research?

How significant is the source and context of the records?

Is the information unique?

How usable are the records?

Do these records serve as a finding aid to other permanent records?

Do the records document decisions that set precedents?

Are the records related to other permanent records?

Do the files contain nonarchival records?

What are the cost considerations for long-term maintenance of the records?

What is the volume of records?

Is sampling an appropriate appraisal tool?[6]

General Comments on Appraisal of Digital Files

Cost is an appropriate appraisal consideration. Digital record programs are expensive. When cost is mentioned, the typical response is that storage costs have gone down. The expense is not just for storage but also for continuous management: creating description and preservation metadata; refreshing, reformatting, or migrating data; and skilled personnel to perform these tasks. Digital records are not processed once and then done, unlike many analog records. Increasingly, this work requires specialized software to automate ingest of new files, processing tasks, and delivery of files to researchers and to run regular fixity checks so that personnel can keep up with the volume of records and work. Processing digital files requires additional tasks that are unnecessary for analog records. If they are performed manually one file at a time, they require more time than if they can be automated. Additional technical support may be required internally from the organization's IT department or externally from a vender. Digital files require both a preservation master and an access copy, increasing storage requirements, and the preservation masters should also be backed up. Additionally, research room personnel may require additional skills to assist researchers in the use of digital records.

Given the cost to acquire, process, and actively manage digital files in order to preserve them, it is reasonable to ask whether the research value of the digital files merit this expense. "If it is neither feasible nor desirable to preserve a digital resource across various changes in technology, then its acquisition may need to be re-evaluated."[7] Should an archives accept a resource it is unable to preserve once the present format or software is obsolete? The "Acquisition and Appraisal" section of the Digital Preservation Coalition's *Digital Preservation Handbook* contains an interactive decision tree. According to the decision tree, there may be instances when a digital file is acquired but the archives will be unable to preserve it once the current format is no longer functional. If the archives knows this, it should both document this fact and inform the source of acquisition.[8] Another option raised in the "Microappraisal of Digital Records" section of this chapter is whether the value is such that reformatting should be considered. There are times a paper copy will be a more affordable, equally acceptable option. Assess the potential functional requirements for the resource and whether they would override the reformatting option.

Macroappraisal of Digital Records

Appraisal of digital records starts the same as for analog records. The archivist appraises the information contents. In many cases, the records he appraises may well be the same records that were previously collected in analog form, except that now they are born digitally. Photographs, annual reports, and meeting minutes are good examples. The archivist assesses the informational value: its completeness; whether it duplicates, supplements, or builds on other records already held; whether the information is available elsewhere; whether there are intellectual property or privacy issues; and more.

The archivist needs to talk with the donor or records creator to gather information, especially if a significant quantity of digital records is involved. Discussion should focus on the records creator's file management practices. What are the records about? What do they document? Activities of the records creator? Work-related files? Do they fall within the archives' collection policy? What is the likelihood of file duplication, deleted files, personally identifiable or sensitive information, or pirated files? What is the donor's preference regarding attempts to recover deleted files? What types of personally identifiable information (PII) are anticipated? How should sensitive information be handled? Is the donor comfortable with materials, like oral history interviews, being posted to the web? Does the archives want to obtain written permission to duplicate files to create preservation and access copies and possibly even backup copies?

Some have suggested that functional appraisal may be more useful for digital records, focusing first on identifying the more significant functions of the records creator and second on the records that best illustrate those functions. Proponents of this appraisal method argue that functions are relatively stable over time. It also shifts the focus from the content of a record to the function that generates it.[9] This approach has been used for organizational records and may work well for high volumes of records. Instead of sifting through all the records presented for consideration, it says, "Here are the records we want. Are they present in this set of records?"

In contrast to organizational records, there is cause for concern regarding acquisition of personal digital records. Private individuals do not have records retention schedules to guide their decisions regarding what to retain or dispose of and when. They lack IT departments to assess when software and technology has peaked and is going to be replaced or that force them to upgrade software, replace aging software or hardware, or routinely backup data for them. No records manager trains them on developing good file organization structure or file-naming conventions. Left to their own natural tendency for order or disorder, private donors may have file formats from old software, files stored on old hardware or external devices, no organizational structure to their files, or vaguely named files. Good information resides alongside useless junk. They may have kept everything or lost significant files due to mistakes and accidents. Active use of social media, cloud storage, multiple e-mail accounts, or multiple devices can further complicate the challenge of locating a coherent and representative body of records due to distributed storage locations.[10] In 2015, Australian professor of library science Ross Harvey challenged archivists and librarians to educate individuals about best practices for digital records creation.[11] It remains to be seen whether enough digital personal archives will survive to be appraised and collected.

Microappraisal of Digital Records[12]

Once a body of digital records has successfully passed a macroappraisal of the information content and it is determined to be a candidate for acquisition, it is time to assess its technical qualities. It is likely that some level of technical appraisal was conducted in the predigital age for audio and visual analog formats, but it is even more crucial for digital records. Digital records have four essential characteristics—authenticity, integrity, usability, and reliability—which must be maintained for successful digital preservation. InterPARES 1 defines an authentic electronic record as one "that is what it purports to be" and a record with integrity as one that is "complete and unaltered in any essential respects." Authenticity, integrity, and usability can be assessed during appraisal. Reliability derives from how the records are managed in order to maintain the other three qualities. To assess a record's authenticity, the archivist "must be able to establish its identity and demonstrate its integrity." Authenticity includes content, context (the circumstances of creation and use, which may be external to the content), and structure (the logical attributes, like hierarchy and subparts; how the information is structured or organized; how the parts interact to convey content and meaning).[13] Authenticity is derived in part by metadata the archivist adds and is monitored through fixity checks but also partially derives from the file itself and its inherent metadata. As such, the inherent authenticity, integrity, and usability can be assessed during appraisal.

Start with Basic Mechanical Questions

Can the file be opened? Do you have the requisite hardware and software, or are they obsolete? If the software is proprietary, can you get a license to view the file(s)? Are the files encrypted or password protected, and is the key or password available? Are they contaminated or corrupted?[14]

Assess the Content

If you are able to open the file, does it make intellectual sense? Is the information understandable?[15] Does it have a title, headings, dates, clear guidance on what the information is, and how any parts relate?

How well organized are the files? Are they grouped intellectually? Do they only make sense to the creator but not to others?

Were the files intended to be kept or simply neglected or not weeded?

How complete are the files? Do they represent a portion or a complete record? What portion of a function or program do they document? Do they document the whole population or a subset? Have records been destroyed or lost? Will there be additional accretions?[16]

Assess the Context

How complete is the metadata? Can you determine who created the file, file size, format, dates created, and last modified?

Further Assess the Authenticity

How secure was the record-keeping system? Were files stored in a filing system that was properly maintained? Are files in their original format? Were they created or used during the normal course of business? Have custody and file modifications and migration been documented over time?[17]

Are the contents authentic? Are they what they purport to be? For example, does the photograph date from the camera metadata contradict a datable, unique event in the photo image itself? If the camera battery dies and the internal date isn't reset when the battery is replaced, the camera can provide false information.

If the files can't be opened due to hardware, software, or security barriers, it is going to be a problem to access, appraise, or use them. If these issues can't be readily resolved, the files may be useless. Or they may be resolvable but not inexpensively. Assuming barriers can be resolved with minimal effort and the files are functional, the subsequent questions focus heavily on appraising the authenticity of the files. The cumulative answer is not "Yes, they are authentic" or "No, they are not" but a sliding scale of authenticity. Some files are not as authentic as others. This means a point value can be assigned for the quality of authenticity and an impartial, relative comparison made of different sets of digital records.

Assess Volume[18]

Must raw data be kept, or is there a summary or statistics that will suffice? If there is more than one data set, is there a summary?

Are there duplicates? Is this source the best source of this content?

Will there be more accretions? Does the repository have sufficient storage capacity? Must some files be compressed? For example what is more important for videos: functionality or their storage cost?

Assess Custody

Where are the files located? Are they even on the institution's computers or servers or someone else's? This applies not just to social media, but also academic athletics websites, yearbooks, and student newspapers, which are often hosted elsewhere.

Will files remain in the office of creation (e.g., GIS files or student grades and transcripts) or transferred to the archives? If they remain with their creator, does that office need advice on preservation?

Does the archives or institution have its own preservation server, or is it outsourced?

What happens if any of the venders close, are bought out, or the records creator decides to change venders?[19] Do you own your files and data, and can you get them back, or will that cost extra?

Assess Preservation Issues

Is the file functional? Does functionality need to be retained; for example, spreadsheet formulas? The answer to this question affects the format used for the preservation copy. It may mean a functional preservation copy is retained in lieu of or in addition to a format that is more desirable for preservation purposes.[20]

Consider the file formats in which the files are received. Can you support the file formats? Some are better for long-term preservation than others.[21]

Are files compressed or contaminated?

Should the file be reformatted to microfilm or paper? Would this affect functionality, access, presentation, or authenticity?[22] Is the cost to reformat less than for maintaining digitally? Weigh these potential consequences against the intellectual value of the resource.

Assess Accessibility, Usage, and Costs

Are files open, closed, or restricted? Are they in the public domain or copyrighted? Do they require proprietary or open software?

Do the files require difficult-to-use software or specialized or advanced knowledge to access the data?[23]

Are the records still actively used? What is the usage rate? Will the creator provide reference service for the records?

What is the cost for storage and backup of the preservation master and access copies;[24] continuous technical support for lifelong maintenance of the master; hosting fees; a delivery system for access copies; appraising, accessioning, and processing digital files?

The questions regarding volume demonstrate good, basic appraisal. Are these the right records? Are they the monthly financial details or the annual summary report? Is this the most authoritative, complete source of this information? They also touch on costs. While the preservation questions are intended to identify potential problems, the answers have cost implications. Accessibility can present barriers or potential expenses. Questions of custody can mean a problem of identifying, locating, and gathering records scattered across numerous locations before appraisal can even begin. They may represent technical problems to retrieve, ownership problems, or a potential data loss if a vender folds. To some extent, these questions also assess present and future usability, one of the four essential characteristics of digital files.

The digital data itself needs additional analysis based on whether it is structured or unstructured data. Data contained in databases, document management and imaging systems, or created by geographic information systems (GIS) and computer-aided design (CAD) software are examples of structured data.[25]

Determine:[26]

How the information is collected and organized.

Whether all the information is retained for the same duration (retention period).

Whether retention is based on trigger dates, like graduation, inactivity, or something else.

Whether expired data and metadata can be separated from active data and metadata.

Whether the data and metadata can be exported.

Whether it is necessary to preserve all data or just aggregate statistics, if lesser-value data fields can be removed, and if there is confidential data.

Whether documents, program books, keys, or codes need to be preserved to maintain the meaning and usefulness of the data.

Examples of unstructured data include word-processed documents, spreadsheets, PowerPoint presentations, digital images, e-mail, instant messages, tweets, blogs, social media, and web pages.[27] Unstructured data is the most difficult to appraise because:

It tends to be unorganized.

Modern offices decentralize records among a number of creators; creators who share server or network space result in more than one records creator filing documents in a single shared digital folder. In some cases, more than one person works on the same document. Such practices make provenance difficult to determine and tend to result in records that document business functions being interfiled with those created by general administrative activities.[28]

Creators frequently store records in many disparate locations—e-mail, shared network, hard drive, external drives, and paper files—leading to problems of retrieval and redundancy.

IT and records creators tend to manage files by different qualities than archivists. IT focuses on creators and format (like e-mail), not business functions or content (policies or reports). Creators are not trained to organize files by function or record series.[29]

These practices cause problems:

Records creators fail to purge inactive records, while IT identifies records to purge based on file size or age, not content.[30]

Shared storage locations challenge file authenticity and integrity.

E-mail header information capturing who sent a message and when is not always complete.[31]

How do you identify the small percentage of records worth preserving among the chaff?

Software Tools to Help

At some point during appraisal, files may need to be opened or at least the file directory examined. Any of these actions alters the file contents. When it is determined these activities need to be done, before proceeding, an unaltered copy of the original files should be made. This may require the use of a write-blocking software or device, depending on the storage location or source of the files to be analyzed. After making a working copy that does not alter the original, assess the risk and run a virus check and malware check as appropriate on the working copies. Now proceed using the clean working copy. During the technical analysis, the file formats of the digital records need to be surveyed and assessed. There are registries and software tools available to help perform and interpret your survey. See appendix B for suggested software and a brief description of tasks they can do. Archivists have turned to the field of forensics in particular for software tools to analyze digital files. Archivists have also developed software and systems themselves to obtain products that respect archival principles, apply archival standards, and perform the requisite tasks. Appendix B includes open-source and commercial software, some of which perform a narrow range of tasks, while others are more comprehensive systems that perform multiple functions. The POWRR [Preserving (Digital) Objects with Restricted Resources] website provides a handy visual chart listing which OAIS functions each software performs.

The Impact of Decisions

Lest the weight of appraisal decisions, mechanical problems accessing files, poor metadata, and other hurdles overwhelm, there is hope. Figure 4.1 is based on research on preserving interactive multimedia art. Although text documents and photographs are less similar, web pages, social media, and some other file types are more similar to interactive art.

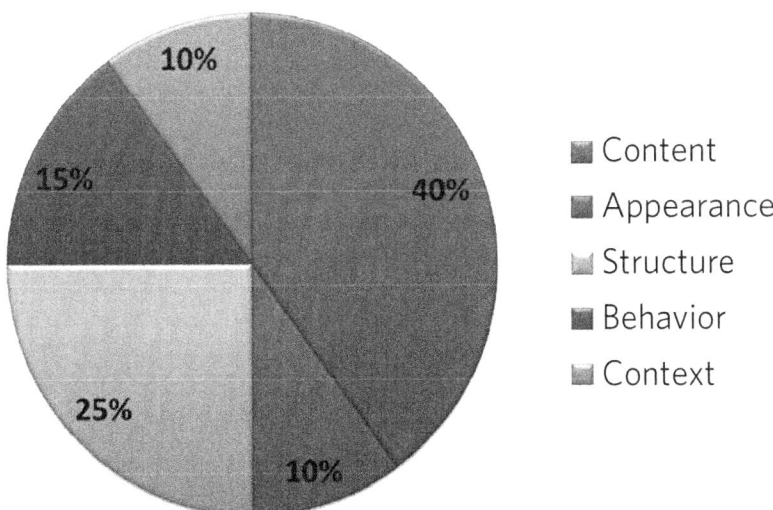

Figure 4.1 Importance of Object Characteristics. *Source*: Christoph Becker, Günther Kolar, Josef Küng, Andreas Rauber, "Preserving Interactive Multimedia Art: A Case Study in Preservation Planning," paper presented at International Conference on Asian Digital Libraries, Hanoi, Vietnam, December 10–13, 2007, accessed July 16, 2016, http://www.planets-project.eu/docs/presentations/ICADL_2007_ChristophBecker_Interactiveart.pdf.

Note that, according to Becker, Kolar, Küng, and Rauber's study, the most important quality to preserve is the file content, followed by its structure. These are qualities that archivists have a reasonably good chance of capturing and preserving. When context is added, these three qualities account for 75 percent of the interpretation of a file. While a great deal of concern is attached to appearance and behavior, even when added together, they account for only 25 percent of what is significant about a file. This is encouraging news for those who may be concerned about the challenge of preserving digital files. Archivists have stressed content, context, and structure as vital qualities to capture, regardless of whether records are analog or digital. This is something archivists understand and can do. We are three-quarters of the way there. The question is, How much of the limited resources available should we expend to more fully preserve any given file or digital object? Which files are worth expending extra resources to reach 80 or 90 percent or more? Also, what will be the impact on successive future iterations of file migration if the first iteration only captures 75 percent of the file characteristics?

Program Considerations

If an archives intends to develop a digital program, there are several tasks that would support not only appraisal and acquisition but also a larger integrated approach. As part of its collection policy, the archives would develop a list of file formats that it can support and will accept, a list of those it is unable to accept, and possibly a list of formats it will accept but is unable to preserve. Similar decisions may be made about storage devices on which files are stored. A visual chart can be created with a green heading for acceptable formats, yellow for those accepted but not to be preserved, and red for unacceptable formats. Formats could be further grouped by function: text, audio, still image, and so on. Acceptable formats would be based on file sustainability qualities. These could also be formats to which other less preferred formats are migrated or normalized. Potential donors would be advised of preferred formats, while institutional records creators would be advised to use preferred formats for permanent records creation.

Chapter 2 already raises the question of developing an appraisal tool or matrix evaluating a body of records against a standard set of qualities chosen by the archives, qualities that are assigned a scoring value and potentially prioritized. The score for higher-ranked qualities are higher compared to lower-ranked qualities. The benefit of such a matrix would be to improve appraisal consistency, potentially set a minimum quality level for new acquisitions, and objectively assess preservation needs or issues and prioritize processing work. In 2004, Stanford University conducted research on an automated appraisal matrix for digital files. The project said it conducted a preservation assessment, but it could equally be called micro or technical appraisal. The matrix rated the digital files on five sustainability factors identified by the LC (see "Additional Reading and Resources" at the end of this chapter). Other factors could be added to the matrix for a fuller technical appraisal.

Notes

1. F. Gerald Ham, *Selecting and Appraising Archives and Manuscripts*, Archival Fundamentals Series (Chicago: Society of American Archivists, 1993), 95; University of Oxford and University of Manchester, "Appraisal and Disposal," chap. 4 in *Paradigm: Workbook on Digital Private Papers*, last modified January 2, 2008, http://www.paradigm.ac.uk/workbook/appraisal/appraisal-approaches.html.

2. See Richard Pearce-Moses, *A Glossary of Archival and Records Terminology* (Chicago: Society of American Archivists, 2005), s.v. "macro appraisal," accessed July 8, 2016. I use the term *macroappraisal* here as

a contrast to microappraisal or technical appraisal of the packaging or carrier of digital content. Another definition of *macroappraisal* focuses on the role of the records creators and why and how the records were created in contrast to Schellenberg's assessment of the informational value.

3. Pearce-Moses, *Glossary*, s.v. "record copy," accessed July 8, 2016, http://www2.archivists.org/glossary/terms/r/record-copy#.V3_XVKIYFHo.

4. Mark J. Myers, "Appraisal of Electronic Records," Society of American Archivists, Digital Archives Specialist workshop, Richmond, KY, June 21, 2013, course booklet, 11.

5. Mark J. Myers, "Electronic Records: The Next Step," Society of American Archivists Digital Archives Specialist webinar, April 13, 2015, 90.

6. National Archives and Records Administration, *Appraisal Policy of the National Archives and Records Administration* (Washington, DC: National Archives and Records Administration, n.d.), accessed June 26, 2016, https://www.archives.gov/records-mgmt/publications/appraisal-policy.pdf.

7. Neil Beagrie, ed., "Acquisition and Appraisal," in *Digital Preservation Coalition*, rev. 2nd ed. (Glasgow: Digital Preservation Coalition, 2015), accessed June 19, 2016, http://handbook.dpconline.org/organisational-activities/acquisition-and-appraisal.

8. Beagrie, "Acquisition and Appraisal."

9. University of Oxford and University of Manchester, "Appraisal and Disposal."

10. Myers, "Appraisal of Electronic Records," 19–20.

11. Ross Harvey, "Keeping, Forgetting, and Misreading Digital Material: Libraries Learning from Archives and Recordkeeping Practice," Whyte memorial lecture, Monash University, Melbourne, Australia, September 15, 2015, accessed January 1, 2016, https://rossharveynet2016.files.wordpress.com/2016/01/harvey_whyte_lecture_2015.pdf.

12. I first heard Mark J. Myers use the terms *macroappraisal* and *microappraisal* to distinguish the two types of appraisal for digital records while attending the SAA Appraisal of Electronic Records workshop, June 2013.

13. "Information and Documentation—Records Management—Part 1: General," *International Standard Organization*, ref. no. ISO 15489-1, 2001, 7, accessed October 15, 2016, http://www.wgarm.net/ccarm/docs-repository/doc/doc402817.PDF; Authenticity Task Force, "Appendix 2: Requirements for Assessing and Maintaining the Authenticity of Electronic Records," *InterPARES Project*, March 2002, 1, accessed November 24, 2016, http://www.interpares.org/display_file.cfm?doc=interpares_book_k_app02.pdf; Myers, "Appraisal of Electronic Records," 5.

14. Myers, "Electronic Records"; Myers, "Appraisal of Electronic Records," 37.

15. Myers, "Electronic Records."

16. Myers, "Appraisal of Electronic Records," 36.

17. Myers, "Appraisal of Electronic Records," 34–35.

18. Myers, "Appraisal of Electronic Records," 36, and oral lecture.

19. Myers, "Appraisal of Electronic Records," 34.

20. Myers, "Appraisal of Electronic Records," oral lecture.

21. Myers, "Electronic Records."

22. Myers, "Appraisal of Electronic Records," 37.

23. Myers, "Appraisal of Electronic Records," 37.

24. Myers, "Appraisal of Electronic Records," 38.

25. Myers, "Appraisal of Electronic Records," 22.

26. Myers, "Appraisal of Electronic Records," 22.

27. Myers, "Appraisal of Electronic Records," 22.

28. Myers, "Appraisal of Electronic Records," 25.

29. Myers, "Appraisal of Electronic Records," 25.

30. Myers, "Appraisal of Electronic Records," 25.

31. Myers, "Appraisal of Electronic Records," oral lecture.

Additional Reading and Resources

AIMS Team. *Born Digital Archives Blog*. Accessed August 28, 2016. http://born-digital-archives. blogspot.com. This blog was created as part of the work of the AIMS project to communicate with the digital archives community. Older posts may interest those who are new to digital preservation, as was the author, who shares his learning experience.

AIMS Work Group. *AIMS Born-Digital Collections: An Inter-Institutional Model for Stewardship*. 2012. Accessed August 2, 2016. http://www2.lib.virginia.edu/aims/whitepaper/AIMS_final .pdf. Pages 108–12 in appendix F include a thorough range of questions to ask a private do- nor about their practices for digital file creation, storage, and usage. Some questions would certainly also apply to organizational offices or users. Stanford University shares their work- flow sequence and digital tools, from preaccessioning through delivery and access, on pages 120–23. Appendix G describes several software tools for gathering information about files for appraisal, accessioning, and writing a processing plan (AccessData FTK Imager, Karen's Directory Printer) and possible solutions in case of difficulty reading 5¼" floppy disks.

Anderson, Richard, Hannah Frost, Nancy Hoebelheinrich, and Keith Johnson. "The AIHT at Stan- ford University Automated Preservation Assessment of Heterogeneous Digital Collections." *DLib* 12 (December 2005). Accessed August 14, 2016. doi:10.1045/december2005-johnson. This article describes a test to automate the preservation assessment of digital files (i.e., technical appraisal) to determine the long-term sustainability of their file formats. Designed by the LC, five of their sustainability factors are used for the assessment. A better view of Stan- ford's "Format Scoring Matrix" is available at http://www.dlib.org/dlib/december05/johnson/

Table1.pdf. Even without software to execute this work, the matrix illustrates how digital file appraisal might be standardized based on recognized factors.

"ArchivesSpace-Archivematica-DSpace Workflow Integration." *Bentley Historical Library, University of Michigan.* Accessed August 27, 2016. http://archival-integration.blogspot.com. The grant project blog talks about the team's work on Archivematica. Read Mike Shallcross's June 15, 2015, post in particular, with specifics of their appraisal process, including software tools and illustrations.

AV Preserve (Bertram Lyons). "An Introduction to Using Command Line Interface (CLI) to Work with Files and Directories (AV Preserve)." *Council of State Archivists (CoSA).* Last modified October 20, 2015. https://www.statearchivists.org/resource-center/resource-library/introduction -using-command-line-interface-cli-work-files-and-directories-av-preserve. The native command line interface in Windows or Mac is a tool that can be used to help organize metadata about digital files that may be produced by software mentioned in this chapter in order to better appraise the files. There are separate versions of the tutorial for Windows and Mac.

Barrera-Gomez, Julianna, and Ricky Erway. *Walk This Way: Detailed Steps for Transferring Born Digital Content from Media You Can Read In-House.* Dublin, OH: OCLC Reports, 2013. Accessed June 16, 2016. http://www.oclc.org/research/publications/library/born-digital-reports.html #walkthisway. This follow-up report to *You've Got to Walk before You Can Run* provides more detailed step-by-step directions for novices on how to transfer files from external media storage to a computer, with links to appropriate software tools and additional research suited for each particular step or task. This is very practically oriented guidance.

Beagrie, Neil, ed. "Acquisition and Appraisal." In *Digital Preservation Handbook.* Rev. 2nd ed. Glasgow: Digital Preservation Coalition, 2015. Accessed June 19, 2016. http://handbook .dpconline.org/organisational-activities/acquisition-and-appraisal. This section of the handbook addresses acquisition and appraisal, including policies, workflows, an interactive decision tree, ingest of digital files, and resources.

Boles, Frank, and Julia Marks Young. "Exploring the Black Box: The Appraisal of University Administrative Records." *American Archivist* 48 (Spring 1985): 121–40. This frequently cited article on appraisal theory discusses measuring the information value of a set of records against the cost to preserve it.

"Comparison of Early Word Processors." *Wikipedia.* Accessed August 9, 2016. https://en.wikipedia .org/wiki/Comparison_of_early_word_processors. This page lists word-processing software in 1985 with the computers that used them.

"Deep Blue Preservation and Format Support Policy." *University of Michigan.* Last update March 9, 2011. Accessed November 12, 2016. https://deepblue.lib.umich.edu/static/about/deepblue preservation.html. Although this is dated, it is often cited and is an example of a policy about which support will be given to categories of file formats.

Erway, Ricky. *You've Got to Walk before You Can Run: First Steps for Managing Born-Digital Content Received on Physical Media.* Dublin, OH: OCLC Reports, 2012. Accessed June 16, 2016. http:// www.oclc.org/content/dam/research/publications/library/2012/2012-06.pdf. Beginners should read this report before Barrera-Gomez and Erway's *Walk This Way.* This is a more basic companion that starts with inventorying. It also instructs how to transfer digital files from external media to a computer in eleven steps.

Esteva, Maria, Weijia Xu, Suyog Dutt Jain, Jennifer L. Lee, and Wendy K. Martin. "Assessing the Preservation Condition of Large and Heterogeneous Electronic Records Collections with Visualization." *International Journal of Digital Curation* 6, no. 1 (2011): 45–57. Accessed August 9, 2016. http://www.ijdc.net/index.php/ijdc/article/view/162/230. This article discusses using visualization techniques to assess the preservation condition of large collections of digital files. The same general concept of visualization can be applied to appraisal. Several software applications that create tree maps are mentioned in other entries here.

National Archives and Records Administration. *Appraisal Policy of the National Archives and Records Administration.* Washington, DC: National Archives and Records Administration, n.d. Accessed June 26, 2016. https://www.archives.gov/records-mgmt/publications/appraisal-policy.pdf. This brochure includes appraisal questions to ask in general and also for a few specific types of information.

———. "Bulletin 2015-04: Metadata Guidance for the Transfer of Permanent Electronic Records." *National Archives.* September 15, 2015. Accessed October 26, 2016. https://www.archives.gov/records-mgmt/bulletins/2015/2015-04.html. This NARA bulletin details the Dublin Core metadata fields recommended for use to describe digital records about to be transferred to the archives.

Nelson, Naomi L., Seth Shaw, Nancy Deromedi, Michael Shallcross, Cynthia Ghering, Lisa Schmidt, Michelle Belden, Jackie R. Esposito, Ben Goldman, and Tim Pyatt. *Managing Born-Digital Special Collections and Archival Materials.* SPEC Kit 329. Washington, DC: Association of Research Libraries, 2012. Four universities share their policies on file formats on pages 127–52.

NISO Framework Working Group. *A Framework of Guidance on Building Good Digital Collections.* 3rd ed. Baltimore, MD: National Information Standards Organization, 2007. Accessed August 15, 2016. http://www.niso.org/publications/rp/framework3.pdf. Section 2 of this report, "Objects," also discusses format registries, good formats, and related standards for those formats. Text, photographs, and audio and video formats are all included.

"PERTTS Portal." *Council of State Archivists (CoSA).* 2017. Accessed August 6, 2016. https://www.statearchivists.org/pertts. The PERTTS portal, or Program for Electronic Records Training, Tools, and Standards, includes a lot of training and education resources for digital records. Look at the self-directed training modules in particular for digital tools and guides (https://www.statearchivists.org/pertts/education-training). A resource guide (https://www.statearchivists.org/resource-center/resource-library) includes tools, policies, forms, educational resources, and more.

"Sustainability of Digital Formats: Planning for Library of Congress Collections." *Library of Congress.* Accessed August 14, 2016 http://www.digitalpreservation.gov/formats/index.shtml. This useful site discusses formats; sustainability; factors for specific types of records, like still and moving images and sound, among other types; and specific format descriptions. It aids technical appraisal of digital files by identifying format obsolescence and guiding which formats to (not) accept.

"The Tufts University Transfer Agreement Form: User Guide." *Tufts University*. September 2011. Accessed August 14, 2016. http://dca.lib.tufts.edu/taper-docs/taf_user-guide.pdf. This is the user guide for the Tufts Submission Agreement Builder Tool, a software tool Tufts developed to automate the process of transferring digital files to their archives while collecting mandatory information. The software is available at https://github.com/TuftsUniversity/sabt. The Digital Curation Centre provides additional details at http://www.dcc.ac.uk/resources/external/tufts-submission-agreement-builder-tool.

University of Oxford and University of Manchester. *Paradigm: Workbook on Digital Private Papers*. Last modified January 2, 2008. http://www.paradigm.ac.uk/workbook/index.html. Chapter 4 on appraisal of digital records is the most pertinent for this book's chapter. The section titled "Appraising Digital Records: A Worthwhile Exercise?" debates the pros and cons of appraisal for digital records. Note that this project is British, and there are variations between British and American archival practice. This project focuses on personal papers, not institutional or public records.

5

Accessioning Archival Records

Accessioning is the process of taking physical and legal custody of a new acquisition and documenting its receipt in a register, log, or database of the organization's holdings.[1] Records received from an external source need to be accessioned to document their receipt. Records created internally already belong to the organization. Typically, a transfer form documents their arrival. However, it may be useful to also assign an accession number to track that particular set of records. If the transfer includes digital records, it will require a unique identification number (UID). Accession numbers are frequently used for this purpose.

Many archivists consider description to begin when accessioning a body of records starts. This is truer now than ever before with the availability of collection management software designed for archives. Information about the records' source, type, quantity, information content, and storage location entered for accessioning can automatically populate fields used by the control or donor files, finding aid, and other access tools and description. This automation will save time that can be used for other tasks.

The same types of information typically recorded for analog records are still collected for digital records but with additional information required for the latter. Different tools are used to gather information on digital files, and this information can be recorded and used in new ways. New uses include creating a submission information package (SIP) for the open archival information system (OAIS) framework or a record in a digital or institutional repository.

Accession information can be recorded in a word-processed form, a spreadsheet, or the accession module of a content management system. Paper accession forms can be collected in a binder. Although a basic, low-tech method, it doesn't allow for easy searching across forms to identify multiple accessions for the same record group or collection. Electronic spreadsheets are available from a variety of software and can be kept in a common digital location accessible by all staff. This option provides easy searches based on any characteristic recorded in a field. Spreadsheet information might be linkable to other software or descriptive tools, depending on one's technical skills, time, and software compatibility. When both the accession information and the descriptive tools reside in the same software system, they are already designed to automatically reuse the appropriate accessioning information in the description. Such systems require funds and technical support. Some institutions choose to use their accession record as their minimum description for the materials and make both the accession record and the archival materials available to researchers once the accession record is completed.

"Accessioning has four main functions: physical and administrative transfer of records; review of general content and condition of records; creation of initial control tools; and assessment of future needs for arrangement, description, and preservation."[2] During accessioning, a number of tasks are performed. If a control or donor file has not yet been established, it is created now. The deed of gift is filed there. An accession record is created, capturing the information the archives has determined to be important. A copy can also go in the control file to link the donor to specific accessions. In order to complete the accession form, the archivist needs to examine the acquisition. For analog materials, this includes a review of the information content, dates, format types, and quantities and a determination of whether the materials need to be rehoused in order to safely store them or make them fit shelving configurations. One might note the presence of excessive quantities of a single item for weeding. An assessment of the physical condition of the records themselves with an eye toward preservation needs might occur now. Once the accession record is completed and the records are shelved, they may sit there for years before they receive further work.

In the case of digital files, their nature necessitates a shift in the analog workflow sequence. A preservation assessment must be done much sooner for digital records in order to prevent data loss or the inability to access the data due to software or hardware changes. Major issues with a new acquisition should already have been identified during appraisal and potentially determined that they are not acquired; however, issues will remain. The short lifespan for software and hardware dominate potential tasks. Files need to be moved from external media with a short lifespan to a safer, more stable preservation environment. Media formats that are obsolete or nearing obsolescence should be a high priority. The same is true of older file formats, but those may be unknown until the files themselves are analyzed, hence the importance of conducting a preservation assessment early on.

Open Archival Information System (OAIS) Framework

The Consultative Committee for Space Data Systems is an international body of space agencies for developing data-handling standards to support space research. They were asked by the International Organization for Standardization (ISO) to develop archival standards for long-term storage of digital data. The Consultative Committee for Space Data Systems developed a conceptual framework called the OAIS model. The first draft was released in 1997, and the framework was approved in January 2002 as ISO standard 14721.[3]

The OAIS reference model, shown in figure 5.1, has six functions: ingest, archival storage, data management, administration, access, and preservation planning. The ingest function is discussed here due to its relevance to accessioning. Ingest is the process for transferring digital files from their creator and preparing them for archival storage and management within an OAIS. Tufts University's *Ingest Guide* describes ingest as the "entire process involved in moving records from a record keeping system to a preservation system." The digital files and metadata, as received from the producer, as well as metadata added during accessioning are called a SIP.[4] Ingest starts with development of and agreement to a submission agreement detailing which records will be transferred, acceptable file formats, file decryption and password resolution, required metadata and documentation, and the manner of their transfer. The total file size may influence the transfer method, or there may be a maximum capacity determined by system limitations. Once details are agreed on, the actual transfer occurs.

Files to be transferred internally or accepted from an external donor may be stored in a variety of locations. The transfer process aims to copy those files from these diverse locations to a location

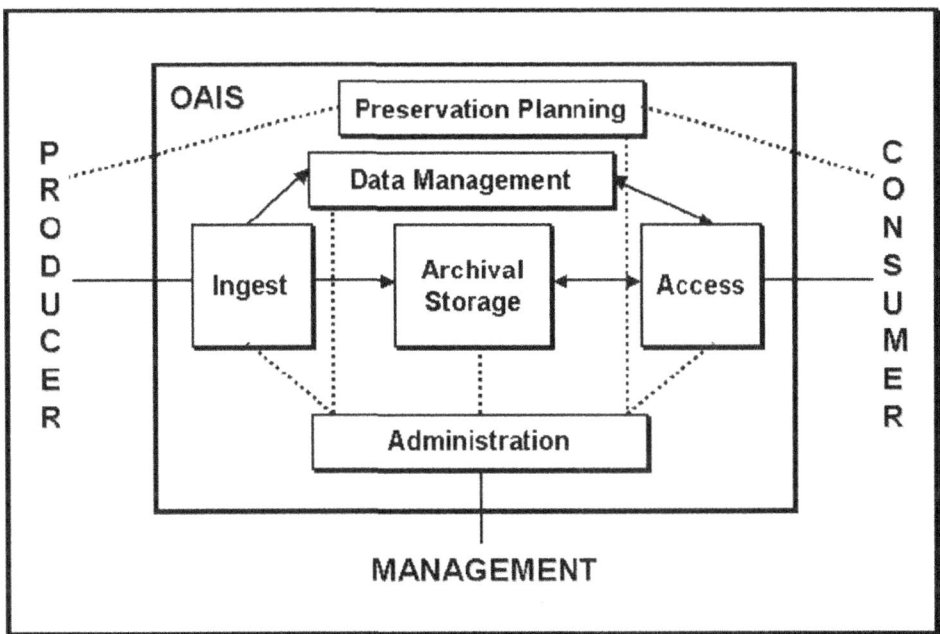

Figure 5.1 OAIS Reference Model. *Source*: Brian F. Lavoie, *The Open Archival Information System Reference Model: An Introductory Guide* (Dublin, OH: Office of Research, Online Computer Library Center, January 2004), 8, accessed September 27, 2016, http://www.dpconline.org/docman/technology-watch-reports/91-introduction-to-oais/file.

chosen by the archives in the manner least likely to alter the files while simultaneously capturing metadata and file structure. The easiest original sources to work with are external storage devices, preferably of a current type. This would include laptops, external hard drives, CDs and DVDs, probably Zip and 3½" floppy disks, and maybe flash drives. OCLC's reports *Walk This Way* and *You've Got to Walk before You Can Run* (see "Additional Reading and Resources" at the end of this chapter) provide excellent guidance on how to transfer files from external media. A single file can be transferred as an e-mail attachment, but file transfer protocol (FTP), Dropbox, or Google Drive are methods that have the capacity to transfer more or larger files.[5] Web crawlers or web archiving software may capture files on websites or social media. "A simple and easy-to-use application for remotely and safely transferring any born-digital material from a sender to a recipient" is Exactly. The recipient can "create customized metadata templates for the sender to fill out before submission." Exactly begins the "activities of establishing provenance and fixity early in the process of acquisition." It uses the BagIt file packaging format, an Internet Engineering Task Force standard developed by the Library of Congress and others.[6]

Once transferred, the files require immediate validation to determine whether everything that was sent was received, uncorrupted, and complete.[7] If not, this step is repeated until successful or canceled. Validation tasks include running virus and malware checks and calculating a checksum for the transfer as a whole and for individual files. If a digital "bag" was used to transfer the files, it will include a pretransfer checksum to which the posttransfer checksum can be compared. If there is no pretransfer checksum for the transfer, the checksums from this step will be used going forward to document that no data has been lost or corrupted. Once validation is completed, depending on the media source for the files, a disk image can be created. A working or access set of files should be made and put in a clearly labeled folder separate from the originally transferred files. The original files after validation should be treated as preservation masters, put in their own clearly labeled folder, and kept unused and therefore unaltered. The next step is to stabilize the working copies of the files. This is comparable to a preliminary preservation assessment, the check for insects or mold, or the reboxing that might be done for analog records upon receipt. This would include identifying file format types, including obsolete or unknown formats; determining date created and last modified; and capturing the file structure and directory paths and possibly a high-level file name list.[8] This technical metadata needs to be recorded and stored with or linked to the files being preserved. The SIP also requires a unique identifier to link the files with its metadata. Based on institution policies and requirements of its archival storage system or software, there may be additional tasks required to make the SIP acceptable to the system.[9] The final step in creating a stabilized SIP is to transfer the files to be preserved and their metadata to archival storage. Although archival records and their description or metadata are a logical unit, they are not typically stored together. A software wrapper can combine all the components of the SIP together while in storage until there is time to process and convert it to an archival information package (AIP). Bagger software developed by the Library of Congress for file transfer is often used for this purpose. While stabilized SIPS sit in storage until they can be processed, maintenance functions should be performed to keep their authenticity, integrity, reliability, and usability intact.

Table 5.1 shows a sample workflow to accession a new digital acquisition and create a stable SIP. Column 1 lists the tasks sequentially. Column 3 identifies the accession functions, qualities desirable for digital preservation, and archival function with which the task is associated. Column 4 lists the OAIS functions with which a task is associated.

Table 5.1. Sample Workflow to Accession and Create a Stable SIP

Task	Record Here	Archival Task	OAIS Requirement	Notes
Accession				
Transfer files. See separate list for methods.		Accession: Physical transfer or control[†]		
Log receipt of file transfers.	Where?	Accession: Physical transfer or control[†]		
Connect to processing station.				Stand alone, write blockers, antivirus and malware.
Run virus scan and malware check if not done during appraisal.		Preservation		
Run checksum on files as received.	AIP>PDI> manifests	Preservation	Technical; Fixity	Get checksum for whole transfer or media and also each file. If you don't calculate file level now, complete prior to finalizing accessioning.

(continued)

Task	Record Here	Archival Task	OAIS Requirement	Notes
Confirm all files transferred successfully.		Preservation; Ingest: Validation*; Authenticity‡		If yes, then notify internal transfers that it is OK to delete their copy. If no, then repeat transfer process.
Assign unique ID or accession number.	SIP/AIP> PDI> Reference	Accession: Control tool†	Reference	Must link to description. Link to accession log?
Create accession record or transfer form.	Accession log; also SIP/ AIP>PDI> provenance/ control file?			
Set up new AIP template for this accession.				
Create SIP/AIP> PDI>original_files_ locked folder and populate with transferred or donated files.	SIP/AIP>- original_ files_locked (folder of masters as received and accessioned only)	Appraisal; Preservation; Authenticity‡		If not done during appraisal, then create a disk image, a preservation or master copy of the digital files, or both. Do not use unless all copies are lost. Maintain in secure, backed-up location!
Create work copies.	SIP/AIP> processed_ work_copies folder	Appraisal; Preservation		Work copies may have been created during appraisal. If not, create now, and use these work copies for all future tasks. Initially, files are unprocessed despite folder label. Determine where to store folder until processed.
Which tasks fulfill the OAIS technical metadata?	SIP/AIP>- Content Informa- tion>Rep- resentation Information		Technical metadata	Which software, hardware, or other is needed to use and view files? Authenticity: Is file what it purports to be? Formats: rights owners and control of access.
Identify file format types (and ver- sions), quantity, and storage size.	AIP>PDI> manifests; accession record	Context: Authenticity‡; Accession: Records condition and preservation needs†	Technical metadata	Metadata recorded as structured data (XML or spreadsheet) could be ingested into an archival data management repository per AIMS, chap. 2, p. 28, obj. 3. File format also called preservation metadata in non-OAIS systems.
Determine file creation dates and date last modified (range for all files).	SIP/AIP> PDI>mani- fests; acces- sion form	Context: Authenticity‡	Technical metadata	Metadata recorded as structured data (XML or spreadsheet) could be ingested into an archival data management repository per AIMS, chap. 2, p. 28, obj. 3.

(continued)

Task	Record Here	Archival Task	OAIS Requirement	Notes
Record the above information.	Determine where.			As a start to collection control file? To use as accession record? Save in SIP/AIP>PDI>provenance/control folder; add to "Jump-In" spreadsheet for repository digital file inventory?
Identify obsolete or unknown file formats.	Record? Where?	Accession: Records condition and preservation needs[†]; Usability[‡]		Note presence and need to migrate or normalize during processing.
Check for personally identifiable information.	Record? Where?	Confidentiality		Mark or segregate or delete?
Determine rights and record.	SIP/AIP>PDI>Access Rights	Copyright: Access	Technical metadata?	Administrative metadata in non-OAIS models.
Run software to capture file directory paths.	SIP/AIP>PDI>manifests	Authenticity[‡]: Context? Structure[‡]	Structural metadata; also technical? Also descriptive.	How records are organized, how parts relate to whole, path, and folder structures. Other software? Tasks? Does this capture high-level file name list? Per AIMS, chap. 2, p. 27, obj. 2, get this. Metadata recorded as structured data (XML or spreadsheet) could be ingested into an archival data management repository per AIMS, chap. 2, p. 28, obj. 3.
Analyze file structure sufficiently to briefly describe content for accession record?	Accession record and?	Accession: Content review[†]		
Any other tasks required to create SIP?				
Can normalize original and work copies now or when processing.	SIP/AIP>PDI>log and "Notes" element DACS 7 and PREMIS	Preservation	Preservation	Record preservation actions, like migration, in "Notes" element DACS 7 and in PREMIS as event and PDI>log. AIMS, p. 30, tasks.
Check for duplicate files now or later?				Use checksums to identify duplicates.

(continued)

Task	Record Here	Archival Task	OAIS Requirement	Notes
Files should be copied from original media by this point; what to do with the media?				Photograph labels on the media if disposing of original media or routinely capture?
If accession record is external, save a copy in SIP to use later for processing.	Where? SIP/AIP>PDI>provenance/control	Processing		
Bundle all files now and create SIP?				Leave in one package or split files, or copy part and move to workspace?
Assign processing priority for the accession, collection, or AIP?	Master holdings management log, Archives Space	Management		
Transfer stabilized SIP to preservation storage.				
Verify transfer by checksums in preservation storage location.		Authenticity‡; Integrity‡; Reliability‡; Usability‡		

Sources: Seth E. Shaw, "Arrangement and Description of Electronic Records, Part I," Society of American Archivists Digital Archives Specialist workshop, Chapel Hill, NC, June 11, 2015, course booklet 134, 94, 114, 136, 78, 134, 104, 92, 99, 102; Shawn Averkamp, "Overview of Metadata for Archivists," Society of American Archivists Digital Archives Specialist webinar, June 19, 2015, slide 15; Seth E. Shaw, "Arrangement and Description of Electronic Records, Part II," Society of American Archivists Digital Archives Specialist workshop, Chapel Hill, NC, June 12, 2015, course booklet 16, 24, 22, 20, 118; Erin Faulder, "Accessioning and Ingest of Electronic Records," Society of American Archivists Digital Archives Specialist workshop, Lexington, KY, May 6, 2015, slide 9; Consultative Committee for Space Data Systems (CCSDS), *Reference Model for an Open Archival Information System (OAIS) Recommended Practice CCSDS 650.0-M-2* (Washington, DC: CCSDS Secretariat, June 2012), 2-6–2-7, accessed January 15, 2017, https://public.ccsds.org/Pubs/650x0m2.pdf; OCLC/RLG Working Group on Preservation Metadata, *Preservation Metadata and the OAIS Information Model: A Metadata Framework to Support the Preservation of Digital Objects* (Dublin, OH:OCLC/RLG Working Group on Preservation Metadata, 2002), 40, accessed May 12, 2016, http://www.oclc.org/content/dam/research/activities/pmwg/pm_framework.pdf; J. Gordon Daines III, "Module 2: Processing Digital Records and Manuscripts," in *Archival Arrangement and Description*, edited and introduced by Christopher J. Prom and Thomas J. Frusciano, Trends in Archives Practice series (Chicago: Society of American Archivists, 2013), 117.

*Ingest functions
†Accession functions
‡Four qualities necessary to preserve digital files

If accessioning is seen as the first step the institution takes to manage a new acquisition, as preliminary work that lays the groundwork for additional work (like arrangement and description), its parallel can clearly be seen in the work performed during ingest to create a SIP. Whenever the ingest process is continued to transform the SIP into an AIP, the work in this phase parallels traditional archival processing, meaning at its core arranging and describing the records so they are ready for use. It is the equivalent of processing a collection or a new accretion to a record group.

Just as archivists perform tasks on analog records that stop short of fully processing them, whether that is an abbreviated MPLP version or something more complete, it is possible to perform essential tasks on a SIP to create a stabilized SIP and safely store it without having transformed it into an AIP.[10] This is an option that institutions should consider in order to prevent data loss pending the age and quantity of digital files waiting to be addressed. Obviously, SIPs would require further work to convert them to or make them a usable AIP.

Submission Information Package or Archival Information Package

As is described later in this chapter, figure 5.2 shows an OAIS-compliant AIP with its components. This figure may look intimidating initially, but much of it is information archivists understand with a different label. On the left is the content information; on the right, the preservation description information (PDI). The content information contains the content data object. This is the digital information to be preserved, the files received from their producer during ingest. The representation information is the information required "to render and make visible the Content Data [Object]."[11] It provides the necessary information that ensures the content can be understood. This could include hardware and software information and file extensions that may indicate the software used to create or read the file. It may include definitions, a key code, or other information to correctly interpret research data; a spreadsheet; or other information that may be known to the original creators but becomes less well-known, secondhand information to subsequent users.

The preservation description information is the value added by the archivist, the preservation metadata. It includes the content, context, and structure that help authenticate digital files. They

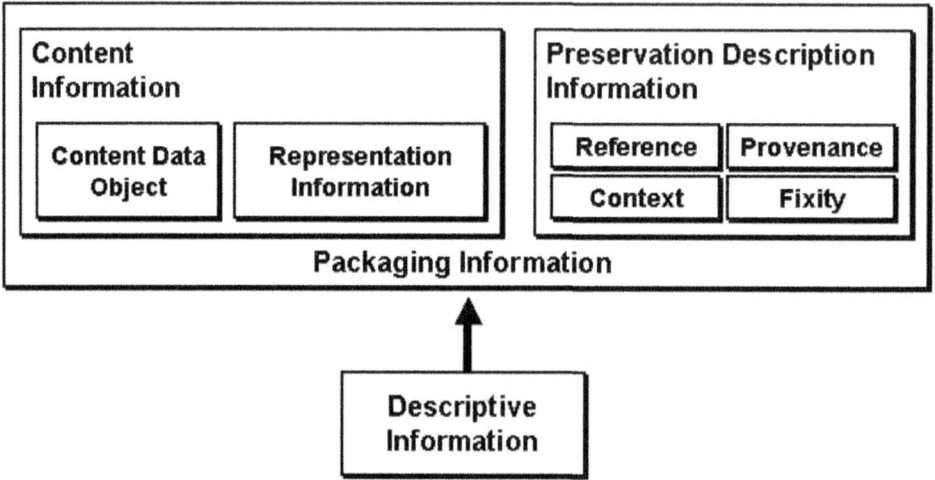

Figure 5.2 Submission Information Package or Archival Information Package. *Source*: Brian F. Lavoie, *The Open Archival Information System Reference Model: An Introductory Guide* (Dublin, OH: Office of Research, Online Computer Library Center, January 2004), 12, accessed September 27, 2016, http:// www.dpconline.org/docman/technology-watch-reports/91-introduction-to-oais/file.

are obtained from new sources, with new tools, and expressed differently than for analog records, but the concepts, their value, and use remain consistent.

The reference information is the most important component of the PDI. It is the unique identifier that links all metadata and description to the content information. The unique identifier is locally generated. Often the accession number is used as the unique identifier or unique ID number, although other numbering systems are acceptable, as long as each number is unique. Finding aids, catalog records, and other description or access tools for analog records are stored separately from the collections themselves. The same is generally true for digital records. The unique identifier is the crucial link between the two parts. If this link is broken, the content information is less useful and more difficult to understand and preserve.

Provenance is familiar. This includes the history of the records and other information that might be included in a donor or control file. Fixity is where all the checksums or hashtags that are generated are preserved. Fixity, checksums, and hashtags (ignoring Twitter) all refer to the same concept, a mathematical computation generated for comparison at future times to determine whether the digital file associated with it has been altered and possibly damaged. Context information documents the relationships to other information objects, files, or records. This may be the file structure of all the files in one AIP or the relationship to other accessions, SIPS, AIPS, or parts of a record group or collection. Access rights documents the terms for access, including any restrictions governing access and use of the content information.[12]

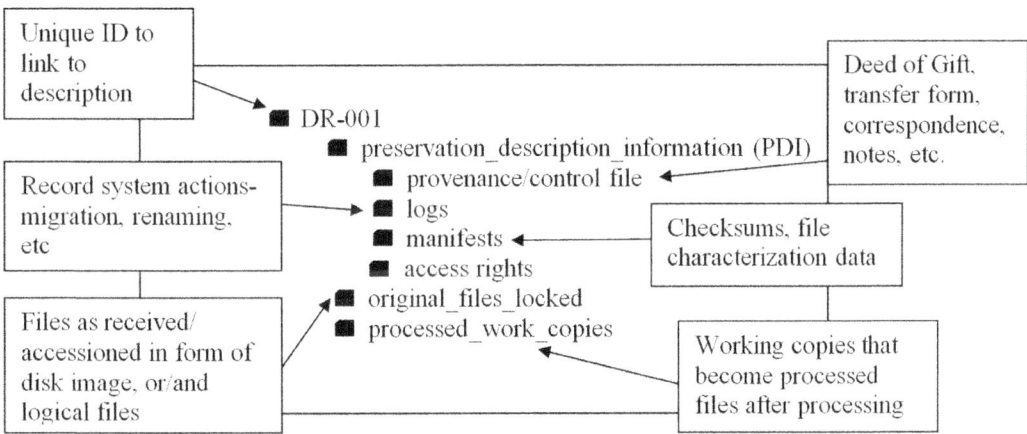

Figure 5.3 Template of Digital File Structure for Components in PDI. *Sources*: Seth E. Shaw, "Arrangement and Description of Electronic Records, Part I," Society of American Archivists Digital Archives Specialist workshop, Chapel Hill, NC, June 11, 2015, course booklet, 114, 138; J. Gordon Daines III, "Module 2: Processing Digital Records and Manuscripts," in *Archival Arrangement and Description*, edited and introduced by Christopher J. Prom and Thomas J. Frusciano, Trends in Archives Practice series (Chicago: Society of American Archivists, 2013), 117; Consultative Committee for Space Data Systems (CCSDS), *Reference Model for an Open Archival Information System (OAIS) Recommended Practice CCSDS 650.0-M-2* (Washington, DC: CCSDS Secretariat, June 2012), 4-30, accessed January 15, 2017, https://public.ccsds.org/Pubs/650x0m2 .pdf; OCLC/RLG Working Group on Preservation Metadata, *Preservation Metadata and the OAIS Information Model: A Metadata Framework to Support the Preservation of Digital Objects* (Dublin, OH:OCLC/RLG Working Group on Preservation Metadata, 2002), 40, accessed May 12, 2016, http://www.oclc.org/content/dam/ research/activities/pmwg/pm_framework.pdf.

Creating a PDI can be as simple as representing each component with a clearly labeled digital file folder in a template for digital processing. See figure 5.3. As initial ingest tasks are performed to create the accession record and stabilize the SIP, information can also be recorded in the AIP template. Refer back to table 5.1, column 2. This tells where to record information from the accession tasks to develop the SIP. The locations named in column 2 are shown in the digital file structure illustrated in figure 5.3. More information will be added later as the SIP is transformed into a processed, complete AIP. It is expected that eventually, when the digital records in figure 5.3 are processed, the whole unit as illustrated will be wrapped and stored in a preservation location to remain untouched except for preservation tasks (running periodic checksums, format migration, or similar). It means that nothing within the wrapper may be accessed or changed, or it invalidates the checksums, which will have to be rerun, and a note may be required to document what was changed. The inability to constantly access wrapped files to update information contained therein should be a consideration in deciding what to include or exclude from the wrapper. For example, this is one reason description should only be linked to rather than included inside the stabilized SIP or processed AIP. Description is frequently revised.

Table 5.2. Template for Components in PDI

Location	Components	Notes
Wrapped in BagIt	• original_files_locked • logs • checksums from manifest • processed_work_copies (optional preservation copy)	Include unique ID.
Provenance/control file	• stored separately in paper or digital control file or in archival collection management system	Associate the unique ID with the record group or collection in documentation in one of these locations.
Accession log	• accession number/unique ID • remainder of manifest except checksums? • access rights	
Description	• stored separately in archives normal location	Associate the unique ID with the description. In "Immediate Source of Acquisition" if using accession number for unique ID.

Table 5.2 shows an alternate version in which more minimal information is contained in the wrapper. Donor or control files (provenance) are maintained in the paper or digital locations normally used for all archival records rather than duplicated in the AIP. Information likely to be recorded in an accession record, accession log, or archival collection management system would also be retained there and not duplicated in the AIP. This alternate method is more likely to fit actual practice but requires careful adherence to linking all key components in order to ensure that the required information for managing digital files is still available at a future date when none of us are around in person to provide it. Recording decisions like the use of this alternate version, how the other components can be identified, and where they are located helps ensure those intellectual links are maintained.[13]

Chapter 5

Program Considerations

Standardization of acceptable file formats is discussed in chapter 4. Another programmatic task is development of processes by which the archives receives or accepts transfers of digital records. Variations on a general workflow are potentially affected by the original source of the files (computer hard drive versus institutional server, external server, external storage device), the file type (Word document, web page, CAD file, social media site, outdated software file), or even simply the quantity of files. As mentioned, files from private donors might not have been as actively managed and include damaged, outdated, and redundant files with personally identifiable or confidential information. Different management practices might require additional work or tasks for personal digital archives. The transfer process for private records may be dependent on the technical skill level of the donor. The transfer or donation process needs to collect standardized information and metadata about the records, particularly if the transfer process is automated.

As with analog records, sometimes the decisions archivists make depend on the quantity of records involved. In the case of a high volume of digital files on a regular basis, it is desirable to automate work as much as possible rather than perform it manually. The use of software tools to bulk process groups of digital records might also be seen as philosophically compatible with the MPLP trend that started about 2004 or 2005. Although the software would deal with records at the computer-file level, which in terms of archival arrangement is equivalent to the item level, the software could analyze large quantities of records rapidly, which might structurally be the equivalent of a file or series.

Both OCLC reports *You've Got to Walk before You Can Run* and *Walk This Way* discuss setting up a separate, dedicated workstation for processing digital records. This enables the practice of segregating incoming digital files until they have been checked for viruses and malware. Incoming analog records are checked to determine whether they will contaminate existing collections before they share storage space. It is the same concept. This workstation is likely to also have specialized software appropriate to the work. Decisions need to be made about where to hold transferred files, where to store them once they are SIPS, and which kind of backup will be created for files in these various stages. The process for running checksums needs to be determined. Will it be done manually, or can it be automated, and how frequently?

Another question is whether to accept SIPs, stabilize and store them, then return later to transform them into AIPs, or to complete all the necessary tasks at once to convert a SIP into an AIP before moving on to the next SIP.

Once files are transferred from external media, there is the question of what to do with the external media. I have hundreds of DVDs with photos from the university photographer. The photos on any given DVD may or may not relate to each other. The creation date is likely to be when they were put on the DVD, not when they were originally taken. I also know that the dates on some photos by this photographer are unreliable based on analysis of the visual contents. I suspect that, when his battery died, he didn't always reset the camera's date stamp. In this example, the file arrangement is not helpful, so I am also not planning on making disk images. I am considering transferring all photos on DVDs for a single calendar year into a single digital folder, running checksums to de-duplicate images, then stabilizing and setting aside for processing later. The DVDs are close to nine years old minimum. The amount of work necessary to provide access to the images on the DVDs would be better spent organizing the copies transferred to server space. In this case, I anticipate discarding the external media. If the disks were only a few years old and limited to two or three record series, I would be more likely to consider using them as access copies.

Finally, institutions should seriously weigh whether to normalize obsolete files when they stabilize SIPS or wait until processing. Is the risk of data loss so much greater now because of the quantity of digital records requiring work and the age of their current storage media that haste must be made and the risk of dealing with obsolete formats later is acceptable? Or can obsolete formats be dealt with now, with the result that stabilized SIPS may sit in storage for a while before they are processed into AIPs? The archives may decide on a case-by-case basis or make a blanket decision one way or the other. There is also the question of which file formats to normalize. Is normalization limited to obsolete formats, or are all text documents, for example, converted to PDF or PDF/A files?

Notes

1. Richard Pearce-Moses, *A Glossary of Archival and Records Terminology* (Chicago: Society of American Archivists, 2005), s.v. "accession," accessed September 26, 2016, http://www2.archivists.org/glossary/terms/a/accession.

2. AIMS Work Group, *AIMS Born-Digital Collections: An Inter-Institutional Model for Stewardship*, 2012, 17, accessed August 6, 2016, http://dcs.library.virginia.edu/files/2013/02/AIMS_final.pdf. In the print version, each of these four functions has its own symbol to distinguish them in column 3 of table 5.2 to help highlight these functions as applied to digital records. In the electronic version, these four functions are also color-coded.

3. Brian F. Lavoie, *The Open Archival Information System Reference Model: An Introductory Guide* (Dublin, OH: Office of Research, OCLC, January 2004), 3, accessed September 27, 2016, http://www.dpconline.org/docman/technology-watch-reports/91-introduction-to-oais/file. This is the Digital Preservation Coalition Technology Watch Report, 04-01 version.

4. Brian Lavoie, "Meeting the Challenges of Digital Preservation: The OAIS Reference Model," *OCLC Newsletter*, no. 243 (January/February 2000): 26–30, accessed September 27, 2016, http://www.oclc.org/research/publications/library/2000/lavoie-oais.html; Kevin Glick and Eliot Wilczek, *Fedora and the Preservation of University Records Project, 2.1 Ingest Guide, Version 1.0* (Medford, MA: Tufts University and Yale University, September 2006), 1, accessed September 29, 2016, http://dl.tufts.edu/catalog/tufts:UA069.004.001.00006; AIMS Work Group, appendix A, s.v. "SIP," in *AIMS Born-Digital Collections*, 30.

5. Mark J. Myers, "Electronic Records: The Next Step," Society of American Archivists Digital Archives Specialist webinar, April 13, 2015, slide 22.

6. "Tools," *AVPreserve*, accessed December 26, 2016, https://www.avpreserve.com/avpsresources/tools.

7. Lavoie, *Open Archival Information System*, 8.

8. AIMS Work Group, *AIMS Born-Digital Collections*, 27, 30. AIMS recommends normalizing both the preservation and access copies. Ben Goldman, "Bridging the Gap: Taking Practical Steps towards Managing Born-Digital Collections in Manuscript Repositories," *RBM: A Journal of Rare Books, Manuscripts, and Cultural Heritage* 12 (2011): 17, says the preservation copies "should be completely restricted, never accessed or opened by anyone, not even repository staff." Work copies are made for the staff, which eventually are used to create copies for researchers.

9. Lavoie, *Open Archival Information System*, 8.

10. Per AIMS Work Group, *AIMS Born-Digital Collections*, 30, the SIP can be stabilized and put into storage for processing later on.

11. Seth E. Shaw, "Arrangement and Description of Electronic Records, Part I," Society of American Archivists Digital Archives Specialist workshop, Chapel Hill, NC, June 11, 2015, course booklet, 72.

12. Shaw, "Arrangement and Description, Part I," 78; OCLC/RLG Working Group on Preservation Metadata, *Preservation Metadata and the OAIS Information Model: A Metadata Framework to Support the Preservation of Digital Objects* (Dublin, OH: OCLC/RLG Working Group on Preservation Metadata, 2002), 40, accessed May 12, 2016, http://www.oclc.org/content/dam/research/activities/pmwg/pm_framework.pdf; Consultative Committee for Space Data Systems (CCSDS), *Reference Model for an Open Archival Information System (OAIS), Magenta Book*, no. 2, CCSDS 650.0-M-2 (Washington, DC: CCSDS Secretariat, June 2012), 2-7.

13. Thanks to Seth Shaw for helping me clarify my thinking about what to include in the AIP wrapper.

Additional Reading and Resources

AIMS Work Group. *AIMS Born-Digital Collections: An Inter-Institutional Model for Stewardship.* 2012. Accessed June 26, 2016. http://dcs.library.virginia.edu/aims/white-paper. Section 2 is about accessioning and includes good information. Appendix F.1 includes a thorough range of questions to ask a private donor about their practices for digital file creation, storage, and usage. Some questions also apply to organizational offices or users. Appendix F.2 from the British University of Hull has a nice sample accessioning workflow indicating which steps to take depending on the format of the external media carrying digital files. Appendix F.5 provides guidance from Stanford University on agreements for acquisition of digital records. This is followed by Stanford's workflow for processing digital records. Appendix G.1:

> AccessData FTK (Forensic ToolKit) generates summary information on a collection (single floppy disk or a collection with floppy, Zip, CD, and hard disks) of files and provides different views of files, sophisticated search, bookmarking and labeling functions. This software can be used in the accessioning, arrangement and description phases of the AIMS framework for born digital material (AIMS Work Group, appendix G, in *AIMS Born-Digital Collections*, 125).

Appendix G.4: Karen's Directory Printer—"This software can be used to create a manifest of the files that have been transferred" to an archives before processing begins "that is within the accession phase of the AIMS framework, and can be used in conjunction with write-blockers" (AIMS Work Group, appendix G, in *AIMS Born-Digital Collections*, 4).

"Bagger." *World Digital Library*. Accessed October 9, 2016. https://project.wdl.org/arab_peninsula/workshop2012/en/doha_workshop_2012_bagger_en.pdf. This is an illustrated tutorial for both PCs and Macs on how to use Bagger software to transfer files.

Barrera-Gomez, Julianna, and Ricky Erway. *Walk This Way: Detailed Steps for Transferring Born-Digital Content from Media You Can Read In-House*. Dublin, OH: OCLC Reports, 2013. Accessed June 16, 2016. http://www.oclc.org/research/publications/library/born-digital-reports.html #walkthisway. This follow-up report to *You've Got to Walk before You Can Run* provides more detailed step-by-step directions for novices on how to transfer files from external media storage to a computer, with links to appropriate software tools and additional research suited for each particular step and task. This is very practically oriented guidance.

"Digital File Transfer Guidelines." *State Archives of North Carolina*. Last updated April 2015. http://www.archives.ncdcr.gov/Portals/3/PDF/guidelines/Transfer_Guidelines_Electronic_Records_2015.pdf. This document explains what to do to transfer files, including preferred formats and using Bagger software for the transfer.

Erway, Ricky. *You've Got to Walk before You Can Run: First Steps for Managing Born-Digital Content Received on Physical Media*. Dublin, OH: OCLC Reports, 2012. Accessed June 16, 2016. http://www.oclc.org/content/dam/research/publications/library/2012/2012-06.pdf. Beginners should read this report before *Walk This Way*. This is a more basic companion that starts with inventorying. It also instructs how to transfer digital files from external media to a computer in eleven steps.

Glick, Kevin, and Eliot Wilczek. *Fedora and the Preservation of University Records Project, 2.1 Ingest Guide, Version 1.0*. Medford, MA: Tufts University and Yale University, September 2006. Accessed September 29, 2016. http://dl.tufts.edu/catalog/tufts:UA069.004.001.00006. This is the ingest guide for the TAPER project. It describes a submission agreement and the tasks performed during ingest. It is based on the PAIMAS standard for ingest.

———. *Fedora and the Preservation of University Records Project, 3.1 Maintain Guide, Version 1.0*. Medford, MA: Tufts University and Yale University, September 2006. Accessed September 29, 2016. http://dl.tufts.edu/catalog/tufts:UA069.004.001.00009. This guide describes maintenance activities to perform after a stabilized SIP or AIP is placed in the archival storage component of an OAIS model.

Goldman, Ben. "Bridging the Gap: Taking Practical Steps toward Managing Born-Digital Collections in Manuscript Repositories." *RBM: A Journal of Rare Books, Manuscripts, and Cultural Heritage* 1 (2011): 11–24. Accessed June 16, 2016. http://rbm.acrl.org/content/12/1/11.full.pdf.

Huc, C., D. Boucon, D. M. Sawyer, and J. G. Garrett. "Producer-Archive-Interface Methodology Abstract Standard (PAIMAS)." Presentation at SpaceOps, Montreal, Canada, May 15, 2004. *https://nssdc.gsfc.nasa.gov/nost/isoas/presentations/paimas-spaceops2004.ppt*. This Power-Point explains the PAIMAS standard for ingest of digital files and details the steps in this process.

Kussman, Carol. "Bag-It and Bagger." *Minnesota Historical Society*. May 30, 2013. Accessed November 17, 2016. http://www.mnhs.org/preserve/records/docs_pdfs/BagIt-Bagger.pdf. This document presents information on how to use BagIt.

Nelson, Naomi L., Seth Shaw, Nancy Deromedi, Michael Shallcross, Cynthia Ghering, Lisa Schmidt, Michelle Belden, Jackie R. Esposito, Ben Goldman, and Tim Pyatt. *Managing Born-Digital Special Collections and Archival Materials*. SPEC Kit 329. Washington, DC: Association of Research Libraries, 2012. Duke University shares its accessioning workflow on page 154; Michigan State University, on page 179–80; and Yale, on page 196.

"North Carolina Digital Repository." *State Archives of North Carolina*. Accessed November 17, 2016. http://archives.ncdcr.gov/For-Government/Digital-Records/State-Archives-Digital-Repository#formats. This includes YouTube videos on the Bagger and BagIt process for digital file transfer.

"Princeton University Archives Transfer Form." *Princeton University Library, The Department of Rare Books and Special Collections*. 2016. Accessed December 17, 2016. http://rbsc.princeton.edu/princeton-university-archives-transfer-form. This is a good form that collects basic information the archives needs yet doesn't seem mysterious or onerous for the transferring office staff. It also asks one or two questions about access restrictions.

"SAN Bagging: How to Install and Use the BagIt Library to Create and Validate Bags." *North Carolina Office of Archives and History, Geospacial Multistate Archive and Preservation Partnership*. March 21, 2011. Accessed November 17, 2016. http://www.geomapp.net/docs/Using_BagIt_ver2_geomapp_FINAL_20110321.pdf. This is a detailed explanation of the process of using the BagIt software, including screenshots.

"Submission Agreements: Case Study One." *Tufts University Digital Collections and Archives*. Accessed October 8, 2016. http://sites.tufts.edu/dca/about-us/research-initiatives/taper-tufts-accessioning-program-for-electronic-records/project-documentation/submission-agreements-case-study-one. This case study is a nice example of how to analyze a prospective records transfer that is a hybrid of analog and digital records, and it presents useful information to capture in the submission agreement.

"TAPER: Tufts Accessioning Program for Electronic Records." *Tufts University Digital Collections and Archives*. Accessed August 6, 2016. http://sites.tufts.edu/dca/about-us/research-initiatives/taper-tufts-accessioning-program-for-electronic-records. Tufts University developed this software to create machine-readable submission agreements for electronic records. TAPER is flexible enough to apply to many types of born-digital materials.

University of Minnesota Libraries. *Electronic Records Task Force Final Report*. Minneapolis: University of Minnesota Electronic Records Task Force, 2015. Accessed January 1, 2016. http://hdl.handle.net/11299/174097. This excellent report provides a good practical model for starting a digital records program with steps, workflow, forms, and more.

"Web Archiving." *International Internet Preservation Consortium*. Accessed October 9, 2016. http://www.netpreserve.org/web-archiving/overview. This consortium was formed in 2003 to develop methods, tools, and standards for preserving portions of the World Wide Web. This is an informative primer on the topic and includes details on current software tools.

6

Archival Arrangement of Digital Records

Arrangement and description has been defined as the "process undertaken by an institution to establish intellectual control of the material following the physical control secured during accessioning. It also prepares the material for discovery by providing the user with information and context about the records, and prepares for access by applying appropriate restrictions."[1]

Chapter 2 presents the principles, theories, and notable concepts for the functions of arrangement and description. They are valid not only for analog formats but also for digital records. In chapter 3, an example of the workflow for processing, including arrangement and description, is detailed by function and then tasks within each function as performed for analog records. This same set of functions and tasks is then reordered to illustrate a new workflow for digital records based on needs dictated by their unique qualities.

Provenance remains relevant and important. Recall that it is one of four components in the preservation description information (PDI) of the OAIS framework for digital records. (Review figure 5.2.) Original order is more fluid with digital files. The creator can specify the electronic folder in which a file is located, but their order within the folder is determined by the file name, not the intellectual contents or its relationship to other files within the same folder. If the file creator is unorganized, the original order will be even more ambiguous because there will be fewer folders indicating any type of structure or degree of relatedness.

An archival record is defined as "data or information that has been fixed on some medium; that has content, context and structure."[2] Records in paper, photographic, audio, video, film, and digital format all meet this definition. Digital records share these qualities with their technological predecessors. In fact, it is the qualities of content, context, and structure, among others, that define a digital file as a record, not its digital format. Not all digital files are records, and not all digital files merit preservation. Authenticity is another important quality of archival records, regardless of format. Content, context, and structure are measures of authenticity for digital records, so they continue to help define archival records in general and play a specific role for digital records. Much of what archivists already know from managing analog records still defines, applies to, and is valid for this newest format—the digital record. Hybrid collections existed before digital records did, and now they include this format as well.

In chapter 3, the comparison of a possible workflow for analog and digital records shows the same functions and tasks for arrangement in both formats:

4. Decide intellectual arrangement

    4.a. Determine whether there is an original order.

    4.b. Identify relationships between the groups of materials within the record group or collection.

5. Arrange records, physically if necessary

    5.a. Arrange into subgroups, series, and subseries.

The manner and method of implementing arrangement, however, varies between the two formats.

Canadian archivist Terry Eastwood says provenance and original order reveal structural information about records. Provenance speaks to external structure, which distinguishes one record group from another, while original order reveals internal structure, how documents were ordered during the conduct of business affairs, and the relationships between them.[3] Paper-based records are physically organized in files labeled according to a classification scheme, linking the physical and contextual aspects of records. This has resulted in the association between original order and physical arrangement.

The use of electronic information technology does not alter the basic purpose of record making (i.e., to document the occurrence of a transaction),[4] but it is clearly challenging the concept of original order and how it is expressed. Digital records lack a physical manifestation. They cannot physically be put in a single sequence. "At its most fundamental, arrangement in the digital world is the representation of relationships between items. The organization of material into a 'folder' and 'file' is representational only—the data of the digital items themselves are not organized this way on the physical hard disk or other storage medium." "Most of the contextual information of electronic records is controlled by software" and is not visible to users. The logical relationships between digital data is reflected in file structures, data directories, and metadata in general.[5] Respect for original order of digital files requires that metadata captured during accessioning or early stages of processing be reused during arrangement to represent and preserve these relationships.

Importance of Prearrangement Tasks to Successful Digital Arrangement

The ability to successfully arrange digital files is dependent on the quality and completeness of work performed before arrangement even begins. Digital files must be successfully captured and stabilized. Metadata documenting the context, structure, and content of the digital records must be captured and recorded. Work processes and documentation must attest to their authenticity, reliability, and integrity. The archives collection policy, appraisal techniques, digital file transfer methods, accession records, and workflows for collecting, organizing, and preserving pertinent metadata all affect the ability to successfully arrange the digital records.[6]

How to Begin: Technical Analysis and Planning

Some hybrid record groups or collections include both analog and digital records. The digital records may be analog records that have been digitized to increase access or reuse or born-digital records. As time goes by, new accretions to existing record groups or new collections will have increased percentages of born-digital records.

The previous chapter presents the OAIS model and argues for performing the tasks necessary to create a stabilized SIP, then setting it aside to await arrangement and description or transformation into an AIP at a later time. Removal of files from at-risk storage media should be prioritized ahead of arranging and describing digital files. Because the point is to stabilize the files and prevent deterioration, the SIP should be monitored like a full AIP. See table 6.1.

Table 6.1. Maintenance Tasks for Stabilized SIP in Storage

Task	Record/ Found Here	Archival Task	OAIS Requirement	Notes
Maintenance			Archival storage	See Kevin Glick and Eliot Wilczek, *Fedora and the Preservation of University Records Project, 3.1 Maintain Guide, Version 1.0* (Medford, MA: Tufts University and Yale University, September 2006), accessed September 29, 2016, http://dl.tufts.edu/catalog/tufts:UA069.004.001.00009.
Run checksums on a regular schedule.		Authenticity[‡]; Integrity[‡]; Reliability[‡]; Usability[‡]	Data maintenance	Once an accession is finished, if there is a break before processing, it must be maintained.
Monitor file formats for obsolescence.		Usability[‡]	Data maintenance	
Perform incremental and full data backups.		Authenticity[‡]; Integrity[‡]; Reliability[‡]; Usability[‡]	Preservation; Data maintenance	
Other tasks?			Data maintenance	

Source: Seth E. Shaw, "Arrangement and Description of Electronic Records, Part II," Society of American Archivists Digital Archives Specialist workshop, Chapel Hill, NC, June 12, 2015, course booklet, 52.

[‡]Four qualities necessary to preserve digital files

When staff are ready to arrange and describe digital files, locate stabilized SIPs, confirm they remained unchanged in storage by running checksums, unwrap the digital storage bag or wrapper, and proceed with arrangement. Work on digital files that were ingested, developed into SIPS, and are going to be processed into AIPs immediately or in the near future will also pick up with completed SIPs.

Many analog archival collections have been hybrids, consisting of a mix of paper files; photographs; oversized maps, blueprints, drawings, or posters; objects; audio, film, or video recordings; or even textiles and art. It is common to arrange the various formats based on the intellectual contents, respecting existing original order. Series initially created in paper—speeches, reports, meeting agendas and minutes, photographic prints—that morph into digitally created versions of the same information are arranged in the same series. Intellectually, changing to digital files is the same as starting a new manuscript box. The only difference is the finding aid listing for the location of the digital files. A DVD inserted in a file of a series that is largely analog can be treated the same as an inserted photo, oversized blueprint, audiocassette, or other dissimilar format. The materials are intellectually included in the series or file arrangement but physically removed. Depending on whether the original media is retained and how and where the researcher accesses a copy of the files, a separation sheet should guide the researcher to the files. If original media is to be discarded, make a note in the finding aid and discard the media once at least two backup versions of the files in the new digital location have been made.

Sometimes a format has been separated into its own series by the creator: Blueprints or drawings are separated from office files for the same project. Family photographs are saved in photo albums. At other times a collection is received with minimal to no discernable original order. In such cases, some archivists choose to create series based on format rather than try to arrange materials based on intellectual qualities. Photographs are a format that is frequently put into its own series, even if they may have been included with a specific letter or other document. Some archivists have applied this pattern to digital records or even new accretions rather than arrange them based on content. This suggests discomfort with integrating dissimilar formats or a preference for a quick, easy solution.

As always, institutional variations exist due to differences in personnel; their training, skills, and experience; available equipment; existing software systems, archival and otherwise; IT support; available time; backlog size; and more. Decisions also vary based on the quantity of digital files in total, as well as relative to the rest of the record group or collection. This does not imply that every action listed should be executed. Please read the preface for more on this point if you skipped it. That said, table 6.2 presents a spreadsheet of sequentially ordered tasks for arranging digital files (column 1); where to record or save information from most actions (column 2); and where each task relates to general archival arrangement activities, OAIS requirements, and additional notes (columns 3 through 5). Column 2 in the spreadsheet refers to the digital file structure illustrated in figure 5.3. This spreadsheet is based on the OAIS model, which is software-independent.

Table 6.2. Arrangement Tasks for Digital Records

Task	Record/Found Here	Archival Task	OAIS Requirement	Notes
Process				
Retrieve accessioned but unprocessed SIP or AIP located on a dark server?				
Open SIP/AIP> unprocessed_work_ copies folder.				
Reconfirm checksums if necessary.		Preservation		
Examine file structure and contents in detail.		Examine records		

(continued)

Task	Record/Found Here	Archival Task	OAIS Requirement	Notes
Assess or identify and record preservation and access issues.	SIP/AIP>PDI>log?			Just identify at this stage while examining the files; address and resolve later on.
Conduct contextual and other research.	Record in work notes or processing plan?	Conduct background research		Review accession form, macroappraisal information, and other pertinent resources; contact donor or creator if needed.
Collect any digital information about provenance, donor, deed of gift, or other information normally in Control/Donor file, including rights.	SIP/AIP>PDI>Provenance/Control	Authenticity[*]	Administrative metadata	May choose to maintain any sensitive or key information in paper Donor/Control file pending security and backup of digital files.
Get file extent, (identify file format types, quantity, and storage size), and record.	Record file formats and extensions only in Content Information>Representation Information; record all in SIP/AIP>PDI>manifests and accession form.	Context	File formats = Representation information; Technical metadata	Can record representation information in PDI>manifests, readme.txt file, or Physical/Technical Access notesobtained at accessioning; review and analyze for context, and record in description research notes.
Review file directory or path structure.	SIP/AIP>PDI>manifests	Context	Structural metadata	Captured during accessioning; analyze for record groupings, relationship between records, and original order.
Create processing plan.				

(continued)

Task	Record/Found Here	Archival Task	OAIS Requirement	Notes
Normalize previously identified obsolete formats.	SIP/AIP>PDI>log and Notes element DACS 7 and PREMIS; may include in PDI>Provenance	Preservation	Preservation	Record preservation actions, like migration, in Notes element DACS 7 and in PREMIS as event and PDI>log; OAIS includes events regarding preservation in PDI>Provenance.
Research previously identified unknown file formats, and attempt to normalize.	SIP/AIP>PDI>log and Notes element DACS 7 and PREMIS	Preservation	Preservation	
Look for hidden or deleted files, and resolve.	SIP/AIP>PDI>log and Notes element DACS 7 and PREMIS	Privacy? Access?		
Check for duplicate files.		Weeding		
Identify other files to weed or deaccession.	SIP/AIP>PDI>log?	Weeding		Complete deaccession form, or record as appropriate.
Identify and address closed or restricted files.	SIP/AIP>PDI>Access Rights and Notes element DACS 7 and PREMIS	Confidentiality		OAIS includes events regarding preservation in PDI>Provenance; rights in PDI> Access Rights.
Check for personally identifiable information, and address.	SIP/AIP>PDI>log and Notes element DACS 7 and PREMIS	Confidentiality		
Create access copies, reformat if necessary, and generate new checksums.	SIP/AIP>PDI>log and Notes element DACS 7 and PREMIS	Access		Create JPGs, etc., format affected by delivery method, software, or system; watermark images?
Arrange digital files intellectually.		Arrangement		If files need new or revised arrangement, create or rename digital folders, and group files per new arrangement.

(continued)

Task	Record/Found Here	Archival Task	OAIS Requirement	Notes
Physically arrange digital files.		Arrangement		Create or rename folders; move files as needed.
Rename files if necessary.		Arrangement		
Monitor date last modified on files.	??	Preservation		If there are changes, copy date from original locked files.
Address disposition of original media used to transfer digital files.	SIP/AIP>PDI>log			Retain?Rehouse?

Sources: J. Gordon Daines III, "Module 2: Processing Digital Records and Manuscripts," in *Archival Arrangement and Description*, edited and introduced by Christopher J. Prom and Thomas J. Frusciano, Trends in Archives Practice series (Chicago: Society of American Archivists, 2013), 121; Consultative Committee for Space Data Systems (CCSDS), *Reference Model for an Open Archival Information System (OAIS) Recommended Practice CCSDS 650.0-M-2* (Washington, DC: CCSDS Secretariat, June 2012), accessed January 15, 2017, https://public.ccsds.org/Pubs/650x0m2.pdf, 4-30, 2-6, 2-7; Seth E. Shaw, "Arrangement and Description of Electronic Records, Part II" Society of American Archivists Digital Archives Specialist workshop, Chapel Hill, NC, June 12, 2015, course booklet, 16, 126, 24; OCLC/RLG Working Group on Preservation Metadata, *Preservation Metadata and the OAIS Information Model: A Metadata Framework to Support the Preservation of Digital Objects* (Dublin, OH: OCLC/RLG Working Group on Preservation Metadata, 2002), 40, 38, accessed May 12, 2016, http://www.oclc.org/content/dam/research/activities/pmwg/pm_framework.pdf; Seth E. Shaw, "Arrangement and Description of Electronic Records, Part I" Society of American Archivists Digital Archives Specialist workshop, Chapel Hill, NC, June 11, 2015, course booklet, 114, 104.

Whether starting with stabilized SIPs retrieved from storage or newly created SIPs, the first step is to locate the unprocessed work copies of the digital files. Refer back to the submission information package and archival information package in figures 5.2 and 5.3 as necessary. Figure 5.3 shows a folder labeled "processed_work_copies." For a stabilized SIP, this could be labeled "unprocessed_work_copies." It may be desirable to have an unprocessed work copies folder and a processed_work_copies folder during processing until the SIP is fully converted to an AIP. In any case, do not work off the originals labeled "original_files_locked" in figure 5.3.

During accessioning, information about file format types, quantity, and size were captured and stored in the SIP/AIP>PDI>manifests, as were file creation dates, dates last modified, and file directory paths. This information may be recorded in a spreadsheet or in the form of a report created by one of the software tools. This previously captured information can now be used for analysis. Start by examining the file structure and contents in detail to identify preservation or access issues, such as unidentified file formats, old formats for which you may not have software, or formats that need to be migrated. A derivative list of obsolete or unknown file formats may already be in the PDI. At this point, simply identify possible issues, and record them; do not try to resolve them yet. Conduct background research for the files, considering information about their context—when, how, and why they were created and used—and function. Questions of context need to examine the relationships not just among the digital records but also between digital records and their related analog records. Software tools like Irfan View, Quick View Plus, and TreeSize Pro may help with analyzing digital context. See appendix B for a brief description of these software tools and others that may help with file analysis. Pending its sensitivity and the security provided by the systems you are using, available digital information about the donor or transferee, provenance, the deed of gift typically filed in the donor or control file can be stored in the SIP/AIP>PDI>Provenance folder. Dig deeper into file format types, the number of each type, and their storage size; determine file creation dates and dates last modified, and record this information; review the file directory path and structure to get a sense of what the files are, how they are structured, and their relationships. Some software tools present their results in a traditional text style, while others, like TreeSize and WinDirStat, create visual tree maps. Some of the software tools used for appraisal are also useful now for analysis. Refer to appendix B.

Command line interface skills may be useful to manipulate raw data into a more understandable, useful format or to manipulate it to make analysis easier, especially for large quantities of files. Raw metadata extracted from files using some of the software tools can be saved as comma-separated values (CSV). Save it first, then open Excel or another spreadsheet software, and import the CSV data for manipulation and analysis. If you open the file directly with Excel, it will try to determine the data formats itself. Dates in particular may be corrupted, being misinterpreted as numbers. Import them as text, not numbers or dates, to avoid this problem.[7] Because the command line interface talks to a computer's operating system, commands for PCs and MACs are not identical. The command line interface works with FITS and Exiftool and is necessary to run the BagIt software, among others.

Analysis may include the normal practice of actually reading a sampling of files. All materials, digital and analog, in the unprocessed collection, record group, or new accretion being processed require analysis. The archivist determines the best sequence and method by which to examine the materials in order to develop a comprehensive arrangement that considers the provenance, original order, and information content in a format-neutral arrangement. Both the AIMS project and the Paradigm project recommend respecting the information content and context first when combining and arranging hybrid collections.[8] In making decisions about how to arrange analog materials, the quantity and nature of the materials involved are factors. How a single photograph, video, or bound volume is handled is different from a quantity that is significant in proportion to the other collection materials. This is still true of hybrid collections that include digital formats.[9]

Upon completion of all research and analysis, create a processing plan that includes documentation of the background and contextual research; notes restrictions; identifies preservation issues and proposed material to separate or discard; records the existing arrangement; outlines the proposed arrangement, including the level to which the records will be arranged (and described); addresses restrictions on the materials and how they will be addressed; and other details. Note, sections of the processing plan, like the background research, can be completed as that work is being conducted rather than waiting to write the entire plan at once. This approach also allows for work to be done in phases over time or among several specialists working on different aspects. Once the processing plan is developed, what remains is its execution, although it is possible that implementation will reveal new information that requires modification of the original processing plan decisions.

At this point, a variety of tasks may be performed depending on the needs of the digital records being arranged, policies in effect, and practices for the level at which work will be performed. Potential tasks include normalizing previously identified obsolete formats, researching previously identified unknown file formats, attempting to open them and normalizing if successful in opening, looking for hidden or deleted files and resolving their status based on policies or donor agreements and discussions, checking for duplicate files and removing them, renaming files, identifying other files to weed or deaccession, identifying and addressing closed or restricted files, checking for and addressing personally identifiable information, and performing any other locally determined tasks. FTK Imager, EnCase, or other similar software can search for personally identifiable information. Once files are identified, make a copy of all the files in question, and re-name them to indicate they are redacted copies. Each file must be examined individually to delete the personally identifiable information. The redacted files are the version used to create access copies. As these tasks are being performed, make note of them in the SIP/AIP>PDI>log shown in figure 5.3. Decide whether to include the information in the Notes element of the respective finding aid (DACS 7) and PREMIS pending their application at your archives.

Once the approved set of tasks has been performed, the question is whether to create access copies next or to arrange the digital work files intellectually. If there are only a few digital copies, it may make sense to create the access copies before arrangement, arrange the digital work cop-ies, and then replicate the file structure with the access copies. If there are a substantial number of digital files, it may make more sense to arrange them first, replicate the folder structure, then create the access copies, and drop them into the appropriate digital folder. The original files as received during transfer are preserved and set aside in SIP/AIP>PDI>original_files_locked. They have received minimal work in order to preserve the original file structure, dates, and more. The "processed_work_copies" are just that. They potentially represent a considerable amount of work, in which case they should also be preserved. An optional copy can be included in the final AIP. A second working copy should be located outside the AIP to use in re-creating a new set of access files if anything should happen to the access copies. Hopefully backup copies are main-tained of copy 2. Actual access copies of the processed files should be created and stored in a third location, separate from the "processed_work_copies," for delivery to researchers.

Intellectual arrangement entails creating well-named digital folders in which to place digital files based on the overall collection provenance and original order; or put differently, the structure, context, and content. Anne Gilliland-Swetland argues that intellectual integration of digital files with analog records provides better context and understanding of the materials. It unites content that is related.[10] In a hybrid collection, the archival subgroup, series, and file structure of the ana-log records are mirrored by the digital folder structure. Digital files are placed in their respective folder based on standard archival arrangement principles and practice. One of the differences with arranging digital files is that the archivist has less control over item-level arrangement within folders. Unless intentional file naming is used to force items to be ordered as the archivist wishes, the order will be controlled by the computer, which places numbers sequentially before alpha-betized file names. In any case, the arrangement is purely intellectual and in no way correlates to where the bits and bytes physically comprising any given file are located.

Archival arrangement for digital files involves using a variety of software tools to gain access to file contents, analyze and capture file structure and context, and determine an appropriate intel-lectual arrangement. Although during arrangement digital files should be integrated with other formats in the record group or collection, that does not happen in a physical manner. During arrangement, preservation issues are typically addressed, depending on what the problems are, their extent and severity, and the archival staff's ability to address them. This also applies to digital records, but the preservation problems are manifested as different problems requiring different skills from those of analog formats. The traditional activity of relabeling and numbering file folders, at least for this segment of a record group or collection, is not required but is a task frequently delegated to less experienced employees; however, digital preservation problems require more advanced skills and experience to resolve them. Actions taken to preserve digital files need to be recorded to help maintain file integrity and authenticity and to better understand file behavior during such future preservation actions as migration. Preservation tasks, as noted earlier, can be recorded in the Notes element of a DACS-compliant finding aid (DACS 7), in the appropriate PREMIS element, in archival collections management systems like ArchivesSpace, or in a simple spreadsheet.

A parting question upon completion of digital file arrangement is storage. First, what will be the disposition of any storage devices or media used to transfer digital files to the archives? This question is raised in the last chapter. Now that the files have been arranged, it is appropriate to deal with them. Will they be retained, rehoused, and arranged to serve as access or backup copies or repurposed (external hard drives) and disposed of (disks and flash drives)? The answer may vary depending on device and age or follow a blanket policy. If disposing of the original media, do wait for at least two backup versions of the files in the new digital location to be created.

Whether access copies are created after intellectual arrangement or before, there should be an arranged set of work copies and an arranged set of access copies. They should be stored in two separate locations, both of which have backup processes in place to protect them. The question is where, and the answer is based on many variables. Institutions with a relatively small quantity of digital files or that have minimal technical resources could consider maintaining preservation and working copies on an external hard drive, with access copies on DVDs. If greater capacity is required, the computer provided to researchers could also have an external hard drive. If there is a need for stand-alone storage to deliver copyright-protected files on-site to researchers beyond the capacity of one external hard drive, a Drobo storage system has the ability to grow with time.[11] All these storage devices require close and frequent monitoring to ensure no file degradation or loss. It is recommended that checksums be run half as often as the expected life of the storage media. Another storage option is a cloud-based account. This option requires consideration of confidentiality requirements for the stored files and whether the selected cloud storage vender practices current standards for cloud-based security. Some institutions may use software systems, like Archivematica, Preservica, or Chronopolis, or a hosted product, like DuraCloud, to store or manage preservation files. An institutional repository accepts, stores, and delivers access copies. Software systems like DSpace; Fedora; Hydra combined with other software; and Islandora, which like Hydra is also based on Fedora but with a different combination of added software; and Bepress are used to develop institutional repositories. Some of these systems can be hosted, others cannot, and some require a very high level of technical skill to develop. Other less robust products are more specialized. ContentDM delivers images, media files, and text via the web. Omeka focuses on presenting exhibits and collections also via the web.

Implementation Based on the Organization's Resources

Much of the discussion so far and to come is about the tasks to perform, their sequence, and factors to consider. A range of software tools has been mentioned that varies in price from free to expensive and in skill level from beginner to quite advanced. Developing a digital records program does require resources and support. How much of these are available is likely to determine whether the archives is able to generally care for a reasonable quantity of digital records or develop a more formal system that is able to actively solicit, manage, and preserve larger quantities of records on a larger scale. An institution can build a program gradually, acquiring one component at a time, mastering it, and then building on what it has.

My institution started by acquiring server space. As we digitized photographs on demand, we established written standards for access and preservation copies and file-naming conventions and stored the files in two separate intellectual locations on the server. The file structure for both copies mirrors each other and the physical photographic prints. Next, we began to develop an institutional repository as a way to deliver digital content. Based on the library's and the university's technical capabilities, our repository is hosted and is being developed in concert with other library units. While we continued to prepare content to add to the repository, we wrote a document on which file formats we can support. The next step will be developing the digital file transfer workflow to acquire digital files from university offices and devices, to be followed by other policy work. A new computer has been designated as our digital records processing workstation and set up with some initial digital tools. We have conducted research, obtained some training, participated in SAA's Jump In 3 program, and will continue inventorying digital holdings. The overall goal is to gradually develop an OAIS-compliant digital program.

As our case demonstrates, it is necessary to assess the technical knowledge and skills of the archives personnel and any other units within the organization that might provide this support.[12] For personnel outside the archives with the necessary expertise, one also has to ask what the likelihood is that their time will be made available to support development of your program. Another possibility is additional training for department personnel. Depending on the results of this assessment, informed decisions can be made about achievable goals. Plan for what is possible with current resources and skills based on what is already in place in the department. Look ahead several steps for what can be done to build on the present. Try to avoid options that create barriers or future problems for building in the direction you want to go. Suppose you know you'd like to obtain a particular preservation software in the future; however, you currently need to select a digital repository or archival collection management system. Try to select a system now that works well with or at least is compatible with the future software.

Program Considerations

The archives should consider the larger organizational picture regarding digital records. Does your organization have a mandatory records management program? Can you argue for resources you need to develop a digital program in order to meet compliance requirements for permanent records in digital format? Do goals for development of a digital program fit the organization's strategic plan? Academic research and grants offices may support development of a digital repository to deliver government-funded research to the public. Do your academic librarians help grant applicants write the data management plan for their applications? What guidance is included for acceptable file formats, data organization, the final disposition of the research data, and reports? Some of these details relate to archival digital programs and what they can support. What is the role of big data in your organization, and who is involved with it? There are potential allies for the archives within your organization who may develop policies that are compatible with the archives' perspective on digital files, may require compliance with a records management program that includes digital records, or may support development of components of your program because it meets mutual goals. Explore your options, and seek allies.

As has already been said, a good working relationship between the archives and the institution's information technology department increases the effectiveness and success of a digital records preservation program. Running software checks for viruses, malware, credit card numbers, and other confidential information is likely to set off warning bells at the organizational level. It is wise to have a conversation with IT during planning stages about your program's development and plans to perform various actions likely to trigger system-level flags. They may be able to recommend software already in use.

If the archives stores preservation masters, working copies, stabilized SIPs, or other key digital files on your organization's server space, another important question for IT is, What is its policy regarding backup of those locations? What is their status in IT's disaster recovery plan? Speaking of permanent files maintained on server space, can IT run system-level fixity checks for those locations? Although intellectually your access and preservation copies may appear to be in different server locations to you, it is wise to confirm that information with the manager of your server space. If they are not actually on different servers, then you do not have a valid backup copy. Also, confirm exactly what is and is not backed up. Many people make false assumptions about what IT really backs up and how far back they can recover lost information. Developing a good relationship with your IT department is likely to benefit the growth of your digital records program.

During arrangement, a common task is to check for confidential, restricted, or personally identifiable information. Information can be redacted, whether analog or digital. What may be less expected is the ability to recover deleted or hidden digital files through disk images or other techniques. While discussions with donors are not part of arrangement and description, the archivist has to deal with what she finds when she processes. On the other hand, the donor has no way of knowing which methods the archives uses to perform its work and may not imagine that information he thought was gone is recoverable. Policies should be developed for handling confidential, restricted, or personally identifiable information regardless of format. They then support discussions with donors on this topic and revised language in donor agreements and deeds of gift. See "Additional Reading and Resources" at the end of this chapter for an example.

Also consider having all employees, student employees, and even volunteers sign a confidentiality agreement, not just to protect information in collections they handle, but also department passwords or other similar information. Northern Kentucky University's archives received a large collection consisting primarily of paper records but that included a small quantity of electronic records. The donor required the collection to be closed for ten years. The digital files were put on server space, but a written agreement was also executed between the university library and the IT department restricting who managed or accessed the server space where the restricted files were stored.

While a number of potential tasks were listed for execution during the arrangement process, each archives must determine which of these tasks it can support, what its minimum requirements are for arrangement, and under which conditions additional tasks are performed. These decisions consider the availability of personnel, time, technology, the quantity of digital files, how much of the process can be automated, processing backlogs, and more in a balancing act. Time permitting, recording these decisions in policies and related guidelines in a processing manual will assist personnel in carrying out this work.

Notes

1. AIMS Work Group, *AIMS Born-Digital Collections: An Inter-Institutional Model for Stewardship*, 2012, 31, accessed August 6, 2016, http://dcs.library.virginia.edu/files/2013/02/AIMS_final.pdf.

2. Richard Pearce-Moses, *A Glossary of Archival and Records Terminology* (Chicago: Society of American Archivists, 2005), s.v. "record," accessed May 8, 2016, http://www2.archivists.org/glossary/terms/r/record.

3. Heather MacNeil, "Archival Theory and Practice: Between Two Paradigms," *Archivaria* 37 (1994): 9-10.

4. Charles Dollar, *Archival Theory and Information Technologies: The Impact of Information Technologies on Archival Principles and Methods*, ed. Oddo Bucci (Macerata, Italy: University of Macerata, 1992), 47.

5. AIMS Work Group, *AIMS Born-Digital Collections*, 31; Dollar, *Archival Theory*, 48, 50; see also MacNeil, "Between Two Paradigms," 10.

6. AIMS Work Group, *AIMS Born-Digital Collections*, 32.

7. Bertram Lyons and Josh Ranger, "Hard Skills for Managing Digital Collections in Archives," lectures, Midwest Archives Conference's Fall Symposium, Minneapolis, MN, September 18-19, 2015.

8. AIMS Work Group, *AIMS Born-Digital Collections*, 40; University of Oxford and University of Manchester, *Paradigm: Workbook on Digital Private Papers*, last modified January 2, 2008, http://www.paradigm.ac.uk/ workbook.

9. AIMS Work Group, *AIMS Born-Digital Collections*, 40.

10. Anne J. Gilliland-Swetland, *Enduring Paradigms, New Opportunities: The Value of the Archival Perspective in the Digital Environment* (Washington, DC: Council on Library and Information Resources, 2000), 14.

11. Thanks to Seth Shaw, who offered this solution during a consultation to assess development of Northern Kentucky University's digital records preservation program and recommend next steps.

12. Catherine Stollar Peters, "When Not All Papers Are Paper: A Case Study in Digital Archivy," *Provenance: Journal of the Society of Georgia Archivists* 24 (January 2006): 33. Peters agrees that digital preservation requires specialized knowledge and specialized staff.

Additional Reading and Resources

"About Drobo." *Drobo*. Accessed November 12, 2016. http://www.drobo.com/about-drobo. This is a storage device system that can grow in capacity as needed.

AIMS Work Group. *AIMS Born-Digital Collections: An Inter-Institutional Model for Stewardship*. 2012. Accessed August 27, 2016. http://dcs.library.virginia.edu/files/2013/02/AIMS_final .pdf. Appendix E has sample processing plans for digital records.

"ArchivesSpace-Archivematica-DSpace Workflow Integration Project." *Bentley Historical Library, University of Michigan*. Accessed November 17, 2016. http://archival-integration.blogspot.com. This blog discusses work about the Bentley Historical Society's Mellon-funded project to im- prove workflow between these three software systems and shares details of how they dealt with some of the issues that arose. They created an "Appraisal and Arrangement" tab that will hopefully be made available in Archivematica version 1.6.

Beagrie, Neil, ed. *Digital Preservation Handbook*. Rev. 2nd ed. Glasgow: Digital Preservation Coali- tion, 2015. Accessed June 19, 2016. http://handbook.dpconline.org/organisational-activities/ storage; http://handbook.dpconline.org/organisational-activities/legacy-media; and http:// handbook.dpconline.org/digital-preservation/preservation-issues. The sections within "Orga- nizational Activities" on storage and legacy media, the "Technical Solutions" section on digital forensics and cloud computing, and the "Digital Preservation Briefing" section on preservation issues apply to topics in this chapter.

Chaos—Order: Four Archivists' Battles with Masses of Legacy Description. Accessed December 23, 2015. https://icantiemyownshoes.wordpress.com. This blog is about processing issues. Particularly note Carrie Hintz's December 15, 2015, post on determining processing levels; Christie Peterson's November 5, 2015, post on access restrictions; and Rachel Searcy's November 8, 2015, post on accessioning.

"How Toy Story 2 Almost Got Deleted: Stories from Pixar Animation: ENTV." YouTube video, posted May 19, 2012, by Hollywood. Accessed November 13, 2016. https://www.youtube.com/watch?v=8dhp_20j0Ys. An example of why communication is important, even in big businesses, so that decisions made by one department do not unknowingly have a negative impact on another.

"Introduction to Digital Preservation Webinars." *Association of Southeastern Research Libraries (ASERL). Spring 2013.*" Accessed October 30, 2016. http://www.aserl.org/intro-dp-2013. This series of webinars presents an introduction to PREMIS, capturing metadata, managing born-digital collections, and using FITS. The webinars include a recorded video presentation and handouts for each topic.

"An Introduction to Using Command Line Interface (CLI) to Work with Files and Directories (AV Preserve)." *Council of State Archivists (CoSA).* Last modified October 20, 2015. https://www.statearchivists.org/resource-center/resource-library/introduction-using-command-line-interface-cli-work-files-and-directories-av-preserve. This is also mentioned in chapter 4. The native command line interface in Windows or Mac is a tool that can be used to organize metadata about digital files that are produced by some of software mentioned in this chapter in order to better appraise the files. There are separate versions of the tutorial for Windows and Macintosh.

"Jump-In Initiative." *Society of American Archivists.* Accessed November 16, 2016. http://www2.archivists.org/groups/manuscript-repositories-section/jump-in-initiative. This initiative to get started with managing digital records began in 2013. It was designed to be very achievable and was so successful that it ran for three years.

Lyons, Bertram. "Try5—Guest Blogger: Bertram Lyons." *Off the Record.* October 31, 2016. Accessed November 12, 2016. https://offtherecord.archivists.org/2016/10/31/try5-guest-blogger-bertram-lyons. The blog is by Society of American Archivists leaders. Lyons's guest post is chock full of tutorials on command line interface, checksums, digital file packing, and more.

McGrath, Gary. *Mad File Format Science.* Accessed July 1, 2015. https://madfileformatscience.garymcgath.com. This blog provides helpful information about file formats. McGrath also authored a short course at Udemy on this topic.

Nelson, Naomi L., Seth Shaw, Nancy Deromedi, Michael Shallcross, Cynthia Ghering, Lisa Schmidt, Michelle Belden, Jackie R. Esposito, Ben Goldman, and Tim Pyatt. *Managing Born-Digital Special Collections and Archival Materials.* SPEC Kit 329. Washington, DC: Association of Research Libraries, 2012. The Bentley Historical Library, University of Michigan, *Digital Processing Manual* on pages 155–61 provides details of tasks to be performed for digital records. The full manual is available at https://deepblue.lib.umich.edu/bitstream/handle/2027.42/96439/ BHL_DigitalProcessingGuidelines_20111116-DRAFT.pdf?sequence=1, but note that the Bentley no longer uses this manual. It may have been superseded by this manual: https://sites .google.com/a/umich.edu/bhl-archival-curation/processing-archival-collections.

"A Processing Manual for the Special Collections Technical Services Department at the University of North Carolina at Chapel Hill." *Special Collections Technical Services Department of the Louis Round Wilson Special Collections Library*. Accessed November 12, 2016. http://www2.lib.unc .edu/wikis/archproc/index.php/How_to_Proceed:_Preparing_to_Process#Writing_a_Pro cessing_Plan. This section discusses preparing a processing plan.

Pyatt, Timothy D. "Penn State Electronic Records Addenda." Accessed November 15, 2016. https://scholarsphere.psu.edu/downloads/0k225b067. This deed of gift addendum addresses electronic records issues related to possible confidential or private information.

University of Oxford and University of Manchester. *Paradigm: Workbook on Digital Private Papers*. Last modified January 2, 2008. http://www.paradigm.ac.uk/workbook/cataloguing/ead-ex emplars.html. This section of the workbook addresses arrangement of digital and hybrid collections, including guidance and examples.

7

Digital Description

Description is the second of two archival functions so closely related and interdependent that a single word, *processing*, is used to encompass them both.[1] "Arrangement and description: the process undertaken by an institution to establish intellectual control of the material following the physical control secured during accessioning. It also prepares the material for discovery by providing the user with information and context about the records, and prepares for access by applying appropriate restrictions."[2] This definition assigns three functions to description: to further establish intellectual control over the records in question, to add context and information that will prepare them for discovery, and to prepare them for access.

In many ways, description is performed the same for digital records as for analog. Refer to text-boxes 3.1. and 3.2, task 6, "Describe the records." The action items are the same in both cases, although their sequence has been adjusted slightly. Technical metadata is gathered and recorded in specific locations in an OAIS-compliant model during technical appraisal and arrangement, but description for digital records is performed outside the OAIS model. However, the description must be linked to the digital files in the OAIS storage system. This is the function of the unique identifier or "Reference" component of the PDI. The gradual increase in application of the OAIS framework as a system and standard to address digital records has affected archival appraisal of digital records, their storage, and delivery because these functions are all related to or are a component of the framework. Because description is linked to the OAIS framework but is not a component of it, description has largely continued to be practiced as it was for analog materials. Rather than being affected by the development of OAIS, it has been subject to change from the development and evolution of both the World Wide Web and the Internet; the growth and development of software specifically designed to manage, deliver, and preserve archival materials; the adoption of new descriptive standards; and research into finding aid design, web design, and the archival research process, to name some factors.

Arrangement works to identify the original order in a body of records, to identify logical, intellectual groupings that are hopefully reflected in the physical order of the records and reflect structural relationships between the records in a record group or manuscript collection. Those groupings and their structural relationships are then reflected in the description of those records. "Description is the creation of an accurate representation of" archival records and applies to all archival records, regardless of their form or medium and regardless of whether they were created by a corporate body or an individual or family. It also strives to explain the context and records systems that create the records being described.[3]

Archival descriptions may be presented in a variety of outputs and with varying levels of detail.[4] The traditional and most prevalent method of presenting description continues to be the finding aid. Chapter 2 discusses the creation of finding aids. Textbox 2.1 presents one example, and others are cited in the "Additional Reading and Resources" section. Standards are also discussed in chapter 2. The sample finding aid in textbox 2.1 uses the required DACS fields and additional locally chosen "Added Value" and "Optimum" fields, the Library of Congress or local name authority files, and Library of Congress Subject Headings as standards. What is different for description of digital records?

Description intellectually unites analog and digital records in hybrid record groups or collections.[5] One question is whether digital records will be integrated into series or files based on the intellectual content of both analog and digital materials. Because records should be arranged based on their intellectual contents, not their format or carrier, the records should be integrated.[6] Some will arrive already physically integrated, as in the case of a CD, DVD, or other disk slipped into a file folder. The storage device is removed to process separately. It is replaced with a separation sheet describing the removed storage device, including the disk title if one exists. The archivist should assign a unique identifier to the disk to link it to the contents. Some archives use or include a photo or photocopy of the disk label information. Some files may be transferred as a new accretion to a series that previously existed in paper. These are very easy to integrate in the finding aid. Some electronic files may arrive unassociated with analog records and require analysis to determine whether a relationship exists with other analog or digital records and which ones. The James Welch Papers at Yale (see "Additional Reading and Resources" in this chapter), in "Series 1 Writings," boxes 8 and 9, describe numerous disks with drafts of literary writing. Each entry includes the disk number for the described literary piece. In the case that a collection is predominantly or completely digital, once the files have been analyzed and arranged, description should be straightforward. What may be different is the method for accessing the files. The Chelsea Records at Yale (http://hdl.handle.net/10079/fa/beinecke.chelsea) includes 128 items holding digital records from a small press publisher. The records are arranged by acquisition, although the same series are used throughout as applicable. The number and type of storage device are listed in the appropriate subgroup, but otherwise, the researcher must examine them herself to determine specific contents. The Salman Rushdie Papers at Emory are arranged in a combination of record type and format. Series 11 is born-digital materials (https://findingaids.library.emory.edu/documents /rushdie1000). This series consists of the contents of four computers and one external hard drive, of which only one computer has been processed and for which no description is given except on-site. The "Scope and Content" note for subseries 2.1 does note that drafts and notes for named works are part of the digital files. There is a searchable database of files available on-site.

Digital records, unlike most analog records, are machine- and software-dependent. This means additional information is created and recorded about digital files. This added information is metadata. Capturing some of this metadata is part of description. Chapter 5 discusses important metadata to capture and explains where to record specific pieces of that metadata within the OAIS structure in order to create a SIP. This discussion is independent of any specific archival system or combination of software. Chapter 6 picks up with a stabilized SIP that may have just been created or been in storage for some time and is ready for processing, starting with arrangement. With description, the SIP should become a completed AIP.

Using Standards to Create Finding Aids

As already mentioned, description of digital records being managed in an OAIS-compliant model are performed outside the OAIS structure. In creating, updating, or managing an archival description program, standards play an important role. Chapter 2 introduces the types of standards that apply to archival description—data structure, data content, and data value—and mentions current examples of each and benefits of their use. In applying standards to a finding aid, the archivist starts with a data structure or data content standard, like Dublin Core, DACS, or ISAD(G), to select the fields that will be used to contain the descriptive information. If the end result for the finding aid is to deliver it as a PDF on a web page, any of these standards will work. If, however, the finding aid will be delivered through a single, searchable portal using archival information management software, like ArchivesSpace, Cuadra STAR/Archives, Eloquent, ICA-AtoM, and others or an institutional repository (IR) using software, like DSpace, Fedora, Bepress, Islandora, Hydra combined with different software than in Islandora, or another software, it is advisable to determine which standards the other system uses to improve compatibility and functionality. Standards are written independent of any specific software to provide the greatest applicability; however, specific archival systems tend to be designed around a given set of compatible standards. Use of such systems can increase compliance with descriptive standards. If additional description is going to be created to submit to a library online public access catalog (OPAC), an archival consortium, or an institutional repository combined with an archival management system, again, determine which standards the other systems use, and identify which standards are the most compatible between all the systems being used. While it may not always be possible to use the same standard across all software in play, the more times the description can be reused, the greater staff productivity, and hopefully the better the integration of all systems in use.

For example, we used a 2009–2010 grant to create a digital collection of scans of Kentucky postcards. A custom database was created to deliver the images and description from the library website. The description used Dublin Core (DC). Project members met and defined how each field was to be used, the information source, and applicable content standard by field. A written chart documented the information for consistency. Three years after completing the postcard collection, we began preliminary research on an IR. Based on our technical capacity, a hosted version of DSpace was selected. DSpace also uses DC. Project members met again to define how the fields would be applied in light of anticipated records and created a lengthier written document. After work began on the IR, the software used for the university's website changed. This caused technical problems for delivering the digital postcard collection. Because the postcard collection and the IR both use DC, it was decided to re-create the postcard collection in the IR. Due to the common description standard, this should be relatively easy to implement because most or all of the description should be reusable.

Once a standard is selected, fields may need to be selected for use in the finding aid template. Some standards have more choices than others. Decide which are the minimum required fields. Additional fields may be optional, depending on whether a specific collection requires it. For example, there may be no Related Materials. Even if there are, Related Materials are designated as Added Value, which means the field use is optional. The archives can decide whether it will be used or not. After fields are chosen, a data content standard and data values may need to be selected. We recently revised our finding aid template and made it fully compliant with DACS. Some field labels were changed. While we retained our existing name for other fields, we recorded which DACS field it was in essence. Name selection was partly determined by what we thought researchers would understand. Our minimum record consists of the required fields plus an assortment of the Added Value and Optimum fields based on information we had previously provided in our finding aids and wanted to continue providing. Any field in our template that does not apply to a particular collection is not even shown. A lot of the administrative fields we think researchers are less likely to use were grouped together and moved toward the end of the template. Thesauri were identified for potential use.

Our finding aids are currently delivered in HTML using the university's web software. However, we are about to implement ArchivesSpace, which will eventually automate EAD encoding of our finding aids. Data content standards are often written to work with a particular data structure standard, like DACS and EAD. Some data structure standards are written for a single serialization.[7] The decision to make our finding aid template fully DACS-compliant was made knowing we were about to commit to ArchivesSpace. This improved the alignment between our existing descriptive standards and our newest software. ArchivesSpace was also selected knowing its compatibility with DSpace due to the common DC standard they both use. I identified the need for a collection management software before the decision was made to create a digital repository. The repository was prioritized ahead of the collection management software. I hoped to get Archon and knew it was reasonably compatible with DSpace. Consequently, I recommended using DSpace software for the digital repository because of my future intentions for Archon. Although our pace was such that Archon was no longer on the market when we were ready to buy our collection management software, its successor, ArchivesSpace, actually meets my original goals and more.

Today's choices have implications tomorrow for interoperability, access, and retrieval. They need to be made thoughtfully to allow room for future growth, especially if a program is being built in stages. Try not to make a decision or select a product that greatly reduces future choices. Even if a particular product is not affordable now, if there is a strong possibility of eventually obtaining it or something very similar, try not to eliminate the desired future option by choices made today. This is true of standards, software, and other situations.

Once decisions have been made about which standards will be used and a generic template is designed, then further decisions are made based on the particular record group or collection to be described. Decide the level to which description will be written. A complex record group or collection may be described to the series level, while a smaller, simpler one may be described to the folder level. If using DACS, decide whether to create a collection-level record or to provide multilevel description at lower levels. In the case of multilevel description, the goal is to avoid repeating information from a higher level at a lower level. For example, collection-level information is omitted from the subgroup-, series-, subseries-, or file-level description.

Table 7.1. Description and Remaining Tasks to Form an AIP

Task	Record/ Found Here	Archival Task	OAIS Requirement	Applicable Standard	Notes
Description and Wrap Up					
Prepare finding aid.		Description		Use appropriate standards.	In hybrid collections, integrate with analog materials, or create a separate series?
Create access points.		Description		DACS; name authority records?	

(continued)

Task	Record/ Found Here	Archival Task	OAIS Requirement	Applicable Standard	Notes
Complete Technical Access element.	description/access tools	Description		DACS 4.3	DACS 4.3 is not a mandatory field but is still crucialfor user access; it explains how to access the files.
Record representation information.	AIP>Content Information >Representation Information		Necessary for AIP		Requires file structure file directory or paths; does disk image qualify? Refer to information in manifests and disk image in original_files_locked or duplicate info in this folder too? Describe hardware if possible and software used to create files. May need to explain information, data, formulas, etc., in files.
Attach metadata to individual files if required.		Description			For example, rightsownership that might regulate who can or how to access. Watermark photos? Closed, restricted, or PII files?
Create PREMIS description.		Preservation		PREMIS	Repeat of log recording preservation actions; location where PREMIS is recorded may vary by systems in use by institution.

(continued)

Task	Record/ Found Here	Archival Task	OAIS Requirement	Applicable Standard	Notes
Create EAC-CPF entries.		Access?		EAC-CPF	
Post, publish, or upload access copies of files.	AIP>Processed_ work_copies				
Load new records or data into description, access tools, and software.					
Make finding aids public, and link digital description to content.					
Create new checksums for processed version of files.	AIP>PDI>manifests		Fixity;Preservation		
Confirm content information, PDI, and descriptive metadata are all linked if stored separately.					
Package completed AIP.					
Store preservation copy of packaged AIP appropriately.					Place in dark server in appropriate record group or collection.
Backup finding aid and or other key components of accession record and description.					

Sources: Seth E. Shaw, "Arrangement and Description of Electronic Records, Part I" Society of American Archivists Digital Archives Specialist workshop, Chapel Hill, NC, June 11, 2015, course booklet, 94, 122; Seth E. Shaw, "Arrangement and Description of Electronic Records, Part II" Society of American Archivists Digital Archives Specialist workshop, Chapel Hill, NC, June 12, 2015, course booklet, 120.

Table 7.1 includes both description tasks and tasks to complete the formation of an AIP. Some description is included in the finding aid, while some is in the metadata. Some metadata should have been collected already during accessioning, ingest, and SIP creation or arrangement and start of AIP creation and may be used to complete DACS fields, like Conditions Governing Access (DACS 4.1) or Technical Access (4.3). Part of description includes creating access points, terms used to search for records in archival description.[8] There are no designated DACS fields for access points; they are included where they fit intellectually. The fields most likely to include vocabulary that qualifies as an access point are Name of Creator(s) (2.6), Title (2.3), Scope and Content (3.1), Administrative/Biographical History (2.7), Custodial History (5.1), and Immediate Source of Acquisition (5.2).[9] They can be included in a DACS-compliant finding aid, a web-accessible PDF file, or in other types of description in software systems. Depending on the sophistication level of the description program, PREMIS or EAC-CPF records might be created. If these are beyond current capabilities, information about appraisal (weeding) and processing decisions, removal of restricted or personal files, files that could not be opened, whether and how files were normalized, and similar activity should be recorded. Alternate options include recording them in DACS fields for Appraisal, Destruction, and Scheduling Information (5.3); Processing Notes (7.1.8) in a finding aid; the processing plan for the record group or collection; a spreadsheet for the record group or collection stored in an ordinary electronic file for the record group or collection; the donor or control file; or an archival collection management system. Be sure the finding aid records the unique ID for all digital files. If the accession number was used to create the unique ID, record it in the Immediate Source of Acquisition element (5.2).

Once the finding aid is finalized, the AIP can be completed. Our archives practices creating links in both directions whenever we associate two items. If none of the documentation in the AIP indicates the record group or collection to which the files belong, an optional text file can be included to record that information and strengthen the link between the two bodies of records. Part of arrangement includes analysis of the digital file formats. This should have yielded information about the software or possibly hardware required to view the files. Be sure this is recorded in "AIP>Content Information>Representation Information." Metadata may need to be associated with specific files for intellectual rights. Note it in documents like the deed of gift; accession record, form, or spreadsheet; the finding aid field Conditions Governing Reproduction and Use (DACS 4.4); and the pertinent field in other description standards used for institutional repositories or other access systems. Create new checksums for the now processed working copy of the "processed_work_copies"; this is the copy of the processed files from which the access copies will be made and delivered elsewhere. It is *neither* the "original_files_locked" raw SIP received from the creator or donor nor the optional preservation copy of the "processed_work_copies" to be included in the AIP. File the checksums in "API>PDI>manifests," clearly labeling them as for "processed_work_copies." If the content information, PDI, and descriptive metadata are stored in separate software, make sure they are all linked to one another by means of the unique identifier assigned to the original SIP. Create the access copies from the working version of the "now processed_work_copies" and descriptive metadata and post, upload, or otherwise deliver them to the location from which researchers will access them. Once all work is completed within the AIP, it can be wrapped or packaged and stored in the preservation system or location.

Assuming related analog materials have also been processed, the finished finding aid can now be published; description can be added to archival collection management systems, digital repositories, or other software. Where possible, link digital files to their finding aid. A paper copy of the finding aid can also be put on file in the research room. Back up the finding aid, accession record, and other key components for the now-processed record group or collection that are not in the preserved AIP.

The Function of the Finding Aid or Problems with Description

The tension between the finding aid as a discovery tool for researchers and as a management tool for the archival staff is well known.[10] As archivists have delved into new areas or they have become more important due to digital records (e.g., access restrictions or rights management), we have tried to make finding aids do more. User studies have demonstrated researchers' confusion when using finding aids.[11] Much discussion has occurred regarding their design, the use of insider lingo and technical jargon, which fields to present, and how and in which sequence. Certainly, flipping the sequence of fields to push researcher-oriented fields toward the top or front and clustering fields more heavily used for collection management together toward the end is a logical option (see textbox 2.1 as one example). Another little-discussed aspect to this researcher confusion is the lack of archival information literacy education. Libraries far outnumber archives. Academic archives are usually located within a library, adding to the confusion. The average citizen is far more familiar with how libraries manage books than how archives function. Academic librarians argue, however, that even more information literacy instruction is needed to teach college students how to locate and assess quality information. Researchers bring their bibliographic experience with them to the archives and want to apply those same practices to archival records. Archives have a challenge to educate those same researchers that archival records are organized, accessed, and used differently. One possibility is for archivists to work with information literacy librarians when they receive requests for instruction involving the use of primary source documents.

In making decisions about the future of description, the profession needs to be aware of the potential gap between those institutions with better funding; access to more expensive, multiple, or custom software systems; and personnel with greater technical expertise and those institutions without those advantages. This gap is likely to lead to two classes of description: well-formed, good basic finding aids as PDFs delivered via the web and advanced finding aids with many additional, specialized fields, like PREMIS and EAC-CPF, accessed through advanced software systems. While it is important to continue to develop the potential of our descriptive systems, there is still other work that requires attention. User studies need to discern which problems are due to the finding aid and which are due to their visual presentation when delivered via the web, because the web software controls presentation options separately from the finding aid itself. It is clear that language, especially for field labels, is a problem. What is a good solution?

Another problem for researchers' comprehension of archival description is the fact that most archives have not brought their descriptive programs up to a uniform presentation and delivery format for all their analog records, never mind digital records. Consequently, even at a single institution, a researcher has to master several systems to locate relevant material.[12] This means that a researcher must conduct the same search multiple times to survey all processed holdings. This is inefficient and must be frustrating. Archivists recognize the fast pace at which technology is evolving when discussing the problem of accessing data using older software or hardware or stored on older storage devices. That same fast pace also hurts us in description. How can we rewrite or reformat the finding aids of hundreds of record groups and collections every five or ten years to keep up with technology? We cannot or are not, as Prom points out. This alone is a challenge for researchers. As standards increase in number, complexity, and the technical skill required to apply them and the software systems to manage our holdings do the same, the gap in description will widen between institutions. Those archives that are unable to afford technology systems that automate EAD encoding, tasks for creating SIPS or AIPS, and other advanced descriptive tasks may be unable to participate in the latest description projects, practices, and standards unless the work can be done manually with their available resources.

The use of archival collections management software enables an institution to capture the information it requires to manage holdings and store it somewhere other than in finding aids. These systems use relational databases that provide the benefit of a single searchable system that integrates functions that may have been previously recorded in separate systems or by methods lacking a unified search. Will archives using these systems refine their finding aids to minimize details that had been primarily for the archivist and not the researcher? Some archivists have argued for more information in finding aids to inform the researcher of archival decisions that those archivists believe may introduce bias into the collection or its description or for other reasons.[13] DACS provides fields already to communicate some of this information, but the archivist always has the option to share additional unrestricted information from a donor or control file or other staff only resource. The relevant question might be whether users have demonstrated the desire for this information and been unable to obtain it. Using collection management software to produce finding aids is one way to use technology to reshape finding aids.

One Potential Future for Archival Description and Finding Aids

Some archivists argue that the profession has not taken advantage of the technology provided by the web to redesign our finding aids and that our finding aid design demonstrates we are still mentally bound by our thinking for finding aids for analog records.[14] The development of hyperlinks was an early advancement for the web. Although simplistic, archivists employed hyperlinks to enhance finding aids by linking between description and digital items or collections. This linking can cross two different software, such as the one presenting the finding aid and a web page, a digital repository, or a digital image library like ArtStor. While linking to a scanned or born-digital text or image is the most common, other examples include links between oral history audio or video and text transcripts or handwritten documents and a print transcript.

Although the MARC AMC format was released in 1984, it was still based on a bibliographic standard that was not designed to describe the hierarchical relationships between sets of records that have been a defining quality of archival records.[15] The weaknesses of MARC AMC combined with technical advances by the Internet led to the development and release in 1997 of EAD as the first archival data structure standard. EAD is an extensible markup language that makes it possible to code finding aids for web delivery with a consistent structure and presentation, despite differences in web browsers and other variables outside the control of the archives. This consistency only applies to those finding aids created with the same EAD template, usually limited to an institution or consortium. There are a minimal number of required EAD fields, and as a data structure standard, it does not regulate the formation of the content of any field. This means there are still many variations between EAD-encoded finding aids.

From the beginning, archivists have valued the relationship between archival materials and their creator, to the point that the principle of provenance was developed to arrange records based on their creator. DACS specifies that the creators of archival materials must also be described, not just the records.[16] While corporate or personal histories were written about records creators and data content standards from AACR2 to APPM to DACS (2004 version) prescribed how to form personal and corporate names, there was no standardization in the information recorded about creators. Librarians developed the Library of Congress Registry of Name Authority Files (LCNAF) for bibliographic materials, but archivists never developed a counterpart. In 1999, work began to develop a standard for the information to collect about records creators. Archivists wanted to be able to exchange this information between descriptive systems to improve discoverability and access to related archival records distributed across multiple repositories.[17] This work became the

EAC-CPF communication standard, developed in light of the International Council on Archives' (ICA) ISAAR(CPF) standard originally released in 1996. A second edition was released in 2004, just after the EAC-CPF beta was released. SAA adopted the EAC-CPF standard in January 2011.[18]

Daniel V. Pitti played a key role in the development of both EAD and EAC-CPF. In 2006, he wrote a seminal article discussing the potential opportunities now afforded by technological advancements to reshape archival description. Pitti cites the strengths of two technologies, markup language and databases, each of which takes "different approaches to representation of data."[19] Each technology is best suited to different types of information. The strength of markup languages is their ability to present complex, hierarchical relationships well. EAD was designed to work with SGML and its derivative, XML, for this reason. Markup technologies model traditional documents (letters, journal articles, books, etc.) and are characterized as "document-centric."[20] Document-centric information share common traits, like an irregular number of components (e.g., chapters, paragraphs), the importance of sequence in conveying meaning (chapter 3 must follow chapter 2), a semiregular structure and unbounded hierarchy, random mixed content (markup and data), and an arbitrary number of interrelations within and between documents. Structured query language (SQL) is the primary standard for relational databases. Information best represented in databases is characterized as "data-centric" and comes from all types of forms.[21] Names, addresses, and telephone numbers are examples of data-centric information. Data-centric information tends to have the following common traits: a regular number of fields whose order is not significant, fields restricted to data only, "interrelated fields [with] a fixed or shallow hierarchy, and the data in each field . . . controlled with respect to form and structure." The strength of databases is their ability to both separate data fields and reliably manage the relationships between fields.[22]

Archival description contains information about records creators, the functions or activities that result in the creation of records, and the records themselves. The relationship between these three is not a predictable one-to-one relationship. A creator may have records that are separated in more than one location. A set of records may have more than one creator. Functions and activities can be performed by more than a single creator, which means a specific function or activity can be split between creators, and so on. Pitti says the relationship between creators, functions, and records are "dynamic and complex, and not fixed and simple. Creators are related to other creators. Records are related to other records. Functions and activities are related to other functions and activities. And each of these is interrelated with the others."[23] The choice between using markup language or an SQL database is clear if information is predominantly document-centric or data-centric. However, archival description tends to be a mix of both. Efforts to express the complex relationships as just described benefit from the use of both technologies rather than just one. This presents a significant challenge for archival description; however, Pitti suggests an approach.

Essentially, a finding aid describes three components: the records creator, the functions or activities documented by the records, and the records themselves. EAD and subsequent technological advances have provided a foundation that makes it possible to separate these three components. EAC-CPF enables separation of the description of records creators from the rest of the finding aid. It provides authority or identity control; captures biographical, historical, and important characteristics (essential functions, activities, dates, and places of activity); and provides a way to link the records creator component to the other two, functions and the records, as well as the authority record for other records creators. In 2010, the University of Virginia began a pilot project, Social Networks and Archival Context (SNAC), to test the capability of the new standard. Participating institutions submitted EAD-encoded finding aids, from which SNAC harvested information about records creators to develop a database of archival authority records. New funding through 2017 for a second phase of work makes it possible to "develop new methods and tools for extracting and assembling archival authority descriptions; enhance methods for matching and combining records describing the same entity."[24] This project demonstrates that it is possible to separate description of records creators from the rest of an EAD-encoded finding aid, store it in a database, and add it back to as many properly coded finding aids as is necessary to describe records related to a specific creator.

Some work has been done to describe functions that result in records. Notably, ICA published the *International Standard for Describing Functions* (ISDF) in 2007. It is one of four ICA standards currently under review by the Experts Group on Archival Description (EGAD), chaired by Pitti. The University of Glasgow, Scotland, began an innovative project in 1999 to describe its records by the academic function that resulted in their creation. Archivists from Australia and New Zealand have also tried to describe records at the series level by function.[25]

Pitti believes that, with EAD and the strengths of markup language and relational databases, it is possible to separate the description of creators and the functions they carry out from the description of the resulting records. Through the use of dedicated schemas, creators, functions, and records can be described independently of each other. By interrelating the independent descriptions using machine-readable techniques, they can be combined at the time of use to form a complete archival description.[26]

There is another component to archival finding aids that is subtly expressed through decisions made about arrangement and description but that need to be expressed more intentionally if components of description are separated. This is the *relationship* between each component. In order for software to accurately recombine components, those relationships must be expressed by a machine-readable method. EGAD has started to examine this problem with a draft conceptual model presented in *Records in Context: A Conceptual Model for Archival Description*, released for public comment in September 2016.[27]

Linked Open Data

If archival finding aids or description is to be reframed into descriptive categories of information about records creators, records, and the functions that caused the records to be created, not only do the relationships between each category require defining, but also a method for rejoining or linking the appropriate components is required. Pitti and other members of EGAD propose using linked open data (LOD).[28] Hypertext links have been used to connect or link documents, but there is also a lot of data available on the web that has not been linked as effectively. Methods for making data available have included CSV, XML, or HTML tables. These methods have failed to adequately capture the structure and meaning of the data. Linked data is a "set of best practices for publishing and connecting structured data on the Web," that was designed to address this problem. Linked open data is "linked data which is released under an open license [meaning no copyright restrictions], which does not impede its reuse for free."[29] Linked (open) data is used to expose, share, connect, or link data and information on the Semantic Web in such a way that it can be read by computers. This technology enables links to be made between previously unrelated data or information and for the information to be queried.[30]

EAC-CPF makes use of linked open data. Archivists are encouraged to take the step of using this technology to provide wider access to their collections and to help researchers locate materials unknown to them that are related in some way to the person, family, or organization they are researching. If the description of activities and functions that cause records to be produced can be described in a standardized manner and similarly exposed using linked open data, researchers could potentially locate records related to the same function, regardless of who was responsible for creating them. Arranging and describing records for functions that are moved about among government agencies is not easy; neither is tracking them from a researcher's perspective. This approach would facilitate this type of searching.

Linked open data has been presented as beneficial to researchers from an access perspective, but implementation will require informed decisions about the use of metadata and standards. It will require EAD-encoded finding aids at a minimum. A 2008 survey of 168 respondents revealed that 47 percent were not using EAD.[31] A 2013 article by Katherine M. Wisser and Jackie Dean analyzes the encoding practices of archivists applying EAD. Other than consistently applying the required fields, there was not much else that was consistent about how 108 archival repositories use EAD.[32] It seems likely that, to optimize the benefits of segmenting current finding aids and linking them back together with the linked open data technology, greater standardization in applying EAD is required.[33] Further, because EAD is only a data structure standard, more consistent application of DACS or another data content standard is required.

Program Considerations

To design a cohesive description program, there are many questions to consider, many of which involve standards. Description and processing are iterative tasks. Progress made today can always be built on by taking the next step tomorrow. Determine what is realistically manageable today, prioritize, and then jump in. Designing a finding aid, selecting data structure and content standards, creating a template, and writing a document outlining these decisions in a table or chart, field by field, is a good basic start to a processing manual. Decisions that are made as less common examples arise can be added to the initial document over time. Written documentation of processes, adopted standards, decisions, templates, and illustrative examples improves consistency for tasks and aids employee training.

This work is affected by software systems the archives currently use or hope to acquire through planned growth, such as archival collection management software, an institutional repository, or a preservation system to create, store, and preserve AIPs. Another consideration is bibliographic or consortial systems to which description is contributed.

Notes

1. Archival educator Elizabeth Yakel uses the word *representation* to include both the processes of arrangement and description and the objects produced, whether a finding aid or additional descriptive products. See Elizabeth Yakel, "Archival Representation," *Archival Science* 3 (2003): 1.

2. AIMS Work Group, *AIMS Born-Digital Collections: An Inter-Institutional Model for Stewardship*, 2012, 31, accessed August 6, 2016, http://dcs.library.virginia.edu/files/2013/02/AIMS_final.pdf.; Society of American Archivists, *Describing Archives: A Content Standard* (DACS), 2nd ed. (Chicago: Society of American Archivists, 2013), xvii. Description reflects arrangement.

3. Heather MacNeil, "Archival Theory and Practice: Between Two Paradigms," *Archivaria* 37 (1994): 9; Society of American Archivists, *Describing Archives*, xvi–xviii.

4. Society of American Archivists, *Describing Archives*, xviii.

5. University of Oxford and University of Manchester, "Arranging and Cataloguing Digital and Hybrid Archives," chap. 6 in *Paradigm: Workbook on Digital Private Papers*, accessed November 26, 2016, last modified January 2, 2008, http://www.paradigm.ac.uk/workbook/cataloguing/index.html.

6. AIMS Work Group, *AIMS Born-Digital Collections*, 40. See also University of Oxford and University of Manchester, *Paradigm*; specific citation not provided in the AIMS report, and I didn't find it myself.

7. Shawn Averkamp, "Overview of Metadata for Archivists," Society of American Archivists Digital Archives Specialist webinar, June 19, 2015, slide 39.

8. International Council on Archives, *ISAD(G): General International Standard Archival Description*, 2nd ed. (Stockholm, Sweden: International Council on Archives, 1999), 10, s.v. "access point," accessed January 10, 2017, http://www.ica.org/sites/default/files/CBPS_2000_Guidelines_ISAD(G)_Second-edition_EN.pdf. See Society of American Archivists, *Describing Archives*, xxi–xxiv, on access points.

9. Society of American Archivists, *Describing Archives*, xxiii, but see the whole section on access points, xxi–xxiv.

10. See Anne J. Gilliland-Swetland, "Popularizing the Finding Aid: Exploiting EAD to Enhance Online Discovery and Retrieval in Archival Information Systems by Diverse User Groups," *Journal of Internet Cataloging* 4 (2001): 201-10.

11. Morgan G. Daniels and Elizabeth Yakel, "Seek and You May Find: Successful Search in Online Finding Aid Systems," *American Archivist* 73 (Fall/Winter 2010): 535-68; Christopher J. Prom, "User Interactions with Electronic Finding Aids in a Controlled Setting," *American Archivist* 67 (Fall/Winter 2005): 234-68, to name a few.

12. Christopher J. Prom, "Optimum Access? Processing in College and University Archives," *American Archivist* 73 (Spring/Summer 2010): 166; Michele Combs, Mark A. Matienzo, Merrilee Proffitt, and Lisa Spiro, *Over, Under, Around, and Through: Getting around Barriers to EAD Implementation* (Dublin, OH: OCLC, 2010), 9-10, accessed December 17, 2016, www.oclc.org/research/publications/library/2010/2010-04.pdf. Combs, et al., state, "Consistency of content and presentation eases the use of collection descriptions for inexperienced researchers. Finding aids that are exposed online are far more likely to be found by inexperienced researchers . . . than collection descriptions that are only available locally."

13. Michelle Light and Tom Hyry, "Colophons and Annotations: New Directions for the Finding Aid," *American Archivist* 65 (Fall/Winter 2002): 216-30.

14. See Light and Hyry, "Colophons and Annotations," 216-30; Jefferson Bailey, "Disrespect des Fonds: Rethinking Arrangement and Description in Born-Digital Archives," *Archival Journal* 3 (Summer 2013), accessed November 29, 2016, http://www.archivejournal.net/issue/3/archives---remixed/disrespect---des---fonds---rethinking---arrangement---and---description---in---born---digital---archives; J. Gordon Daines III and Cory L. Nimer, "Re-Imagining Archival Display: Creating User-Friendly Finding Aids," *Journal of Archival Organization* 9 (2011): 4-31, accessed November 29, 2016, http://dx.doi.org/10.1080/15332748.2011.574019.

15. Sibyl Schaefer and and Janet M. Bunde, "Module 1: Standards for Archival Description," in *Archival Arrangement and Description*, Trends in Archives Practice series (Chicago: Society of American Archivists, 2013), 24.

16. Society of American Archivists, *Describing Archives*, xviii.

17. Daniel V. Pitti, "Technology and the Transformation of Archival Description," *Journal of Archival Organization* 3 (2006): 18–19; "Announcements: New Funding for the Social Networks and Archival Context Project," *Encoded Archival Context Corporate Bodies, Persons, and Families*, May 18, 2012, accessed November 21, 2016, http://eac.staatsbibliothek-berlin.de/announcements.html.

18. Pitti, "Technology and Transformation," 19; "Encoded Archival Context—Corporate bodies, Persons, and Families (EAC-CPF)," *Society of American Archivists*, last updated August 8, 2012, accessed December 8, 2016, http://www2.archivists.org/groups/technical-subcommittee-on-eac-cpf/encoded-archival-context-corporate-bodies-persons-and-families-eac-cpf.

19. Pitti, "Technology and Transformation," 9–22; Gretchen Gueguen, Vitor Manoel Marques da Fonsecs, Daniel V. Pitti, and Claire Sibille-de Grimoüard, "Toward an International Conceptual Model for Archival Description: A Preliminary Report from the International Council on Archives' Experts Group on Archival Description," *American Archivist* 76 (Fall/Winter 2013): 572.

20. Pitti, "Technology and Transformation," 10–11; Gueguen et al., "Toward an International Conceptual Model," 573; Pitti, "Technology and Transformation," 12, from Ronald Bourret, *XML and Databases*, last updated September 2005, http://www.rpbourret.com/xml/XMLAndDatabases.htm. The terms *document-centric* and *data-centric* were used as early as 1997 on the xml-dev list.

21. Pitti, "Technology and Transformation," 13; Gueguen et al., "Toward an International Conceptual Model," 573; Pitti, "Technology and Transformation," 13. 12; Gueguen et al., "Toward an International Conceptual Model," 573.

22. Pitti, "Technology and Transformation," 12; Gueguen et al., "Toward an International Conceptual Model," 573.

23. Pitti, "Technology and Transformation," 17.

24. Pitti, "Technology and Transformation," 18–19; "Announcements."

25. Experts Group on Archival Description (EGAD), *Records in Contexts: A Conceptual Model for Archival Description*, consultation draft v0.1 (Paris: International Council on Archives, September 2016), 1, accessed November 23, 2016, http://www.ica.org/sites/default/files/RiC-CM-0.1.pdf; "Functions," *GASHE: Gateway to Archives of Scottish Higher Education*, accessed December 2, 2016, http://www.gashe.ac.uk/heicolls/functions.html; Pitti, "Technology and Transformation," 20. See also Chris Hurley, "What, If Anything, Is a Function?" *Archives and Manuscripts: The Journal of the Archives Section, the Library Association of Australia* 21, no. 2 (1993): 208–20. EGAD, *Records in Contexts*, is part 1 of the proposed standard that has been released for public comments.

26. Pitti, "Technology and Transformation," 18.

27. Pitti, "Technology and Transformation," 20; EGAD, *Records in Contexts*, 2, 39–90.

28. EGAD, *Records in Contexts*, 2; Gueguen et al., "Toward an International Conceptual Model," 574.

29. Christian Bizer, Tom Heath, and Tim Berners-Lee, "Linked Data: The Story So Far," *International Journal on Semantic Web and Information Systems* 5 (2009): 3, accessed December 4, 2016, doi:10.4018/jswis.2009081901; Tim Berners-Lee, "Linked Data," last revised June 18, 2009, https://www.w3.org/DesignIssues/LinkedData.html.

30. "Linked Data," *Wikipedia*, accessed December 4, 2016, https://en.wikipedia.org/wiki/Linked_data.

31. Combs et al., *Over, Under*, 5.

32. Katherine M. Wisser and Jackie Dean, "EAD Tag Usage: Community Analysis of the Use of Encoded Archival Description Elements," *American Archivist* 75 (Fall/Winter 2013): 542, 568. The authors found only one other study [Hannah C. Frost, "Guidelines Counseling: A Comparative Analysis and Evaluation of EAD Implementation Guidelines," *Journal of Archival Organization* 1 (2002): 73–86] of how archivists have applied the EAD standard in light of their institution's descriptive practices and recommend further research on the subject.

33. Gilliland-Swetland, "Popularizing the Finding Aid," also argues that more standardized use of EAD is required to improve user-centric search methods. Her article describes those search methods and design strategies that would support them.

Additional Reading and Resources

"09. Description." *Bentley Historical Library, University of Michigan*. Accessed November 17, 2016. https://sites.google.com/a/umich.edu/bhl-archival-curation/processing-archival-collections/09-description. This is the section of the Bentley's processing manual for description.

Combs, Michele, Mark A. Matienzo, Merrilee Proffitt, and Lisa Spiro. *Over, Under, Around, and Through: Getting around Barriers to EAD Implementation*. Dublin, OH: OCLC Research, 2010. Accessed December 4, 2016. www.oclc.org/research/publications/library/2010/2010-04 .pdf. Although a little dated, this report is helpful in overcoming problems implementing EAD. It includes templates and resources.

Forstrom, Michael. "Managing Electronic Records in Manuscript Collections: A Case Study from the Beinecke Rare Book and Manuscript Library." *American Archivist* 72 (Fall/Winter 2009): 460–77. This thoughtful article provides insight into the archivist's thinking about how to process digital records in hybrid collections in a manner that documents and maintains the authenticity of the files through application of DACS fields. The author uses the InterPARES 1 Authenticity Task Force's work as his baseline for defining authenticity.

"Functions." *GASHE: Gateway to Archives of Scottish Higher Education*. Accessed December 2, 2016. http://www.gashe.ac.uk/heicolls/functions.html. This page presents a partial list of functions for higher education with brief descriptions. This innovative project describes records by the academic function that they document.

Gilliland-Swetland, Anne J. "Popularizing the Finding Aid: Exploiting EAD to Enhance Online Discovery and Retrieval in Archival Information Systems by Diverse User Groups." *Journal of Internet Cataloging* 4 (2001): 199–225. Read the Pitti article before this to better imagine the possibilities Gilliland-Swetland suggests for ways to search EAD-encoded finding aids. Includes a good preliminary explanation of the multiple functions of finding aids, as well as design changes to improve finding aids.

International Council on Archives Committee on Best Practices and Standards. *ISDF: International Standard for Describing Functions*. 1st ed. Dresden, Germany: International Council on Archives, May 2–4, 2007. Accessed December 2, 2016. http://www.ica.org/sites/default/files/ CBPS_2007_Guidelines_ISDF_First-edition_EN.pdf. This is the first standard for describing archival functions.

Meissner, Dennis. "First Things First: Reengineering Finding Aids for Implementation of EAD." *American Archivist* 60 (Fall 1997): 372–87.

Pitti, Daniel V. "Technology and the Transformation of Archival Description." *Journal of Archival Organization* 3 (2006): 9–22. Pitti was a key developer of both EAD and EAC-CPF. This article explains how together these standards may revolutionize the twenty-first-century finding aid. I recommend reading this article first, followed by Gretchen Gueguen, Vitor Manoel Marques da Fonsecs, Daniel V. Pitti, and Claire Sibille-de Grimoüard, "Toward an International Conceptual Model for Archival Description: A Preliminary Report from the International Council on Archives' Experts Group on Archival Description," *American Archivist* 76 (Fall/Winter 2013): 567–84, then International Council on Archives, Experts Group on Archival Description, *Records in Contexts: A Conceptual Model for Archival Description*, consultation draft v0.1 (Paris: International Council on Archives, September 2016), http://www.ica.org/sites/default/files/RiC-CM-0.1.pdf. EGAD cites earlier work discussed in Abelardo Santamaria, *Report on the Work of CNEDA (2007-2012): Toward a Conceptual Model for Archival Description in Spain* (Seville, Spain: Ministerio de Educación, Cultura, y Deporte, July 11, 2012). An English version is at http://www.mecd.gob.es/cultura-mecd/dms/mecd/cultura-mecd/areas-cultura/archivos/mc/cneda/documentacion/ReportCNEDA_11_07_2012-pdf/ReportCNEDA_11_07_2012.pdf.

"Social Networks and Archival Context." *Institute for Advanced Technology in the Humanities, University of Virginia.* 2016. Accessed November 21, 2016. http://socialarchive.iath.virginia.edu. This project tested the use of linked open data in archival description and the new EAC-CPF standard.

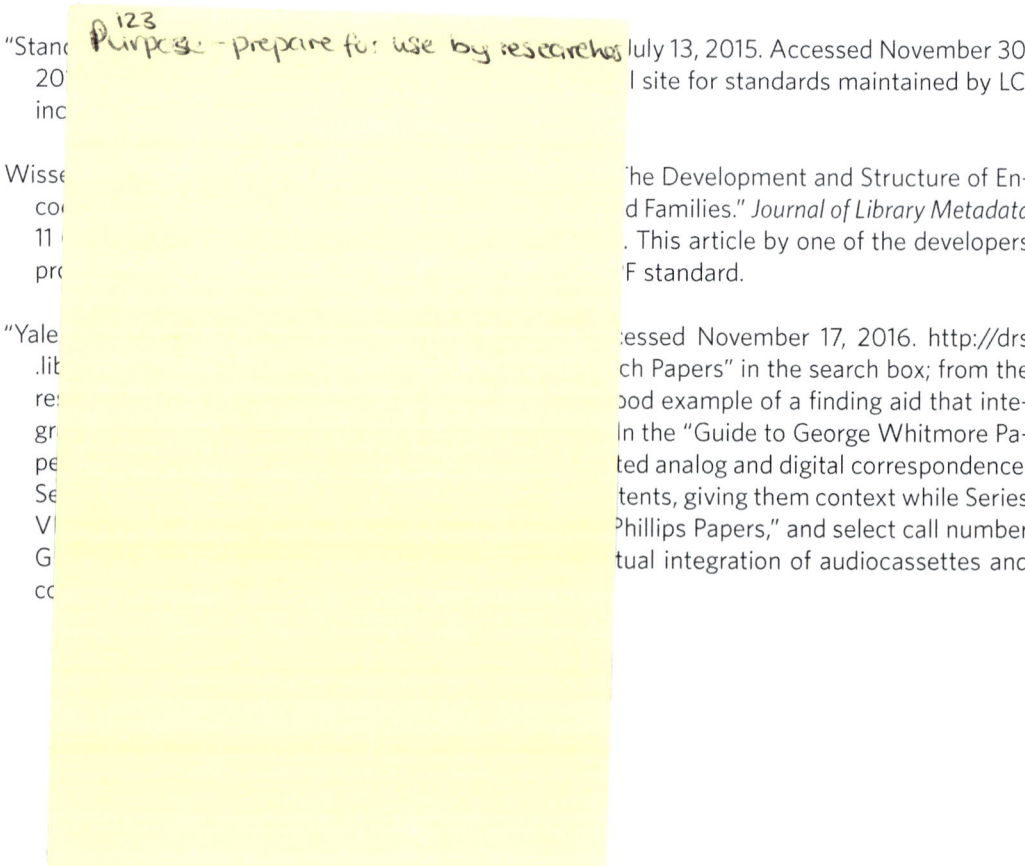

p 123
Purpose - prepare for use by researchers

"Stand[ard] ... July 13, 2015. Accessed November 30, 20[...] site for standards maintained by LC, inc[...]

Wisse[...] he Development and Structure of En- co[...] d Families." *Journal of Library Metadata* 11 [...]. This article by one of the developers pr[...] F standard.

"Yale [...] essed November 17, 2016. http://drs .lib[...] ch Papers" in the search box; from the res[...] od example of a finding aid that inte- gr[...] In the "Guide to George Whitmore Pa- pe[...] ted analog and digital correspondence. Se[...] tents, giving them context while Series V[...] Phillips Papers," and select call number G[...] tual integration of audiocassettes and c[...]

8

Digital Access to Description and Records

The purpose of everything an archivist does to or for a body of records is to prepare it for use by researchers. Description used to be the final step in the process of readying archival records for use. The description was typed to create a paper finding aid that was shown to researchers in the research room or sent by postal mail in advance when requested. The description and the method by which it was delivered were one and the same. Some institutions created bibliographic card files intermingling archival and published materials, also only available in the research room. Select institutions published guides to their collections. Until 1993, the *National Union Catalog of Manuscript Collections* (NUCMC) was a printed union catalog of manuscript collections nationwide; now, it is a searchable database on the web.[1] Other options that developed include the creation of MARC bibliographic records for local library catalogs and then national catalogs like WorldCat; word-processed documents; customized local databases using FileMaker, spreadsheet software, and other database-type software; web pages in plain text or displaying word-processed and, later, PDF documents; customized database software–managed, web-delivered finding aids or collection description; and other variations. The development of commercial software, custom-written based on archival practice, standards, and needs is a very recent development.[2] Today, with the advent of the desktop computer and development and growth of the web, it is possible to separate description from the method by which it is delivered, meaning access. Consequently, access has become a separate and crucial step in making records available for use.

Access Systems to Deliver Description and Records

A review of textbox 3.2 shows the following incomplete tasks:

7. Create access tools

    7.a. Identify the types of access tools to create.

    7.b. Create them.

    New. Load records or metadata into the tools.

Does the delivery system precede design of the descriptive program or dictate the standards to apply, or do decisions about description and standards guide selection of the delivery method or software? Hopefully there is a bit of both. An institution may aspire to automate creation of EAD-encoded, DACS- and EAC-CPF-compliant description but currently only create DACS-compliant finding aids. Several archival management systems (see appendix B) automate EAD encoding once the archivist sets up a template indicating how to code each field in the institution's finding aid, but they may or may not yet automate EAC-CPF description. System variations include the descriptive standards it uses, other functions it performs (besides EAD encoding), and compatibility with existing or hoped-for technology. The final choice may be based on any of these factors, cost, or technology requirements to use the system. The individual priorities of each archives influence its decisions.

Current delivery methods for description still include word-processed finding aids delivered in print, by e-mail, as an HTML web page of text and tables or a PDF document, or in an institutional repository as a PDF file. PDF files are word-searchable. HTML web pages are searchable by web browsers if their access is not restricted at the institutional level for security purposes. Some web pages and PDF finding aids are also more optimized than others for browser discoverability. The physical card catalog has been replaced by MARC records in an online public access (electronic) catalog (OPAC) or is delivered by a newer web-based integrated library (management) system (ILS).[3] Some archives create MARC catalog records at the collection or record group, series, or item level that are delivered via their library catalog system. Some current integrated library management systems still include a search capability, but some are not as effective or well developed as they were previously. To address this issue, there are separate discovery products, like OCLC's Discovery or Ex Libris's Primo, that sit on top of and are designed to work with the ILS, which seem to be producing better search results. They obviously search MARC catalog records in the ILS but can also search finding aids delivered from library web pages.[4]

Some of the access methods and software systems described in this chapter contain description about records but not the records themselves; for example, ArchivesSpace. ArchivesSpace can also digitally describe records that are in an analog format. Some methods are able to deliver not only the description but also the digital object being described. ContentDM delivers item-level description attached to the individual digital object, while DSpace and BePress treat the finding aid like another digital object and deliver both components.

Commercial Systems Managing Digital Objects in Active Use

A number of commercial applications manage current records in active use in business and government. A document management system (DMS) tracks, manages, and stores digital documents. It may track document versions and editing by users. A document management system may be a component of a larger enterprise content management system (ECM) and overlap in function with records management systems.[5] The Association for Information and Image Management (AIIM) defines ECM as the "systematic collection and organization of information that is to be used by a designated audience. It is a dynamic combination of strategies, methods, and tools used to capture, manage, store, preserve, and deliver information supporting key organizational processes through its entire lifecycle."[6] Records and information management (RIM) is management of actively used records, predominantly in business and government, to control risk and compliance and capture evidence of business activities. Sharepoint, OnBase, Open Text, Documentum, and Oracle Content Management are examples of enterprise content management systems.[7] DMSs and ECMs manage, index, store, and retrieve information and records in active use. These systems provide access to the digital objects but not archival description. They have information about the documents to manage copies and versions because the files are being actively used. Some of these records are not intended for permanent retention. The systems are not designed to preserve records for the long term using archival description standards to protect their authenticity, integrity, and interoperability with other archival systems. Records created or managed by business systems like these may eventually be transferred to an archives, but the two types of systems should not be confused with each other. They serve different functions. If digital records managed by a DMS, ECM, or even a records management system can export structured description or metadata as XML, it is a usable start to describing that body of records.[8]

Archival Collection Management Systems

Initial software applications for managing archival holdings tended to focus on managing analog collections and often were originally designed for libraries, businesses, or other nonarchival users. Cuadra Associates appears to have been one of the earliest companies to market their product to archives, starting in the early 1980s, followed by Eloquent in about 1989. Other examples of collection management software include Archon and Archivists' Toolkit, which may still have users but has been replaced by ArchivesSpace; ICA-AtoM, developed for the international archival community; CollectiveAccess for archives and museums; Minisis, also oriented to museums; and PastPerfect, designed for local historical societies, manages archival records, photos, objects, and books. These applications include open-source, proprietary, manage-it-yourself, and hosted options.

The best of these systems includes an accessioning function to capture initial descriptive information that is entered once and reused; capture the relationships between sets of records within a record group or collection; comply with DACS and other descriptive standards; and create finding aids that are deliverable in multiple formats, including XML EAD. They not only create description, but they also deliver it, providing searchable access to the finding aids. These systems use relational database and markup technologies. Researchers access the description in these archival collection management systems from the web. While these systems describe archival records of all formats, the collection materials are likely to be stored elsewhere. Where possible, it is desirable to link from the description of digital records to the digital objects themselves.[9]

Institutional Repositories

An institutional repository accepts, stores, and delivers access copies of digital resources. Each organization decides the type of resources it will include in its IR. Examples include raw research data and archival resources that may be used to create new scholarship and published scholarship. Software like DSpace; Fedora; Hydra combined with other software; and Islandora, which like Hydra is also based on Fedora but combined with different software; and Bepress are used to develop institutional repositories. DSpace and Fedora were designed to create digital archival repositories. Bepress was initially designed for a publishing workflow. Some of these software can be hosted, some cannot, and some require a very high level of technical skill to develop.

IRs are basically custom-designed digital databases, just like the many electronic databases to which libraries subscribe to provide resources for their patrons. In this case, the institution gets to pick its content. Archival records are described and uploaded at the item level. They can be grouped in a hierarchical manner though not too deeply (three to four levels); the names of levels are not all archival terms. Description adheres to accepted standards. This process varies by the software or vender. Northern Kentucky University is using a hosted version of DSpace. It comes with a preset data-entry form that provides some qualified DC fields, but not all. Data-entry field names do not always match the DC field they map to in the display records. At the local level, our department developed a guide documenting how to apply each field, applicable data content standards, and examples based on typical records in our holdings. Like collection materials, finding aids in the form of PDFs can be included in the IR. Both are searchable. It is possible to link between finding aids and digital records stored in the IR or between digital records in an IR and a finding aid in a collection management application. IRs are searchable by Google and should be searchable by library discovery products like Discover and Primo, depending on how the discovery product is configured. Note also that IRs can serve as the delivery system for access copies or DIPS as part of an OAIS framework.

Other software products that are less powerful or more functionally limited have been used to deliver collection materials. OCLC's Contentdm is a digital media management, storage, and retrieval software that can handle any document, image, video, or audio file and deliver it via the web. Contentdm was originally designed for images to replace art slide libraries. It "plays well" with other systems that use Dublin Core. It presents description but is less powerful because it is not a relational database; neither does it perform the wide range of functions of a system like ArchivesSpace.[10] Omeka is a free, open-source web-publishing tool that can present exhibits and collections via the web. It requires little technical skill, is easily set up, and allows user interaction with the content.[11] It, too, is not a fully functional institutional repository but is another tool archivists can consider for content delivery.

Consortial or Portal Databases

Many of the software applications mentioned so far in this chapter are commercial; some are open source. This dichotomy involves choices. Commercial software requires money. Open-source software usually requires a high level of technical skill, even computer programming skills, and time to develop, possibly customize, install, and manage it. This may require a commitment from IT, hiring someone, or a skilled archivist taking time from other archival responsibilities. Salaries may appear to be less of a cost than new funding for software, but the cost includes less productivity in another archival function. Most of the commercial software mentioned is licensed, meaning there is a reoccurring annual expense in library budget parlance. In tight budgetary times, this may be difficult to obtain. The pricing for software may also be tiered depending on the amount of storage used or the number of records, making it more affordable while allowing for growth. In situations where institutional IT support is judged to be minimal, the answer may be a hosted version of the application. The archives, library, or institution needs to ensure that its vender contract obligates the vender to be responsible for updating software, providing equipment and personnel with the requisite skills, backing up data files, and maintaining and protecting servers. The tradeoff for a hosted version is less customization and less independence in managing your instance of the software.

Another option to help balance monetary costs and technical requirements is to participate in a consortium—join a group of other archives who are creating collection description and delivering it. The Online Archive of California (OAC) is a statewide consortium that delivers finding aids through a single, searchable web portal. Contributors may submit EAD-encoded finding aids that comply with the consortium's best practices or MARC21 collection guides or item-level records.[12] How they accomplish that is up to the individual institution, although OAC provides many resources, from online web forms and templates, transformation scripts, and tools to software suggestions and more. Once an institution creates the EAD or MARC21 collection guide, OAC handles the publishing, makes the guides accessible to ArchivesGrid and WorldCat, makes them available to other aggregators through Open Archives Initiative Protocol for Metadata Harvesting (OAI-PMH), links them to Aeon software or Google Analytics for usage statistics, and provides a searchable digital repository for digital items.[13] The Ohio Library and Information Network (*OhioLINK*) is a consortium of Ohio college and university libraries and the State Library of Ohio. Among its resources is a finding aids repository of EAD-encoded finding aids. Support for contributors includes an EAD finding aid creation tool, content guidelines, and resources. These are two examples of geographic-based consortia. Others may focus on a common topic or even format. The Kentucky Oral History Commission created Pass the Word, a discovery portal for oral histories held by organizations in Kentucky.[14] Description submissions follow a template. Collections are searchable and bring the researcher to the contributor's finding aid, catalog, or even the oral history itself.

Depending on institutional decisions regarding the technology it can support to deliver archival description and the selection of and local implementation decisions for description standards, these choices determine which records to create, how to format them, and where they should be entered. Archival software applications, standards manuals, and local practice should provide guidance on how to create descriptive records for specific delivery methods.

Structured versus Unstructured Data or Long-Lived Description

Archivists need to create description that is portable, interoperable, long-lived, and reusable. This is a goal for my archives in order to increase the efficiency of a highly labor-intensive task. Compliance with current descriptive standards, most especially DACS and EAD, also increases efficiency. "EAD is represented in XML (Extensible Markup Language), a platform-neutral data format that ensures . . . data longevity when migrated from one software environment to another." EAD ensures the long-term viability of data by encoding intellectual content unlike HTML, which only encodes presentation. EAD can be produced from or mapped to a variety of formats, including relational databases, MARC, Dublin Core, HTML, and others, which makes it an excellent format for porting data.[15] DACS and EAD are description standards that are designed to work together and are the combination that is the most flexible and interoperable. They support the newer PREMIS standard for preservation and the EAC-CPF standard, which is moving finding aids and archival description in a new direction through linked open data.

Computers can produce EAD-encoded finding aids most readily from description that is formatted as structured data. In *Designing Descriptive and Access Systems*, archivist Daniel A. Santamaria provides numerous examples of exporting or converting description stored in spreadsheets; Microsoft Access, FileMaker, or other local databases; or XML, tab, or other delimited files into MARC so that it can then be converted to EAD. These conversions are possible with varying degrees of difficulty because the description is formatted as structured data. On the other hand, unstructured data is not so readily converted to EAD. The most common example of unstructured data or description is a word-processed finding aid, although word processing is also used for accession records and other forms.[16] The lack of structure makes word-processed finding aids the most difficult format to automate migration out of in order to create EAD. It may be easier and faster to manually encode this category of finding aid.

Because word-processed finding aids are unstructured data, this is a handicap for migrating them to EAD encoding or newer collection management software. However, word-processed finding aids can easily be printed for research room use; mailed or e-mailed to a distant researcher; converted to PDF, which is a searchable, portable, sustainable format; and easily published to the web. They are also easily made DACS-compliant. These qualities make word processing very appealing to a smaller institution or one with limited technological capability or manpower.

"Although today's researchers find collection descriptions using keyword searching on search engines, the Web of the future will be no place for unstructured data. The future is the 'semantic Web' or linked data. Implementing EAD will help to position your institution for the future of internet applications."[17] Unstructured data is unlinkable and consequently may become invisible compared with linked information.

Initially, implementation of EAD encoding was a complicated, technical process usually involving several software applications just to start. Many journal articles and books have been written about EAD, including problems, tips, help, case studies, and more. With the release of EAD3 in mid-2015, some resources are dated. Writing in 2008, Sonia Yaco identifies three hurdles to implementation: technical challenges to encoding finding aids; technical difficulty of a server to deliver encoded finding aids; and desire to improve description before encoding, notably to implement DACS.[18] With the development of archival software applications like Archivists' Toolkit, Archon, and ArchivesSpace, hopefully the first two hurdles are mostly addressed, with much of the work being done by the software. The 2010 OCLC report by Michele Combs and colleagues puts it differently but identifies similar difficulties and offers resources and solutions. Not all archives are able to afford these systems, but a lot of work has been done in the last eighteen years. The University of California consortium has created many resources to assist archivists with a variety of approaches to EAD encoding. See this chapter's "Additional Reading and Resources" for the report by Combs and colleagues, as well as "EAD Toolkit."

Yaco's third hurdle, confirmed by the OCLC report, the desire to upgrade finding aids before EAD encoding, remains. Archival literature and experience confirm that the description created by any individual archives is not consistent for all its holdings. Part of the holdings are described by access system A, part are described in system B, and the remainder in system C. Another possible inconsistency is the use of more than one template for finding aids. As an institution increases its application of standards, for example, its template might be revised and result in descriptive variations. DACS permits creation of collection-level description only and multilevel description. One collection processed to the series level and another to the folder level based on collection differences or MPLP decisions are legitimate reasons for differences in their descriptions; also, not all fields in any given description standard apply to every set of records. Description is iterative. An institution's descriptive program makes progress as the department develops. This is likely to leave a trail of legacy finding aids delivered by different methods during that growth. Many archives hope to eventually implement a collection management system or other advanced technology, but having all finding aids formatted with a single, uniform template and delivery or access system is an equally valid goal.

Notes

1. "NUCMC History Timeline: 1947–Present," *Library of Congress*, accessed December 18, 2016, http://www.loc.gov/coll/nucmc/timeline.html; "NUCMC: National Union Catalog of Manuscript Collections," accessed December 18, 2016, http://www.loc.gov/coll/nucmc.

2. Archon was first released in July 2006, while Archivists' Toolkit was still in early development. "Archon (software)," *Wikipedia*, accessed December 18, 2016, https://en.wikipedia.org/wiki/Archon_(software).

3. See Elizabeth Post, "Embedding Metadata in PDF Finding Aids to Enhance Discoverability," *Boston College University Libraries*, August 2016, accessed December 21, 2016, http://hdl.handle.net/2345/bc-ir:107137; Christopher J. Prom, "Using Web Analytics to Improve Online Access to Archival Resources," *American Archivist* 74 (Spring/Summer 2011): 158–84, especially 178–81. Software for the previous generation of library management systems, like Voyager, resided on the institution's servers. Examples of the new cloud-based, web-delivered ILS systems include OCLC's Worldshare Management Services (WMS), Koha (open source), Ex Libris's Alma, and Innovative Interfaces' Millennium.

4. Daniel A. Santamaria, "Module 3: Designing Descriptive and Access Systems," in *Archival Arrangement and Description*, Trends in Archives Practice series (Chicago: Society of American Archivists, 2013), 198–99.

5. "Document management system," *Wikipedia*, accessed December 18, 2016, https://en.wikipedia.org/wiki/Document_management_system.

6. Association for Information and Image Management (AIIM), *Glossary*, s.v. "enterprise content management," accessed December 18, 2016, http://www.aiim.org/What-is-ECM-Enterprise-Content-Manage ment.aspx#.

7. "Document management system," *Wikipedia*, accessed December 18, 2016, https://en.wikipedia.org/wiki/Document_management_system; Karen A. Hobert, Gavin Tay, and Joe Mariano, *Magic Quadrant for Enterprise Content Management* (Stamford, CT: Gartner, October 31, 2016), accessed December 18, 2016, https://www.gartner.com/doc/reprints?id=1-3KZPGDB&ct=161031&st=sb.

8. Santamaria, "Module 3," 151.

9. Prom, "Using Web Analytics," 174, 177. Recall Prom's finding about the desirability of a tight, two-way link between description and digital content.

10. "Contentdm," *OCLC*, accessed December 22, 2016, http://www.oclc.org/en-US/contentdm.html; Lisa Spiro, "Notes from Interviews with Archivists about Archon, Archivists' Tookit, Cuadra STAR/Archives, Eloquent, and CollectiveAccess," app. 4 in *Archival Management Software: Report for the Council on Library and Information Resources* (Washington, DC: Council on Library and Information Resources, 2009), accessed December 22, 2016, https://www.clir.org/pubs/reports/spiro/append4.htm.

11. "Serious Web Publishing," *Omeka*, accessed December 23, 2016, https://omeka.org/about. See Jason Kucsma, Kevin Reiss, and Angela Sidman, "Using Omeka to Build Digital Collections: The METRO Case Study," *D-Lib Magazine* 16 (March/April 2010), accessed December 23, 2016, doi:10.1045/march2010 -kucsma; Nancy Moussa, "What Is Omeka?" *Library Tech Talk*, July 8, 2015, https://www.lib.umich .edu/blogs/library-tech-talk/what-omeka-0, for additional information, examples of use, strengths, and weaknesses.

12. OAC Working Group, Metadata Standards Subcommittee, *OAC Best Practice Guidelines for EAD (OAC BPG EAD)*, ver. 2.0 (Oakland: University of California, April 2005), accessed December 23, 2016, http://www.cdlib.org/services/access_publishing/dsc/contribute/docs/oacbpgead_v2-0.pdf.

13. "EAD Toolkit," *University of California, California Digital Library*, accessed December 23, 2016, http://www.cdlib.org/services/access_publishing/dsc/tools/ead_toolkit.html; "Dashboard/Administration," *University of California, California Digital Library*, accessed December 23, 2016, http://www.cdlib.org/services/access_publishing/dsc/contribute/administration.html.

14. "OhioLINK EAD Finding Aid Creation Tool," *OEAD Encoded Archival Description*, accessed December 23, 2016, https://ead.library.kent.edu/login.php; "Documentation," *Ohio EAD Task Force*, accessed December

23, 2016, https://sites.google.com/site/ohioead/s; "Guide to Archives Consortia," *Society of American Archivists*, accessed December 23, 2016, http://www2.archivists.org/groups/regional-archival-associations-consortium-raac/guide-to-archives-consortia; "Pass the Word," *Kentucky Oral History Commission*, accessed December 23, 2016, http://passtheword.ky.gov.

15. Sonia Yaco, "It's Complicated: Barriers to EAD Implementation," *American Archivist* 71 (Fall/Winter 2008): 456–75; Michele Combs, Mark A. Matienzo, Merrilee Proffitt, and Lisa Spiro, *Over, Under, Around, and Through: Getting around Barriers to EAD Implementation* (Dublin, OH: OCLC, 2010), 8, accessed December 17, 2016, www.oclc.org/research/publications/library/2010/2010-04.pdf. Description in general is time-consuming; Yaco specifically discusses time for EAD. On page 463, she finds that a minimum staff of four archivists affects an institution's ability to adopt EAD, while on 471, a survey respondent cites the need for uninterrupted time to concentrate on planning, not just execution of encoding.

16. Santamaria, "Module 3," 151, 154–55, 161–62, 168, 152, 164, 169.

17. Combs, *Over, Under*, 10.

18. Yaco, "It's Complicated," 471–72.

Additional Reading and Resources

Combs, Michele, Mark A. Matienzo, Merrilee Proffitt, and Lisa Spiro. *Over, Under, Around, and Through: Getting around Barriers to EAD Implementation*. Dublin, OH: OCLC Research, 2010. Accessed December 17, 2016. www.oclc.org/research/publications/library/2010/2010-04.pdf. This report addresses technical problems with implementing EAD and includes templates, web forms, migration and conversion tools, many other useful tools and added information.

"EAD Encoded Archival Description Official Site." *Library of Congress*. Accessed December 17, 2016. http://www.loc.gov/ead. This is the official website for this standard. This page includes directions to subscribe to the EAD LISTSERV.

"EAditor." *GitHub*. Accessed December 17, 2016. https://github.com/ewg118/eaditor. This is a tool to create and edit EAD finding aids using Xforms for data entry. It also works with content management systems and can include an "easily customizable public interface for searching, sorting, and browsing collections of finding aids" (Santamaria, "Module 3," 163).

"EAD Toolkit." *University of California, California Digital Library*. Accessed December 17, 2016. http://www.cdlib.org/services/access_publishing/dsc/tools/ead_toolkit.html. This rich resource includes a best practices guide for EAD encoding, guidelines for EAD guides created by collection management software, web forms, other software, and more.

"NUCMC: National Union Catalog of Manuscript Collections." *Library of Congress*. Accessed December 18, 2016. http://www.loc.gov/coll/nucmc/eligible.html. Those institutions "unable to contribute national-level cataloging to OCLC WorldCat" may qualify to have LC create and submit bibliographic records for collections to WorldCat and create authority records.

Post, Elizabeth. "Embedding Metadata in PDF Finding Aids to Enhance Discoverability." *Boston College University Libraries*. August 2016. Accessed December 21, 2016. http://hdl.handle.net/2345/bc-ir:107137. This is a brief but interesting document about programming Archivists' Toolkit to beef up the metadata in the PDF finding aids it creates to enhance discoverability in ArchivesGrid and Google.

Reese, Terry. *MarcEdit*. Accessed December 17, 2016. http://marcedit.reeset.net. This is an open-source software that edits MARC records, but it can also convert them to another structured format, like EAD, or export MARC data as delimited text for use in another application. The "Delimited Text Translator" can translate data from Excel, Access, or any delimited format into MARC. MarcEdit can do more. There are also tutorials and other aids for its use.

Santamaria, Daniel A. "Module 3: Designing Descriptive and Access Systems." In *Archival Arrangement and Description*. Trends in Archives Practice series. Chicago: Society of American Archivists, 2013. Appendix A describes options for creating description and delivering it based on ease of performance. Appendix B includes a case study that walks through one possible workflow and names specific tools for each step. The module also provides numerous examples of how to convert information from one format to another with the goal of encoding as EAD.

9

Parting Thoughts

User Studies and Development of Description for Both External and Internal Audiences

User studies will continue to play an important role in the design of archival description for two diverse audiences. The first is external, the researcher who seeks information. The trend to reduce archival mediation in the use of archival materials and the design of software systems that provide access without an archivist is likely to continue. Archives have succeeded in attracting online users from greater distances than those who visit in person. Technology and advertising have increased user expectations of 24/7 access to whatever they want, whether shopping on Amazon or searching on Google. Unfortunately, neither of these has educated the user about the unseen high costs and labor required to build infrastructure to meet unrealistic expectations. Archives don't have the resources of Amazon or Google to deliver at that level.

Archivists like Elizabeth Yakel, Wendy Duff, Christopher Prom, and others have conducted studies of how users discover our resources, how long they stay on websites that deliver finding aids, how they interact with finding aids, some of their (erroneous) expectations, and whether their searches are successful.[1] Users have problems with archival vocabulary. They are unfamiliar with the structure, contents, and purpose of finding aids. They do not grasp archival hierarchies and how records relate or even clearly understand the distinction between archives and libraries.[2] Google or Google-like searches hunting for subject terms combine with software systems that present series descriptions as if they stand alone to bypass context and bring researchers directly to series-level records. As an archivist, I do not always feel I can easily identify related records, and unlike many researchers, I know there should be a hierarchy, but I cannot find it in some systems. Software systems add a layer between the researcher and the finding aid. Their search functions vary in how they work, how limited the search choices are, and the quality of search results.[3] What do researchers make of what they find in some of these systems? In the last ten years or so, Archon, Archivists' Toolkit, and ArchivesSpace have come into use; DACS, ICA-ISDF, and EAC-CPF were adopted; and the web began using linked (open) data. These changes affect how description is written and presented by the finding aid, whether information within the finding aid is standardized, how it is displayed, and search options the delivery system allows. These variables may also affect how the systems search or the quality of the search results they return.

A contributing factor to researchers' confusion is the general absence of education on how to use an archives and its resources and the lack of awareness that, though physically located within libraries, archives and libraries function differently. Library (and Google) search methods, like browsing, don't work in archives. Yakel and Torres studied characteristics users needed to successfully conduct archival research, focusing particularly on their "archival intelligence," and conclude that archivists need to do more in the way of archival user education.[4] Their findings are useful for developing instruction that could improve researchers' skills and their success rates when interacting with archival materials, whether remotely or in person. The challenge may be in getting remote users to even quickly skim instructional information before proceeding to search for materials, but that is a question for another user study.

The second audience to be studied is internal; it is us, the archivists who perform arrangement and description. It is those who have recommended changes to and development of standards, how description is performed and envisioned, and how changes in web technology could reshape archival description. How are these changes working? Are they working? Are there user studies for finding aids using ICA-ISDF and EAC-CPF? Do we know whether implementation of these particular standards has improved researcher success in finding records? Many studies examine the implementation of EAD and the problems institutions have with adopting it. These problems have gradually been eased as applications like Archon, Archivists' Toolkit, and ArchivesSpace were developed and automated some of the implementation work. It was eight years between the release of the first version of EAD and Archon, which automated EAD encoding with a single software. How are archives implementing PREMIS, EAC-CPF, or linked data in general? Manually? Will software like ArchivesSpace eventually be able to encode for these new standards?

Do we know whether archives have been implementing all of these new descriptive standards and technology options? What percent of archives? What problems have they encountered? Are the standards that have been approved or the changes that have been recommended working, making a difference either to researchers or the archivists assisting them? In 1989, the Working Group on Standards for Archival Description linked better automated descriptive system design to verified knowledge of researchers' behavior gained through user studies.[5] The profession has made changes in description. To which degree has it been applied, how effectively (by archivists)? Is it working, according to researchers?

Archives, like libraries, museums, and others, increasingly need to be able to assess their work and justify systems, technology, personnel, and expenses to resource allocators. We need studies to answer questions like these in order to argue effectively to continue to implement additional description or license systems that can.

Issues Regarding the Future of Archival Description

Writing as director for the National Information Systems Task Force (NISTF) in 1983, David Bearman expresses concern about archivists' "frightening level of indifference to information retrieval theory, lack of experience in generalizing from immediate context to broader systems requirements, and woeful ignorance of automation planning methodologies."[6] Bearman recommends archivists remedy this ignorance in order to better design description and access systems of the future.

In discussing the application of standards to description, archivist Michael Rush mentions that standards implementation has led to the need for archivists to develop "programming skills that are not trivial," even though the work to be done is not, in his opinion, really archival. "We must eliminate needless complexity and ease the processes of implementing standards and generating descriptive data."[7] Archivists have reached the stage in technological development of records description that there is a separation between the archival work and the technology that we use to create, manage, or deliver description. Analog materials have been and continue to be physically arranged. Description conveys the written or recorded representation of the physical arrangement. This is one reason bibliographic description fails; it is not tied to this physical or intellectual arrangement. Similarly, the technology (e.g., encoding) that presents, delivers, or links description is not description itself but one of the mechanisms for conveying the description. Care needs to be taken that the technology used to deliver description is not separated from the description itself or the arrangement on which it depends. This was part of the problem with the development of the NUCMC card catalog version. The rules for description and method of delivery (catalog cards) were divorced from archival arrangement and description. Archivists are content specialists. We know our materials and how to describe them. Sometimes we have the requisite technological knowledge for the systems that deliver that description. Sometimes we do not and work with others who are experts in the needed technology. Each specialist contributes his knowledge to create standards-compliant description delivered by software systems chosen by their institution. Just as the archivist who lacks computer programming skills is not an IT specialist, so, too, the technology specialist who lacks an archival education is not qualified to write archival description. Library catalogers, systems librarians, and IT professionals can contribute technical expertise the archivist may lack, but the archivist is the expert on archival description and should take the lead on how description is done or delivered. Enough archivists need to have sufficient technical skill or support from technical specialists to develop software that respects archival principles and practice so that implementation of descriptive standards can be automated. Every archivist should not have to develop the same high degree of technical expertise to implement descriptive standards; otherwise, implementation will not be widespread. I do not know how to build a computer, but I can use one to complete archival tasks.

DACS has twenty-five possible fields with a variety of ways to use them. PREMIS has ninety-five potential fields. EAC-CPF has ninety elements with thirty attributes. ICA's recently released Records in Contexts Conceptual Model describes eighty-three entities and properties with forty-nine pages of options to describe the relationship between entities.[8] That is hundreds of choices, fields with which to have some familiarity. That sounds a bit like the case with EAD. Is there a way to reduce this complexity? Can a worksheet or form, with certain fields reserved for each of these standards that are properly coded to send the input information to the appropriate software or finding aid display, depending on the function of the standard or the individual field, be developed? Archivists decide how many fields to complete for a minimal record; all data entry for the standards they choose are completed in and automated by a single software.

It looks like the description model I present in chapter 7 is very likely to occur. Creators and functions have already been broken off (EAC-CPF, ICA-ISDF, or the draft Records in Contexts Conceptual Model). We've been describing records for decades. The new Records in Contexts Model addresses relationships and linked open data, already functions on the web. Now, how to put it all together? Archival collection management systems or other software for delivering description and content will need updating. Archivists will require training and help to implement. Lessons learned in trying to implement EAD should be considered.

"[T]he archival community is in transition 'from a one-dimensional archival description (focusing almost exclusively on the representations of records), to another multidimensional description, aimed at creating and maintenance [*sic*] of representations of entities of different types (records, agents, business, etc.) and their interrelationships.'"[9] Separating description into components based on its purpose and relinking them has some advantages and may address some of the concerns archivists have had about open records that change creators with time or whose creator changes functions. Some archivists have complained that description has remained bound by the form of finding aids predating the web and that typed finding aids have simply been published on the web. This development in description certainly does not follow that pattern. These components—creator, function, records, entity relationships—focus on researchers. Description has also included information for the archivist to manage the records. Where is that going? Will it be a separate component? Mostly included in the records component? Or will it be relegated to archival collection management software and require use of a unique identifier to maintain links between the records and their management information, like the OAIS framework?

I have two concerns about this potential course of deconstructing finding aids. I have difficulty imagining how this works. Will this method result in each individual component occupying a cell in a universal, master relational database at the institutional or national level? Will there be separate master databases for each of the components, creators, functions, and records? Will only record-group or collection-level or series-level records description exist, with links to creators, functions, and any digital copies of the records? Will the links go off to these master databases to search for related people, functions, or records there? Will the group-level or collection-level or series-level records description have dozens or hundreds of links directly to other related creators, functions, and digital copies?

Based on my unclear image of how this description methodology will work on a practical level, the first concern is for users. As has already been presented in this book, user studies have shown researchers do not understand archival vocabulary, have difficulty grasping our arrangement methods, do not comprehend that their knowledge of how libraries function does not transfer well to archives, struggle to use finding aids, and expect to bypass finding aids and go directly to records that they will somehow search by subject. They attempt to use what they know, library and Google search techniques, in their search strategies because they do not know how to function in an archival environment. Search results that give them what they want and drop them directly in a record series may not really be in their best interest. Yakel and others argue that more education is needed. I agree. That is an excellent proposal. There may be opportunities to collaborate with library information literacy programs.

So, if researchers are struggling with the current formats of finding aids, how will they fare with finding aids that are broken apart into related components? Does this type of design increase the probability of Google taking researchers directly to series-level description over other components? Recall Prom's research that at least partially verifies search engine impact. He documents that Google took 47.8 percent of their users directly to a series-level description, although the location of subject search terms seems to have influenced Google's behavior.[10] How will design variations improve or hinder comprehension of context or the ability to recognize other related records and how they are related to the original set of records? Will researchers realize there are other components? Will linking components from a single collection to components from many different collections create an overwhelming results list? How useful will it be to wade through that much material, if they look past the first twenty-five or fifty results? If they want to go visit an archives after conducting preliminary online research, will they clearly understand which records are at the archives they plan to visit? Will the screen view a researcher sees of a particular set of records always be the same if the same search is repeated? Will his or her view be the same as the archivist at the repository holding the records, or will it be a custom researcher-specific mini–finding aid at the series or file level? If not, how will the archivist assist the researcher? How will they know whether the researcher is looking at their holdings and not another archives? Increasing the complexity of our description is likely to increase researcher confusion and the need for user education and the information to be included in user education. How will this difficulty be addressed, particularly for the remote researchers who wish to use materials in an unmediated style? Will they even locate any educational materials on our websites based on their route to our records? Prom's research shows that only 11.9 percent of users started at the archives' homepage, and he suspects the majority of those were staff members.[11] Will links to helpful material on our sites be included in the archival description they locate?

Table 9.1. Automation of Description Standards

Standard	Date Approved as Standard	Automated Implementation in Software	Interval
EAD	1998	Archon, July 2006	8 years
OAIS framework	May 1999	Some components automated	17 years
PREMIS	May 2005	Not automated yet?	11.5 years
EAC-CPF	January 2011	ArchivesSpace, ver. 0.4, March 2013	2 years

The second concern is for archivists trying to implement all this. Table 9.1 shows the interval between approval as a standard for some recent descriptive standards and the date when software first automated production of description according to that standard. The literature on EAD implementation suggests that, until new and currently proposed descriptive standards and technology can be automated, the greater part of archives will not be able to apply them. Amazingly, DACS and EAC-CPF were rapidly incorporated into software that itself was being newly developed. Timing is likely to account for their rapid adoption by archival software. Compare the progress for implementing PREMIS, which is largely still not automated, with EAD. Archivists who can generate metadata encoding and transmission standard (METS) data or use DROID or JHOVE software can create PREMIS description, which is similar to the stage when EAD was created by using several software tools in combination.[12] Once EAD no longer required combining a series of software and a special server but could be generated as part of one system that handled several archival functions, adoption became much easier time-wise and technically. Archivematica has shown promise in 2016 with the University of Michigan project.[13] It can create PREMIS description as well as further automate more of the work for implementing the OAIS framework.

If use of archival collection management software becomes a requirement for more than basic description, licensing fees will become a minimum hurdle to overcome in order to join the club. The profession needs to be careful of creating the "great descriptive divide," which essentially becomes a case of haves and have-nots: archives with sufficient resources to either obtain the requisite software or manually create standards-compliant description and those who can afford neither so possibly create "old-fashioned," unsegmented, DACS-compliant finding aids without linked open data delivered via web pages. Standards are important, but while we are dazzled by what technology might make possible, let us not create an unattainable ideal for the average archivist and institution. We need to develop options for the average archives so that we can apply them at our institutions as we describe collections.

Digital Curation versus Data Curation versus Records Management versus Data Governance

There are clearly many different professions or even subspecialties that interact with or manage digital information in distinctive functions. Computer scientists and programmers were among the earliest to create, manage, and store digital data. Records managers manage records in all formats during active use, determine when they have reached the end of their retention cycle, identify and retain permanent records, and identify and dispose of nonpermanent records. Records managers managed information in business, government, and education before it became digital and have updated their practices as needed for the new format, including rebranding as records and information managers. Data governance dates to the early 2000s and focuses on the management of the availability, usability, integrity, quality, and security of data employed most often in business but recently also in the academic environment.[14] It focuses on structured digital data that is frequently shared across organizational units. Data curation was first mentioned in 1995 relative to natural history museums and research science databases. It is a subset of digital curation that applies specifically to scientific research data that involves adding metadata to enable its discovery and retrieval as well as its preservation in general, actively managing the data through its lifecycle, and maintaining its quality for the purpose of reuse to create new knowledge by the greater academic community.[15] Digital curation was talked about in the United States in reports between 2003 and 2007 but not actually defined. Digital curation is the active management by information professionals of digital data, including adding metadata; aiding discoverability and access; and preserving authenticity, integrity, reliability, and usability, to make its continued future use possible.[16]

Archivists are some of these information professionals who curate digital data so it can be used in the future. Many of us may say we are managing or preserving digital records, which sounds very ordinary, but it is a monumental task. Digital curation is the jazzy term for what we are doing, even if it is a more rudimentary version of what better-funded archival programs can do. This is what Chris Prom has been discussing in his blog, what DigCCurr is about, what SAA's Digital Archives Specialist program is about. As Jackie Dooley points out in her recent OCLC report *The Archival Advantage: Integrating Archival Expertise into Management of Born-Digital Library Materials*, digital records have many qualities in common with the types of records we are already expert at managing. Our experience with donors, questions of legal ownership, intellectual property, and access and use restrictions; understanding of provenance and context; and skill in appraisal and metadata creation to aid discoverability, access, and preservation are readily transferable and necessary to the successful management of permanent digital records.[17] Although some other professions may have knowledge that partially overlaps that of archivists, this expertise tends to be unique to the archival profession.

In speaking about preservation of born-digital records, archivist Chris Prom concurs with Dooley that archivists have much to contribute to this work. Archivists have a history of preserving document genres that other professions have not.[18] Unpublished materials have distinctive qualities that tend to raise questions other professions do not routinely address. Dooley includes many sample questions in her report. Many digital records are unpublished, created by organizations or individuals during the course of their daily business, and have a relationship to other records, just like analog archival records. Information is appraised, arranged, and preserved based on its content, not its carrier or format. The format, whether digital, acetate film, or reel-to-reel audio, is more important to its care, method of access, and preservation, not the expertise required to manage the information. When the information content is analyzed, a lot of digital content is a continuation of information previously created in analog, just in a new format. For digital information to be of value in the future, it needs to be authentic, reliable, and usable.[19] Authenticity includes context (the circumstances of its creation and use) and structure (the logical attributes, how the information is structured and organized, how the parts interact to convey meaning),[20] questions archivists routinely consider for analog records. The archival concepts of provenance, hierarchical relationships between record sets, and collective description are as applicable for digital records as analog.[21] Archivists clearly are qualified and have much to contribute to the management and preservation of digital information. Our approach to thinking about records and information add value to digital information. We bring skills and expertise with unpublished information that others lack to the digital realm. This is why archival arrangement and description is still relevant in the digital age.

Parting Thoughts

"For now we need to settle for 'good enough' practice and continue to invest time and resources in developing systems and workflows that will prevent a 'digital dark age' for the first part of the 21st century."[22] Much has been written about how to perform archival functions. The literature explains at great length what needs to be done. At times, these writings become "shoulds": What we should do if we are a competent archivist or a professional archivist? Instead of interpreting what is written about preservation or processing or digital records as a list of everything that should or must be done to perform a particular function, perhaps it should be read as, "Here is what best practices recommend be done, in this sequence. You select what you are able to do to the level you can, applying the recommended method or sequence." Not all authors translate their theory into an actual workflow of how to do it and why. Someone needs to provide the practical interpretation of the theoretical. They also need to explain the reasoning behind recommendations so we can determine how well it fits our specific situation or whether it requires modification. If the ideal is to rehouse all paper records in acid-free folders and boxes but in practice it is deemed safe at an institution with a high volume of records to only replace damaged or missing acidic folders for records of average research value, that would be helpful to know. What is the acceptable minimum?

Best practices and standards in particular create a single bar to aim for without adjustment for the differences between institutions in personnel; their technical expertise, skills, and specialties; funding, physical space, volume, and type of records, and so on. Standards generally ask the lone arranger and the staff of twenty to forty archivists to achieve at the same level. Their resources to get there are unequal, including the time that can be spent on any one function.

I support archival standards. I practice excellence in my work and am attentive to details, as they are often at the root of problems that need solving. Aspiring for mediocrity does not result in quality work; it is reached by aspiring for excellence. But, there is a balance between "good enough," as the quote at the beginning of this section says, and perfection. Balance comes from experience and good judgment.

Digital records have ratcheted up the ante for arrangement and description. The photocopier increased the potential number of copies of the same document. The personal computer has increased the potential number of unique documents; the form taken by digital files; and even their location, both on physical devices and virtually on the web. This increased complexity has caused the need for added appraisal of technical qualities; added capture, creation, and documentation of metadata; and mastery of additional technical skills and many new digital tools. All these new extras require more time to complete arrangement and description, assuming that acceptance of transfers and donations of digital records also signals the acceptance of or a commitment to make reasonable efforts to preserve them. Oh, and of course there is still the problem of a bit of a backlog with the analog records.

Those institutions with more resources can afford to be the cutting-edge leaders who test or adopt new standards and practices sooner than others. They design work processes, test software, hire programmers to customize computer code or add functionality, or even develop new software. We are professionally grateful for their leadership. Small to medium-sized archives wait and watch until products and processes mature, overcome initial problems, improve functionality, and possibly become affordable or hosted to reduce required technological support. While the profession desires to improve description to improve the ability of researchers to find and use information, implementation of some options may always be out of reach for some organizations. The more technology-dependent description or preservation of digital files becomes, the longer the lag before some will be able to implement it if at all.

Tiered implementation for a standard is one method for making adoption more approachable for all. For example, DACS has three tiers of description: a minimum record includes nine fields, an optimum record includes ten, and a value-added record includes from eleven to twenty-six fields, of which not all may apply to a particular set of records. DACS can easily be incorporated in manually created, word-processed finding aids, as well as automated in current archival collection management systems. EAD is much more complex with 146 tags, of which many are repeatable but only 5 are required.[23] Much collective work was done to create shared templates and other tools for manual encoding, but now several automated systems exist that handle encoding and delivery. Leading institutions shouldered the responsibility of developing affordable automated systems for other institutions to use. The release of Archon and Archivists' Toolkit enabled previously nonparticipatory institutions to create EAD finding aids. Another example of tiered implementation is the National Digital Stewardship Alliance's Levels of Digital Preservation, a rubric of digital preservation tasks in five categories.[24] There are four levels of preservation tasks for each category. An archives could work incrementally toward performing at level 1 in all categories before proceeding to level 2.

Individual archives need to assess where they are now, identify priorities, and develop incremental goals for progress in arrangement and description, adoption of standards, and managing and preserving digital records. Prioritization, development of workflows, and establishment of the minimum to be done in order to juggle many demands flows in part from risk assessment. What is currently or will soon become the biggest risk if no action is taken? Which need is growing that requires preparation for now? Which resources currently exist or are likely to be received in the same time frame to address these risks and needs? Assess risks, make decisions, document them, and then proceed. Arrangement, description, and preservation are all iterative. Better to set realistic goals, achieve them, set new goals, and repeat. This results in progress.

The profession needs to advance arrangement and descriptive practice for valid reasons, but it needs to be careful of a descriptive divide between the haves and the have-littles. Theory needs to be fleshed out into specific details for examples of implementation. This was done for manual EAD encoding and has started for the OAIS framework with SAA's Arrangement and Description of Electronic Records workshops. Authors and speakers need to be clearer about what the minimum steps are to be good enough work for a task and what readers can work toward iteratively as their resources improve. Those forging ahead must realize not everyone can keep the same pace. If they shoulder some of the extra burden, they can help raise the boat for everyone.[25]

Notes

1. See Morgan G. Daniels and Elizabeth Yakel, "Seek and You May Find: Successful Search in Online Finding Aid Systems," *American Archivist* 73 (Fall/Winter 2010): 535–68; Christopher J. Prom, "User Interactions with Electronic Finding Aids in a Controlled Setting," *American Archivist* 67 (Fall/Winter 2004): 234–68; Christopher J. Prom, "Using Web Analytics to Improve Online Access to Archival Resources," *American Archivist* 74 (Spring/Summer 2011): 158–84, among others.

2. Elizabeth Yakel, "Encoded Archival Description: Are Finding Aids Boundary Spanners or Barriers for Users?" *Journal of Archival Organization* 2, nos. 1–2 (2004): 63, accessed December 28, 2016, doi:10.1300/J201v02n01_0663; Elizabeth Yakel and Deborah A. Torres, "AI: Archival Intelligence and User Expertise," *American Archivist* 66 (Spring/Summer 2003): 51–78.

3. Daniels and Yakel, "Seek and You May Find," 537–38.

4. Yakel and Torres, "AI," 57–60, 63–77.

5. Working Group on Standards for Archival Description, "Recommendations of the Working Group on Standards for Archival Description," *American Archivist* 52 (Fall 1989): 472–73.

6. David Bearman, *Towards National Information Systems for Archives and Manuscript Repositories: The National Information Systems Task Force (NISTF) Papers 1981–1984* (Chicago: Society of American Archivists, 1987), 90.

7. Steven L. Henson, William E. Landis, Kathleen D. Roe, Michael Rush, William Stockting, and Victoria Irons Walch, "Thirty Years On: SAA and Descriptive Standards," *American Archivist* 74 (2011 Supplement): 1–35, accessed November 24, 2015, http://www2.archivists.org/sites/all/files/AAOSv074-Session706.pdf; Michael Rush, "The Archival Network: You Don't Get to Describe Records without Making a Few Standards," *American Archivist* 74 (2011 Supplement): 25–26, 23.

8. PREMIS Editorial Committee, *PREMIS Data Dictionary for Preservation Metadata*, ver. 3.0 (June 2015), 25–27, accessed December 29, 2016, http://www.loc.gov/standards/premis/v3/premis-3-0-final.pdf; Encoded Archival Context Working Group of the Society of American Archivists and the Staatsbibliothek zu Berlin, *Encoded Archival Context—Corporate Bodies, Persons, and Families (EAC-CPF) Tag Library*, version 2010 (initial release), accessed December 29, 2016, http://www3.iath.virginia.edu/eac/cpf/tagLibrary/cpfTagLibrary.html; Experts Group on Archival Description (EGAD), *Records in Contexts: A Conceptual Model for Archival Description*, consultation draft v0.1 (Paris: International Council on Archives, September 2016), accessed December 29, 2016, http://www.ica.org/sites/default/files/RiC-CM-0.1.pdf.

9. Gretchen Gueguen, Vitor Manoel Marques da Fonsecs, Daniel V. Pitti, and Claire Sibille-de Grimoüard, "Toward an International Conceptual Model for Archival Description: A Preliminary Report from the International Council on Archives' Experts Group on Archival Description," *American Archivist* 76 (Fall/Winter 2013): 577; Abelardo Santamaria, *Report on the Work of CNEDA (2007–2012): Toward a Conceptual Model for Archival Description in Spain* (Seville, Spain: Ministerio de Educación, Cultura, y Deporte, July 11, 2012), 7, accessed November 23, 2016, http://www.mecd.gob.es/cultura-mecd/dms/mecd/cultura-mecd/areas-cultura/archivos/mc/cneda/documentacion/ReportCNEDA_11_07_2012-pdf/ReportCNEDA_11_07_2012.pdf.

10. Prom, "Using Web Analytics," 172.

11. Prom, "Using Web Analytics," 172.

12. "PREMIS: Tools for Preservation Metadata Implementation," *Library of Congress*, accessed December 31, 2016, https://www.loc.gov/standards/premis/tools_for_premis.php.

13. "ArchivesSpace-Archivematica-DSpace Workflow Integration Project," *Bentley Historical Library, University of Michigan*, April 2014–October 2016, accessed December 31, 2016, http://archival-integration.blog spot.com; "Development Roadmap: Archivematica," *Archivematica*, accessed December 31, 2016, https://wiki.archivematica.org/Development_roadmap:_Archivematica.

14. "Definition: Data Governance (DG)," *TechTarget*, accessed December 31, 2016, http://searchdataman agement.techtarget.com/definition/data-governance.

15. Carole L. Palmer, Nicholas M. Weber, Trevor Muñoz, and Allen H. Renear, "Foundations of Data Curation: The Pedagogy and Practice of 'Purposeful Work' with Research Data," *Archives Journal* 3 (Summer 2013), accessed January 1, 2017, http://www.archivejournal.net/issue/3/archives-remixed/foundations-of-data -curation-the-pedagogy-and-practice-of-purposeful-work-with-research-data.

16. Elizabeth Yakel, "Digital Curation," *OCLC Systems and Services: International Digital Library Perspectives* 23 (2007): 335. Note, although I base this on Yakel's definition, among several sources, this is not how she defines it.

17. Jackie Dooley, *The Archival Advantage: Integrating Archival Expertise into Management of Born-Digital Library Materials* (Dublin, OH: OCLC, 2015), 3.

18. Christopher Prom, "Making Digital Curation a Systematic Institutional Function," *International Journal of Digital Curation* 6 (2011): 143.

19. Mark J. Myers, "Electronic Records: The Next Step," Society of American Archivists Digital Archives Specialist webinar, April 13, 2015, PowerPoint, 2.

20. Mark J. Myers, "Appraisal of Electronic Records," Society of American Archivists, Digital Archives Specialist workshop, Richmond, KY, June 21, 2013, course booklet, 5.

21. Prom, "Making Digital Curation," 143.

22. Naomi L. Nelson, Seth Shaw, Nancy Deromedi, Michael Shallcross, Cynthia Ghering, Lisa Schmidt, Michelle Belden, Jackie R. Esposito, Ben Goldman, and Tim Pyatt, *Managing Born-Digital Special Collections and Archival Materials*, SPEC Kit 329 (Washington, DC: Association of Research Libraries, 2012), 19.

23. "Encoded Archival Description Tag Library, Version 2002," *EAD Encoded Archival Description Official Site*, accessed January 6, 2017, https://www.loc.gov/ead/tglib/element_index.html; Katherine M. Wisser and Jackie Dean, "EAD Tag Usage: Community Analysis of the Use of Encoded Archival Description Elements," *American Archivist* 75 (Fall/Winter 2013): 565.

24. Trevor Owens, "NDSA Levels of Digital Preservation: Release Candidate One," *The Signal*, November 20, 2012, http://blogs.loc.gov/thesignal/2012/11/ndsa-levels-of-digital-preservation-release-candidate-one.

25. "A rising tide lifts all the boats," *Wikipedia*, accessed January 7, 2017, https://en.wikipedia.org/wiki/A_ rising_tide_lifts_all_boats, attributes this aphorism to the New England Council (the regional chamber of commerce).

Additional Reading and Resources

Some resources already mentioned on preservation, particularly in chapter 4, are applicable here, as are those in chapter 7 on linked data.

"Digital Curation." *Digital Curation Centre (DCC)*. Accessed June 24, 2015. http://www.dcc.ac.uk/ digital-curation/what-digital-curation. This page defines digital curation and presents a life-cycle of activities included in digital curation. Note the "How-To Guides and Checklists" on the "Resources" tab and the "Glossary" on the "Digital Curation" tab. Also note that, as this is a British site, some information does not apply.

"LC Linked Data Service." *Library of Congress*. Accessed November 23, 2016. http://id.loc.gov. This site provides links to standards and controlled vocabularies that can be used to correctly form terms and names that may be used as linked open data.

Lee, Christopher. "DigCCurr Publications and Documentation." *DigCCurr*. Accessed June 24, 2015. https://ils.unc.edu/digccurr/products.html#curriculum. The first two items on this page under "Draft Curriculum Framework Documents"—"Matrix of Digital Curation Knowledge and Competencies" and "High-Level Categories of Digital Curation Functions"—are of particular interest. The first brings up a chart. Item 2 describes the functions and skills involved in digital curation, while item 5 describes prerequisite knowledge. The second document lists and describes digital curation functions from the perspective of educating students to be digital curators.

LOCAH Project: Creating Archival Linked Data since 2010. Accessed November 23, 2016. http:// locah.archiveshub.ac.uk. This project ended in 2011, but there are some thoughtful blog posts with questions still worth considering.

Appendix A

Chronology of Technology Changes Impacting Digital Files

1960s Henriette Avram, computer scientist at LC, developed the MARC format, by 1971 a U.S. bibliographic standard.

1961 Individual users timeshared access to mainframe computers from terminals. Computers communicated with multiple users at terminals simultaneously but could not communicate with each other unless they were part of a small number of closed-network communities. These multiuser systems could file-share, e-mail, and chat.[1]

1968 A computer conference demonstration showed "collaborative editing, videoconferencing, word processing, hypertext links, and a strange pointing device jokingly referred to as a 'mouse.'"[2]

1969 "ARPAnet was the first large-scale, general-purpose computer network to connect different kinds of computers together." Rival networks began to come online internationally within the year.[3]

1970s Competing computer networks used a variety of communication protocols to build national networks; then they started trying to link networks to each other. By mid-decade commercial networks were available to businesses.[4]

1970 NARA accessioned its first electronic records and thus began its work with electronic records.[5]

1971 IBM released the first 8" read-only floppy disk and drive. In 1973, it released the read/write floppy drive, which quickly became an industry standard.[6] E-mail changed from communication within a single timeshared computer to communication anywhere within a networked computer system.[7]

1977 The Apple II, TRS 80 from Tandy Radio Shack, and the Commodore PET, released this year, were the first personal computers sold in larger quantities and were actively sold until the early 1990s.[8]

1978   WordStar, "among the first popular word processing systems for personal computers," was introduced and continued to be used even after Microsoft Word was introduced.[9] The 5¼" floppy drive and disks were introduced for use in desktop PCs. They were popular through the 1980s but were discontinued by the mid-1990s. Initially, disks were single-sided, then double-sided, and eventually high-density.[10]

Late 1970s   Personal computing slowly took off in the United States. By 1990, individual consumers subscribed to early online services, like CompuServ, and bulletin boards, like Prodigy, AOL, and others. Subscribers participated in dial-up group discussions, shopped, chatted, read news, and e-mailed.[11]

ca. 1980–1981   Some businesses still used punch cards to input data to mainframe computers to accomplish work.[12]

1981   The MS-DOS operating system was released.[13] The 3½" floppy drive and disk was introduced and by 1988 became more popular than the 5¼" size. Most PCs continued to have built-in floppy drives until about 2002–2003.[14]

1982   The compact disk was invented. It was first used to distribute recorded music, followed by *Grolier's Electronic Encyclopedia* in 1985.

1983   Cuadra/Star began offering software to manage archives. At that point, it is likely that only the management function was electronic, not the records being managed. Microsoft released Word, which competed against WordPerfect for the word-processing market.[15]

1984   Apple released the Macintosh computer, the "first successful mouse-driven computer with a graphical user interface."[16] The graphical user interface won a lot of supporters but was not available in PCs for another six years. The MARC AMC format was adopted by OCLC.

1986   The structured query language (SQL) standard was released. SQL is the predominant standard used for relational databases.[17] The standard generalized markup language (SGML) standard was released. SGML is important for presentation of text documents.[18]

ca. 1989   Eloquent started offering software for managing archival collections.

1989   Microsoft released Word for Windows, at which point it became a global standard for word processing.[19] Tim Berners-Lee invented the World Wide Web, or Web 1.0, the initial version that presented information to be passively read.[20]

1990   Microsoft released operating system Windows 3.0, which enabled PC users to run multiple programs simultaneously. It also was the first time PCs handled large graphical applications, making the PC more user-friendly. Photoshop, image editing software, was first released.[21]

1992   Charles M. Dollar's book *Archival Theory and Information Technologies: The Impact of Information Technologies on Archival Principles and Methods* is published. This is an early book on the topic of computers and archival theory, raising the question of how they will blend and what it might mean for the future of archives.

1993   Mosaic released the first web browser that accommodates graphics.[22] The Berkeley Finding Aids project headed by Daniel Pitti began.[23]

1994   The Iomega Zip Disk was released. ISAD(G) was adopted as an international standard. Richard J. Cox's book *The First Generation of Electronic Records Archivists in the United States: A Study in Professionalization* was published.

December 1994   Very few websites existed.[24]

1995   The digital video disk (DVD) was released. Its initial usage was movie distribution.[25]

1997   Research began at Cornell to develop Fedora, which was used to create digital or institutional repositories. Fedora was first released in May 2003.[26]

August 1, 1997   New York State Archives Technical Information Series, leaflet no. 22, *Guidelines for Ensuring Long-Term Accessibility and Usability of Records Stored as Digital Images* provided guidance for state agencies and local government for preserving electronic records.

1998   NARA began to address the challenges of electronic records through development of their Electronic Records Archives (ERA) program.[27] EAD version 1.0, a data structure standard for the presentation of archival finding aids, was released.[28] It was the result of the Berkeley Finding Aids project. The extensible markup language (XML) standard, a derivative of standard generalized markup language (SGML), was released by the World Wide Web Consortium (W3C) and widely adopted.[29]

1999   The USB flash drive, USB stick, memory stick, or thumb drive was invented and commercially available in 2000.[30]

May 1999   The draft model for the OAIS framework was released by Consultative Committee for Space Data Systems (CCSDS).[31]

ca. 2000–2002   SAA's annual conference began to be dominated by electronic records sessions compared with earlier conferences.

March 2000   Work started on DSpace to develop an institutional repository for MIT, with its first release in November 2002. Since 2009, DSpace and Fedora, both open-source software with a common function, are now managed by DuraSpace.[32]

December 2002   EAD 2.0 was released.

ca 2003–2005   Web 2.0, an interactive version of the web in which users generate content, began to emerge.[33]

2003   "64-bit CPUs were introduced to the (formerly 32-bit) mainstream personal computer market."[34]

ca. 2004–2006   Web 3.0, or the Semantic Web, which uses linked (open) data to connect structured data, began to emerge.[35]

March 2004   DACS was adopted as an archival data content standard.

April 2005   Microsoft released Windows XP Professional x64 Edition, its first 64-bit operating system.[36]

May 2005   The *PREMIS Data Dictionary for Preservation Metadata* was released.[37]

ca. 2006   Development of Archivists' Toolkit, an archival collection management system, began. Research showed that less than 8 percent of colleges and universities had a formal electronic records management program in place when surveyed.[38]

2006   Microsoft released Windows Vista as a 64-bit system with 32-bit compatibility, its last 32-bit operating system.[39] Amazon launched cloud-based web services, such as file storage.[40]

July 2006   Archon software for the creation and publication of online finding aids was first released. Support and development for Archon ended in January 2014 due to its merger with Archivists' Toolkit to create ArchivesSpace.[41]

2007   Dropbox offers cloud-based file storage, including file sharing by multiple users and access from multiple devices to a single file storage location.[42] Most non-ARL libraries do not have an institutional repository.[43]

2009   The New York University Libraries, University of California, San Diego Libraries, University of Illinois Urbana–Champaign Libraries, and the Andrew W. Mellon Foundation agree to integrate the Archon and Archivists' Toolkit software.[44]

2010   OCLC's report "Taking Our Pulse: The OCLC Research Survey of Special Collections and Archives" finds "management of born-digital archival materials is still in its infancy."[45]

2011   Adobe announced Creative Cloud, its cloud-based subscription model for distributing its software.[46]

January 2011   SAA adopted EAC-CPF as an archival data structure standard.

2012–2013   SAA's Manuscript Repositories Section, inspired by the Erway OCLC report, challenged archivists to "Jump In" to managing their digital records. Results were presented at a session in New Orleans, August 2013.[47]

August 2012   OCLC's report *You've Got to Walk before You Can Run: First Steps for Managing Born-Digital Content Received on Physical Media*, authored by Ricky Erway, is the first in a series of short reports about managing born-digital materials.

2013   Census data showed that 88.4 percent of Americans lived in a household with a computer. However, nearly half the states have lower-than-average ownership while the other half have higher-than-average ownership. Lower ownership is predominant in southern states, like Kentucky, from Arizona east, to the Carolinas. Kentucky's terrain combined with a rural population makes it more expensive to run high-speed Internet cables to areas outside population centers.[48]

January 2013   DACS, second edition, was released.

September 2013   ArchivesSpace 1.0, a merger of the best of Archon and Archivists' Toolkit, was released as the newest archival collection management system.

August 2015   EAD3 1.0 was released.[49]

August 2016   The University of Michigan's project on ArchivesSpace-Archivematica-DSpace Integration ended. The project improved workflow between these three systems and developed the "Appraisal" tab to be released in Archivematica ver. 1.6.[50]

Notes

1. "Timeline of Computer History: Networking and the Web," *Computer History Museum*, accessed May 31, 2016, http://www.computerhistory.org/timeline/networking-the-web.

2. "Timeline: Networking."

3. "Timeline: Networking."

4. "Timeline: Networking."

5. "Electronic Records Archives (ERA): About ERA," *National Archives and Records Administration*, accessed November 8, 2016, https://www.archives.gov/era/about.

6. "Timeline of Computer History: Memory and Storage," *Computer History Museum*, accessed May 30, 2016, http://www.computerhistory.org/timeline/memory-storage.

7. "Timeline: Networking."

8. "Timeline of Computer History: Computers," *Computer History Museum*, accessed May 30, 2016, http://www.computerhistory.org/timeline/computers.

9. "Timeline of Computer History: Software and Languages," *Computer History Museum*, accessed May 30, 2016, http://www.computerhistory.org/timeline/software-languages.

10. "Timeline: Memory"; "Floppy disk," *Wikipedia*, accessed April 5, 2016, https://en.wikipedia.org/wiki/Floppy_disk.

11. "Timeline: Networking."

12. Lisa Perna, telephone conversation with the author, May 29, 2016.

13. "Timeline: Software."

14. "Timeline: Memory"; "Floppy disk."

15. "Timeline: Software."

16. "Timeline: Computers."

17. Daniel V. Pitti, "Technology and the Transformation of Archival Description," *Journal of Archival Organization* 3 (2006): 13, http://dx.doi.org/10.1300/J201v03n02_02.

18. Pitti, "Technology and the Transformation," 10.

19. "Timeline: Software."

20. Mark Frauenfelder, "Computing Sir Tim Berners-Lee," *MIT Technology Review*, October 1, 2004, accessed December 18, 2016, https://www.technologyreview.com/s/403095/sir-tim-berners-lee; Tim Berners-Lee, James Hendler, and Ora Lassila, "The Semantic Web," *Scientific American* (May 2001): 4.

21. "Timeline: Software."

22. "World Wide Web," *Wikipedia*, accessed November 27, 2015, https://en.wikipedia.org/wiki/World_Wide_Web.

23. Daniel V. Pitti, "Development of an Encoding Standard: The Development of an Encoding Standard for Archival Finding Aids," *American Archivist* 60 (Summer 1997): 279.

24. "World Wide Web."

25. "Timeline: Memory."

26. "Fedora Commons," *Wikipedia*, accessed May 27, 2016, https://en.wikipedia.org/wiki/Fedora_Commons.

27. "Electronic Records Archives."

28. Pitti, "Technology and the Transformation," 10.

29. Pitti, "Technology and the Transformation," 10.

30. "USB flash drive," *Wikipedia*, accessed May 30, 2016, https://en.wikipedia.org/wiki/USB_flash_drive.

31. Brian F. Lavoie, "Meeting the Challenges of Digital Preservation: The OAIS Reference Model," *OCLC Newsletter* No. 243 (January/February 2000), accessed May 27, 2016, http://www.oclc.org/research/publications/library/2000/lavoie-oais.html.

32. MacKenzie Smith, Mary Barton, Mick Bass, Margret Branschofsky, Greg McClellan, Dave Stuve, Robert Tansley, and Julie Harford Walker, "DSpace: An Open Source Dynamic Digital Repository," *D-Lib Magazine* 9 (January 2003), accessed May 27, 2016, http://www.dlib.org/dlib/january03/smith/01smith.html; "DSpace," *Wikipedia*, accessed January 24, 2017, https://en.wikipedia.org/wiki/DSpace.

33. "Web 2.0," *Wikipedia*, accessed December 18, 2016, https://en.wikipedia.org/wiki/Web_2.0.

34. "64-bit computing," *Wikipedia*, accessed January 24, 2017, https://en.wikipedia.org/wiki/64-bit_computing.

35. Frauenfelder, "Computing Sir Tim Berners-Lee."

36. "64-bit computing."

37. PREMIS Editorial Committee, *PREMIS Data Dictionary for Preservation Metadata*, ver. 2.0 (March 2008), accessed May 27, 2016, http://www.loc.gov/standards/premis/v2/premis-2-0.pdf.

38. Lisl Zach and Marcia Peri, "Desperately Seeking Solutions: College and University E-Records Management (ERM) Programs," Mid-Atlantic Region Archives Conference, Morristown, NJ, October 27, 2006),

later published as "Practices for College and University Electronic Records Management (ERM) Programs: Then and Now," *American Archivist* 73 (Spring/Summer 2010): 105–28.

39. "64-bit computing."

40. "Timeline: Memory."

41. "Archon (software)," *Wikipedia*, accessed December 18, 2016, https://en.wikipedia.org/wiki/Archon_ (software); "Archon: The Simple Archival Information System," *University of Illinois*, accessed December 18, 2016, http://www.archon.org/doc/2.20/index.html.

42. "Timeline: Memory."

43. DuraSpace, *Managing Digital Collections Survey Results Summary* (Winchester, MA: DuraSpace, 2014), 4. See also Karen Markey, Soo Young Rieh, Beth St. Jean, Jihyun Kim, and Elizabeth Yakel, *Census of Institutional Repositories in the United States: MIRACLE Project Research Findings* (Washington, DC: Council on Library and Information Resources, February 2007), accessed January 24, 2017, https://www.clir.org/pubs/reports/pub140.

44. "Mission and History," *ArchivesSpace*, accessed December 18, 2016, http://archivesspace.org/about/mission-and-history. Chris Prom and Scott Schwartz, "Archon™: Facilitating Access to Special Collections," last modified October 31, 2008, http://www.archon.org/ArchonUpdateOct2008.pdf, makes no mention of the upcoming merger discussions. In June 2009, an agreement to merge became public.

45. Jackie M. Dooley and Katherine Luce, *Taking Our Pulse: The OCLC Research Survey of Special Collections and Archives* (Dublin, OH: OCLC, 2010), 9, accessed May 27, 2016, http://www.oclc.org/content/dam/research/publications/library/2010/2010-11.pdf.

46. "Timeline: Software."

47. "First Steps for Managing Born-Digital Content Report Inspires SAA Jump-In Initiative," *OCLC Research*, last modified June 12, 2013, http://www.oclc.org/research/news/2013/06-12.html.

48. "Deck the Home with High-Speed Trimming," *USA Today, The Enquirer* (Northern Kentucky), November 23, 2014, 7B. Charts cite the most recent census data from the U.S. Census Bureau. Katie Brandenburg, *Bowling Green Daily News*, "Kentucky's Internet Speed Ranks among Slowest of States," *The Enquirer* (Northern Kentucky), approximately August 10, 2014.

49. "EAD3 1.0 Is Available!" *Society of American Archivists*, accessed December 19, 2016, http://www2.archivists.org/groups/technical-subcommittee-on-encoded-archival-description-ead/ead3-10-is-available.

50. Mike Shallcross, "Archivematica Users Group @ SAA," *ArchivesSpace-Archivematica-DSpace Workflow Integration*, August 9, 2016; Mike Shallcross, "Appraisal and Arrangement Tab 101," *ArchivesSpace-Archivematica-DSpace Workflow Integration*, January 17, 2017, accessed January 24, 2017, http://archival-integration.blogspot.com.

Appendix B

Software Tools for Digital Tasks

General Resources for Software Description and Analysis

"Collection Management and Creation Strategies for UC Special Collections and Archives: Summary and Features Matrix." *University of California Digital Library*. Accessed January 4, 2016. http://www.cdlib.org/services/access_publishing/dsc/tools/docs/cdams_summary_report .pdf. This research proceeds from a functional analysis of needs to specific software. The value of its methodology outweighs its age. Many of the products are still in use.

COPTR Contributors. "Main Page." *Community Owned Digital Preservation Tool Registry (COPTR)*. Last modified January 8, 2016. http://coptr.digipres.org/index.php?title=Main_Page&oldid =2795. This collection of more than four hundred tools for long-term digital preservation helps practitioners discover and assess tools for all phases of work on digital files. Some tools focus on a single task, while others are useful for more than one archival function.

"POWRR Preserving (Digital) Objects with Restricted Resources." *Digital POWRR*. Accessed August 2, 2016. http://digitalpowrr.niu.edu/tool-grid. This project ended in 2013, but the visual presentation of the tool grid makes it easier to identify and compare software that performs similar functions. The findings are organized by functions using the OAIS model. The project's final report (http://commons.lib.niu.edu/bitstream/handle/10843/13610/FromTheoryTo Action_POWRR_WhitePaper.pdf?sequence=1&isAllowed=y) provides more detailed information about some of the software. Also see the listing for the COPTR site, where their data is now maintained.

Spiro, Lisa. *Archival Management Software*. Washington, DC: Council on Library and Information Resources, 2009). Appendix 2 compares features in chart form across select collection management software. Appendix 3 provides a more detailed comparison of the same software, and appendix 4 includes the comments of archivists about the software.

Use the software products listed here at your own risk. The author makes no warranty nor endorses any of them. Listings are supplied for informational purposes only.

Categories of Software

Archival Management Software

ArchivesSpace. This collection management software is the result of the merger of Archon and Archivists' Toolkit, which began in 2008 and includes the strengths of each. ArchivesSpace 1.0 was released September 2013.

Archivists' Toolkit. Development of this archival collection management system started in about 2006.[1] Its strength was organization of the wide range of information archivists collect about their holdings for internal management purposes.

Archon. This software designed for the creation and publication of online finding aids was first released in July 2006. It provided a single searchable site for researchers of all of an archives finding aids. Support and development for Archon ended in January 2014 due to its merger with Archivists' Toolkit to create ArchivesSpace.[2]

CollectiveAccess. This is open-source software for managing and publishing museum and archival collections and was released in 2007. As of 2009, there was no hosted version. The software did not publish archival finding aids but did focus heavily on object collections.[3]

Cuadra/STAR Archives STAR. This commercial software has been available to manage archives since 1983. STAR/Archives was released in 2003. It is available as either a perpetual license or hosted subscription. CuadraSTAR was "developed to serve multiple information management needs in libraries, information centers, archives, museums, records centers, and publishing organizations."[4] "Cuadra SKCA software assists archives to accession, catalog and manage collections. It makes catalogs of the collections ('finding aids') visible on the Internet via a secure public access module. The software can generate finding aids in Encoded Archival Description (EAD)."[5]

Eloquent. This was first available more than twenty years ago, around 1989. The cost varies by the amount of service. Eloquent Museum is collections management software (CMS) for cultural institutions of any size.[6]

Filemaker. This is a proprietary relational database application, as is Microsoft Access. Santamaria mentions using Filemaker and Access to create local databases for small institutions that may be unable to afford a more expensive product for collection management to deliver finding aids and to track collection use and metrics.[7]

ICA-AtoM. This was projected to be released in summer 2009 as an open-source, relational database system developed by Artefactual Systems. It is a web-based archival description software that is based on ICA standards.[8]

MINISIS. Developed by a software company with a strength in database management applications, this proprietary software is a tailored application to perform museum management tasks.[9]

Digital Preservation Software Systems

Archivematica. This is a "comprehensive digital preservation system." It "uses a micro-services design pattern to provide an integrated suite of free and open-source tools that allows users to process digital objects from ingest to access in compliance with the ISO-OAIS functional model."[10] The University of Michigan's ArchivesSpace-Archivematica-DSpace Workflow Integration grant project developed a new "Appraisal and Arrangement" tab in Archivematica to "review, appraise, deaccession, and arrange content" and to "load (and create) ArchivesSpace archival object records in the Archivematica Appraisal and Arrangement tab and then drag and drop content onto the appropriate archival objects to define Submission Information Packages (SIPs) that will in turn be described as 'digital objects' in ArchivesSpace and deposited as discrete 'items' in DSpace," and to "create new archival object and digital object records in ArchivesSpace and associate the latter with DSpace handles to provide URIs/'href' values for <dao> elements in exported EADs."[11]

DuraCloud. This is a commercial, cloud-based storage service provided by DuraSpace.

Preservica. This is a commercial, OAIS-compliant preservation software system that handles ingest, data management, storage, access, administration, and preservation. It also provides the ability to open content with the public.[12]

Institutional Repository Software Systems

Digital Commons. This is a commercial, hosted institutional repository developed by BePress. The product particularly focuses on published scholarship and metrics demonstrating its use and can be used to publish electronic journals.[13]

DSpace. This is an open-source software application to create a digital repository. Duraspace offers a commercial hosted version, DSpace Direct, that preserves and provides "open access to all types of digital content including text, images, moving images, mpegs and data sets."[14]

Fedora (Flexible Extensible Digital Object Repository Architecture). This was originally developed at Cornell University for storing, managing, and accessing digital content. This is open source and more complex than DSpace. Fedora performs a number of tasks, some of which are automated.[15]

Hydra. This is a free, open-source solution to provide access to digital content. It employs a combination of Fedora, Solr, Ruby on Rails, and Blacklight software. This is a large, collaborative project of many institutions working together.[16]

Islandora. This is a combination of Drupal, Islandora, and Fedora software used to store, access, and preserve digital content. Lyrasis offers a hosted version.[17]

Specific Software Tools for Digital Tasks

AccessData Forensic Toolkit (FTK) Imager. This is a data visualization and imaging tool created by AccessData Corp, able to recover or decrypt passwords, with optional malware detection and resolution. It creates forensic or logical (deleted files, unallocated space not included) images of local hard drives, floppy diskettes, Zip disks, CDs, DVDs, mobile devices, network data, and Internet storage entire folders. FTK also "offers the ability to conduct pattern searches for things like social security or credit card numbers and keyword searches, including searching on related or fuzzy terms."[18]

Aid4Mail. This software can migrate (large volumes), archive, and analyze e-mail; also convert from one format to another; extract deleted messages; and more. There are free and paid versions.[19] See also http://www.howto-outlook.com/addin/fookes_aid4mail.htm for more details.

Bagger. This graphical software tool wraps or packages a set of data files according to the BagIt specification.[20]

Bit Curator. This is a series of free and open-source digital forensics tools that support a digital curation workflow that starts with digital records located on removable media, whether new acquisitions or preexisting materials within a repository's holdings, and leads to the creation of SIPs or AIPs.[21]

ClamAV. This is an open-source, antivirus tool useful against viruses, malware, trojans, and other threats. It can scan e-mail and popular document formats.[22]

Curator's Workbench. This is a "tool that automates and streamlines the process of preparing collections of digital materials for submission to a repository. The Workbench will capture and stage files, generate manifests that include fixity information, arrange folders and objects, normalize metadata to custom requirements, and finally create a submission package for ingest into the archive."[23]

Data Accessioner. This is a simple tool, with an easy-to-use graphic interface, for migrating content "off disks and onto a file server for basic preservation, further appraisal, arrangement, and description." It integrates common metadata tools for use at the time of migration rather than after the fact. "It is intended to be easily adopted by smaller institutions with little or no IT staff support."[24]

Den4b Renamer. This is a powerful renaming tool that can apply complex renaming changes to batches of files.[25]

DROID. Developed by the United Kingdom's National Archives, this software is one of a number that identify file formats, including version, age, size, and date last modified. It can also help locate duplicates.[26] Carol Kussmann's instructions on how to use DROID are found at http://www.mnhs.org/preserve/records/docs_pdfs/DROID.pdf.

EnCase Forensic. By Guidance Software, this is an alternative to Forensic Toolkit (FTK) Imager. It, too, "offers the ability to conduct pattern searches for things like social security or credit card numbers and keyword searches, including searching on related or fuzzy terms."[27]

Exactly. This is another tool for remotely transferring digital files from a donor to the archives, while confirming provenance and fixity during acquisition.[28]

ExifTool. This is a "platform-independent command-line application for reading, writing, and editing meta information contained in a variety of visual, audio, and video files. ExifTool supports many different metadata formats."[29]

FITS (File Identification Tool Set). This "identifies, validates, and extracts technical metadata for a wide range of file formats." It wraps several third-party open-source tools, normalizes their output to a single common format, and combines their results into a single XML file.[30]

Appendix B

Fixity. This "monitors file integrity through generation and validation of checksums" and can be used for file maintenance by "monitoring digital files in repositories, servers, and other long-term storage locations."[31]

Irfan View. This is an image viewer and editor. It converts quite a few file formats and also plays audio and video files.[32]

JHOVE. This is a "file format identification, validation and characterization tool."[33]

Karen's Directory Printer. This software can print the name of every file on a drive with its file size; date last modified, created, or accessed; and attributes (read-only, hidden, system, and archive), as well as sort the file list by name, size, or dates.[34]

NARA File Analyzer. This software, developed by NARA, can evaluate an entire file directory, including file name validation, counting the number of files by type, creating a directory listing, and generating checksums. These all aid file analysis. The software can be used on a file system or an external hard drive. This is a desktop and command line tool.[35] Carol Kussmann explains how to use this software at http://www.mnhs.org/preserve/records/docs_pdfs/NARAFileAnalyzer.pdf.

OpenRefine. Formerly called *Google Refine*, this is an open-source desktop application for data cleanup and transformation to other formats, also called data wrangling.[36] Data wrangling may be necessary to organize the results of some of the reports produced by other software discussed here or when performing command line work.

QuickView Plus. This software from Avantstar provides a single "interface for browsing, viewing, copying, printing, and searching" "over 300 Windows, Macintosh, Internet, and DOS formats from virtually any source—e-mail attachments, the Web, file servers, and more." "Integrates seamlessly with popular e-mail programs and web browsers." Allows viewing of a file without changing its metadata.[37] For further information, see https://en.wikipedia.org/wiki/Quick View.

TeraCopy. This is a Windows tool for quickly copying files that reports errors, permits pause and resume of file transfer, calculates a checksum, and doesn't change creation dates.[38]

Thunar. This file management software can be used on external devices and will perform bulk file renaming.[39]

TreeSize Free and Professional. This disk space management software uses color-coding and tree maps to visualize file hierarchies and subfolder sizes and reports statistics on file formats, ownership, and last access date by branch. It works on mobile devices and can locate duplicate files on drives, servers, networks, and more.[40]

WinDirStat. This is an open-source disk usage viewer for various versions of Microsoft Windows. It, too, can display information visually as a tree map. Each directory is shown as a colored rectangle containing all its subdirectories and files within it, also as rectangles. The size of each rectangle is proportional to the size of the subtrees or individual files, respectively. The color of individual rectangles indicates the file type, as shown in the extension list.[41]

Notes

1. Lisa Spiro, *Archival Management Software* (Washington, DC: Council on Library and Information Resources, 2009).

2. "Archon (software)," *Wikipedia*, accessed December 18, 2016, https://en.wikipedia.org/wiki/Archon_ (software); "Archon: The Simple Archival Information System," *University of Illinois*, accessed December 18, 2016, http://www.archon.org/doc/2.20/index.html.

3. "CollectiveAccess," *CollectiveAccess*, accessed December 22, 2016, http://www.collectiveaccess.org/; Spiro, *Archival Management Software*, 85.

4. "CuadraStar Information Management Solutions," *Lucidea*, accessed December 22, 2016, http://lucidea .com/cuadrastar.

5. Mount St. Mary's University (Los Angeles, CA), *Procedure Manual for Cuadra Star Knowledge Center for Archives* (Los Angeles: Mount St. Mary's University, March 21, 2015), ix, accessed December 22, 2016, http://www2.archivists.org/sites/all/files/msmu_001.pdf.

6. Spiro, *Archival Management Software*.

7. "Filemaker," *Wikipedia*, accessed December 17, 2017, https://en.wikipedia.org/wiki/FileMaker; Daniel A. Santamaria, "Module 3: Designing Descriptive and Access Systems," in *Archival Arrangement and Description*, Trends in Archives Practice series (Chicago: Society of American Archivists, 2013), 161, 188, 207.

8. *ICA-AtoM*, accessed December 22, 2016, https://www.ica-atom.org; "What Is ICA-AtoM?" *ICA-AtoM*, accessed December 22, 2016, https://wiki.ica-atom.org/What_is_ICA-AtoM%3F. As of March 2017, this software is no longer supported by Artefactual. See *AtoM*, 2015, https://www.accesstomemory.org/en.

9. "Minisis, Inc.," *Minisis*, accessed December 22, 2016, http://www.minisisinc.com/index.html; Bob Schmitt, "Collections Management Systems/Software, ver. 1.2, 2014," March 2014, accessed December 22, 2016, http://carlibrary.org/CMS-Table.htm. This site compares diverse collection management software.

10. "Digital Preservation: Tools," *Library of Congress*, accessed August 27, 2016, http://www.digitalpreser vation.gov/tools.

11. Mike Schallcross, "Archivematica Users Group @ SAA," Bentley Historical Library, University of Michigan, *ArchivesSpace-Archivematica-DSpace Workflow Integration*, August 9, 2016, accessed August 27, 2016, http:// archival-integration.blogspot.com.

12. "How Preservica Works," *Preservica*, accessed March 5, 2017, http://preservica.com/preservica-works.

13. "Home, Products, Digital Commons, Features," *BePress*, accessed March 5, 2017, https://www.bepress .com/products/digital-commons/features.

14. "About DSpace," *DuraSpace*, accessed March 5, 2017, http://www.dspace.org/introducing.

15. AIMS Work Group, "Glossary," s.v. "Fedora," *AIMS Born-Digital Collections: An Inter-Institutional Model for Stewardship*, 2012, accessed August 6, 2016, http://dcs.library.virginia.edu/files/2013/02/AIMS_final.pdf.

16. "Hydra Is a Repository Solution," *Hydra*, accessed March 5, 2017, https://projecthydra.org.

17. Russell Palmer, "Lyrasis Islandora Hosting Services Demonstration," live web presentation, viewed October 20, 2015.

18. "Access Data, Solutions, Forensic Toolkit (FTK)," *Access Data*, accessed November 12, 2016, http://accessdata.com/solutions/digital-forensics/forensic-toolkit-ftk; AIMS Work Group, appendix G, *AIMS Born-Digital Collections*, 127.

19. "Aid4Mail," *Fookes Holding*, accessed March 6, 2017, http://www.aid4mail.com.

20. *NDSA Glossary*, s.v. "Bagger," accessed January 14, 2017, http://ndsa.org/glossary.

21. "BitCurator," *University of North Carolina School of Information and Library Science*, accessed August 27, 2016, http://www.bitcurator.net/bitcurator.

22. "ClamAV," *Cisco*, accessed March 6, 2017, http://www.clamav.net/index.html; "About," *Cicso*, http://www.clamav.net/about.

23. "Community Owned Digital Preservation Tool Registry (COPTR)," *Curator's Workbench*, last modified April 7, 2016, http://coptr.digipres.org/Curator%27s_Workbench.

24. Seth E. Shaw, *Data Accessioner*, accessed August 14, 2016, http://dataaccessioner.org.

25. "Products, ReNamer," *Den4B*, accessed March 6, 2017, http://www.den4b.com/products/renamer. See also http://www.mnhs.org/preserve/records/docs_pdfs/Den4bRenamer.pdf for minimal instructions.

26. "Download DROID: File Format Identification Tool," *National Archives*, accessed November 4, 2016, http://www.nationalarchives.gov.uk/information-management/manage-information/preserving-digital-records/droid.

27. AIMS Work Group, *AIMS Born-Digital Collections*, 38; "EnCase Forensic," *Guidance Software*, accessed November 12, 2016, https://www.guidancesoftware.com/encase-forensic.

28. "Tools, Exactly," *AudioVisual Preservation Solutions*, accessed March 6, 2017, https://www.avpreserve.com/avpsresources/tools.

29. "Community Owned Digital Preservation Tool Registry (COPTR)," *ExifTool*, last modified October 6, 2015, http://coptr.digipres.org/ExifTool.

30. "File Identification Tool Set (FITS)," *Harvard University*, accessed August 27, 2016, http://projects.iq.harvard.edu/fits.

31. "Tools, Fixity," *AudioVisual Preservation Solutions*, accessed March 6, 2017, https://www.avpreserve.com/avpsresources/tools.

32. "Irfanview," *Irfan Skiljan*, accessed November 5, 2016, http://www.irfanview.com.

33. "JHOVE," *Open Preservation Foundation*, accessed March 6, 2017, http://jhove.openpreservation.org.

34. "Karen's Directory Printer 5.3.2," *MajorGeeks*, accessed November 4, 2016, http://www.majorgeeks.com/files/details/karens_directory_printer.html.

35. "Social Media and Web 2.0 at the National Archives," *U.S. National Archives and Records Administration*, accessed March 7, 2017, https://www.archives.gov/social-media/github.html; "NARA File Analyzer and Metadata Harvester," *COPTR*, accessed March 7, 2017, http://coptr.digipres.org/NARA_File_Analyzer_and_Metadata_Harvester; "File-analyzer, File Analyzer and Metadata Harvester," Georgetown University Libraries, accessed March 7, 2017, https://georgetown-university-libraries.github.io/File-Analyzer/.

36. "OpenRefine," *Wikipedia*, accessed December 17, 2016, https://en.wikipedia.org/wiki/OpenRefine.

37. "Avantstar, Products, Quick View Plus Standard Edition, Overview," *Avantstar*, accessed August 27, 2016, http://www.avantstar.com/quick-view-plus-standard-edition#fndtn-overview.

38. "Codesector, TeraCopy for Microsoft Windows," *Code Sector*, accessed November 19, 2016, http://www.codesector.com/teracopy.

39. "Thunar File Manager," *Xfce Development Team*, accessed November 4, 2016, http://docs.xfce.org/xfce/thunar/start.

40. "Jam Software, Products, TreeSize Professional, Overview and Features Tabs," *Jam Software GmbH*, accessed August 27, 2016, https://www.jam-software.com/treesize.

41. "WinDirStat Windows Directory Statistics," *WinDirStat*, last updated June 28, 2016, accessed August 27, 2016, http://windirstat.info.

Glossary

access point. A "name, term, keyword, phrase or code that may be used to search, identify and locate [records in] an archival description." Used in DACS-compliant finding aids, MARC records, and other bibliographic description.[1]

access rights information. One component of preservation description information or PDI in the OAIS reference model.[2] *See also* preservation description information (PDI).

administrative metadata. Comprises both technical and preservation metadata and may include rights metadata; generally used for internal management of digital resources; typically stored separate from the resource. Helps ensure authenticity and integrity.[3] Administrative metadata is captured as part of the OAIS reference model.

archival information package (AIP). Consists of the content information and associated preservation description information (PDI), which is managed, stored, and preserved within one OAIS-compliant system.[4] Previously it was a SIP whose files have now been arranged and described so that it includes the digital files or content to be preserved and their metadata. *See also* dissemination information package (DIP); submission information package (SIP).

archival record. "[D]ata or information that has been fixed on some medium; that has content, context and structure." "It is of a legal or official nature that may be used as evidence," proof or accountability.[5] Whether information is a record depends on the information content, not the carrier (i.e. the manner, format, or medium by which it is recorded).

archival representation. Yakel uses this term instead of *arrangement and description* or *processing*; also refers to the "products," whether a tool, finding aid, system, database; the "work of the archivist in (re)ordering, interpreting, creating surrogates, and designing architectures for representational systems that contain those surrogates to stand in for or represent actual archival materials."[6]

archives. 1. Materials created or received by an organization, person, or family during the conduct of their affairs and preserved because of the enduring value of the information they contain or as evidence of the activities, functions, or responsibilities of their creator. 2. The organization or organizational unit responsible for managing archival records. 3. The physical location that houses archival records.[7]

arrangement. The "process of identifying the logical groupings of materials within the whole as they were established by the creator, of constructing a new organization when the original ordering has been lost, or of establishing an order when one never existed. The archivist then identifies further sub-groupings within each unit down to the level of granularity that is feasible or desirable, even to the individual item. This process creates hierarchical groupings of material, with each step in the hierarchy described as a level"[8] (collection or record group, subgroup, series, file, item).

artificial collection. An "artificial assemblage of documents accumulated on the basis of some common characteristic without regard to the provenance of those documents."[9] ISAD(G) uses the term *collection* as the equivalent to the American *artificial collection*. American archivists contrast a collection (records created by a private individual) and a record group (those created by a government, corporate, or other organization), while ISAD(G) uses *archival fonds* for both.

authenticity. An "authentic record is one that can be proven to be what it professes to be" and is free from tampering or corruption as determined by internal and external evidence, including physical characteristics, structure, content, and context. One of four qualities essential for preserving digital records or files. Checksums are external evidence of digital file authenticity. Descriptive, administrative, structural, and technical metadata help ensure authenticity and integrity.[10] *See also* integrity; reliability; usability.

bag. A package of content that conforms to the BagIt specification. It consists of a base directory containing a small amount of machine-readable text to help automate the content's receipt, storage, and retrieval and a subdirectory that holds the content files.[11]

bagger. A graphical software application tool to produce a package of data files that conforms to the BagIt specification.[12]

BagIt specification. An Internet Engineering Task Force (IETF) specification for a hierarchical file packaging format for the storage and transfer of digital content. Specification available at http://www.digitalpreservation.gov/documents/bagitspec.pdf.[13]

characterization. "[I]dentifying and describing . . . what a file is and what its technical characteristics are," a core activity of digital preservation.[14] File characterization data is recorded in the manifests of the PDI or AIP and includes file format, the creator, time created, information on the creating application, and the application needed to view the digital file or object.

checksum. A checksum or hashtag are different words for the same thing, a numeric value resulting from applying a mathematical algorithm to one or more digital files. Checksums are used to determine whether accidental and unrecorded data loss or file changes and corruption occurred during transfer or storage. The authenticity, integrity, and trustworthiness of files can be determined at any later time by recalculating the checksum and comparing with the initial checksum. MD5 hash and SHA-256 hash are two examples. *See also* fixity check.

classification. In libraries this refers to the "process of assigning materials a code or heading indicating a category to which it belong."[15] Dewey Decimal and Library of Congress call numbers are examples of library classification codes.

conservation. *See* preservation.

content data object. In the OAIS reference model, this is the digital information or object to be preserved.[16]

content information. In the OAIS reference model, this is comprised of the content data object and the representation information. Together with the preservation description information (PDI), it forms a SIP or AIP. *See also* archival information package (AIP); content data object; representation information.[17]

context, context information. Context is one component of preservation description information (PDI) in the OAIS reference model. Context documents the relationships of the records or components in the content data object to each other and to other records and the circumstances of their creation. Context includes the dates created, the dates modified, and file directory paths.[18] *See also* preservation description information (PDI).

dark server. A digital storage area for files not made accessible to the public. Preservation masters and AIPs are kept here in the absence of a preservation software system.

data content standards. Control how to format the information within a data element or "container." Examples include DACS, ISAD(G), ISAAR(CPF), ICA-ISDF, ICA-ISDIAH, RDA. *See also* data structure standards, schema; data value standards.

data curation. A subset of digital curation that applies specifically to scientific research data; it involves adding metadata to enable its discovery and retrieval as well as its preservation in general, actively and continuously managing the data through its lifecycle, and maintaining its quality for the purpose of reuse to create new knowledge by the greater academic community.[19] *See also* digital curation; digital preservation.

data elements, fields. A "discrete component of data"[20] defined by a data structure standard, like MARC or Dublin Core.

data stewardship. Managing a shared resource to preserve data but potentially for only one scholarly community; more narrow in activity that data curation or digital curation.[21] *See also* data curation; digital curation.

data structure standards, schema. Define the data elements, fields, or "containers" in a descriptive standard and how they relate to each other. Individual data fields may be required or optional, (non)repeatable, or have attributes that further describe the field.[22] Examples include PREMIS, EAC-CPF, Dublin Core, EAD, MARC, MODS, MIX. *See also* data content standards; data value standards; serialization.

data value standards. Controlled vocabulary or a preapproved list of terms used to complete specific data fields in order to ensure consistent use of the same term for the same entity or concept across all description. Data value standards include controlled vocabularies, thesauri, and authority files.[23] Examples include Library of Congress Name Authority File, Library of Congress Subject Headings, and Getty Thesaurus of Geographic Names. *See also* data content standards, schema; data structure standards.

delimited text. "[D]elimited files are a simple way to store data and import or export it between various applications. Delimited in essence means data that's separated by specific delimiter characters. Common delimiters are tab, comma and semicolon." A delimited file is not useful "unless it is converted into some form suitable for analysis and study."[24]

description. The process and product of a complex hierarchical and progressive analysis of the intellectual structure, context, and contents of a set of records, during which a somewhat standardized set of information is captured and presented in a standardized form.[25]

descriptive metadata. A specific type of metadata that identifies a resource and describes its intellectual content for purposes such as discovery and identification. Helps ensure authenticity and integrity.[26]

digital curation. The active management by informational professionals of digital data for current and future use, including adding metadata; aiding discoverability and access; and preserving authenticity, integrity, reliability, and usability.[27] *See also* data curation; data stewardship.

digital forensics. A "branch of forensic science encompassing the recovery and investigation of material found on digital devices." Its application for archivists is the knowledge of how to transfer files without changing file properties and forensic imaging during acquisition.[28]

digital objects. A "conceptual term that describes a discrete, aggregated unit of digital content comprised of one or more related digital files (bitstreams). These related files might include metadata, derivative versions and/or a wrapper to bind the pieces together."[29] Examples include photographs and videos.

digital preservation. A "term that encompasses all of the activities, policies, strategies and actions required to ensure that the digital content designated for long-term preservation is maintained in usable formats, for as long as access to that content is needed or desired, and can be made available in meaningful ways to current and future users, for as long as necessary regardless of the challenges of media failure and technological change. Digital preservation goals include ensuring enduring usability, authenticity, discoverability, and accessibility of content over the very long term."[30]

digital repository. 1. An "online, searchable, web-accessible database." 2. A "collection of digital assets and metadata." 3. An "organization that has responsibility for the long-term maintenance of digital resources."[31] *See also* institutional repository.

disk image. A single file or storage device containing the complete contents and structure representing a data storage medium or device, such as a hard drive, tape drive, floppy disk, CD, DVD, BD, or USB flash drive, although an image of an optical disc may be referred to as an optical disk image.[33] *See also* forensic disk image, forensic copy.

dissemination information package (DIP). The package of digital object(s) and metadata that is derived from one or more AIPs, produced or retrieved by an OAIS system as a result of a dissemination request, and delivered to a user.[32] *See also* archival information package (AIP); submission information package (SIP).

emulation. A method for overcoming technological obsolescence of hardware and software by mimicking the functionality of the older hardware or software to re-create the original functionality, look, and feel of a digital object on current computers. Emulation focuses on the hard- and software environment in which the original object was rendered in order to re-create the environment. An example is emulating WordPerfect 1.0 on a Macintosh computer.[34]

extensible. "[I]n information technology, extensible describes something, such as a program, programming language, or protocol that is designed so that users or developers can expand or add to its capabilities. Extensibility can be a primary reason for the system, as in the case of the Extensible Markup Language (XML), or it may be only a minor feature."[35]

fixity. In the OAIS reference model, this is a component of the preservation description information (PDI). Also refers to the "property of a digital object that indicates that it has not changed between two points in time."[36] *See also* content information; preservation description information (PDI).

fixity check. The process of verifying that a file or digital object has "not been altered in an undocumented manner."[37] Fixity checks can be performed manually or automated and should be run twice as often as the anticipated life of the storage device. Fixity checks are evidence of file authenticity and integrity. *See also* checksum.

forensic disk image, forensic copy. A complete sector-by-sector copy of the source medium and thereby perfectly replicating the structure and contents of a storage device.[38] *See also* disk image.

format migration. A narrower term for migration. Includes media migration, which does not change the bitstreams within the files copied, such as moving files from a floppy disk to a CD-ROM. Converting data from an obsolete structure to a new structure to counter software obsolescence is a type of format migration that may cause "changes in the internal structure of a data file to keep pace with changing application versions, such as migration from Word 95 to Word 2000. Or, it may involve a more radical change in structure, such as changes from one application to another, such as Word to WordPerfect. Making changes in a data structure places the original at risk, as the new structure may not accurately capture the form and function of the original."[39] *See also* media migration; migration; reformat; refresh.

hashtag. The same as a checksum. *See also* checksum; fixity check.

ingest. The set of processes responsible for accepting information submitted by producers (SIP) and transforming it into an AIP ready for storage. Includes receipt of the information, validation that the information received is uncorrupted and complete, transformation of the submitted information into a form suitable for storage and management, extraction or creation of descriptive metadata to support the OAIS's search and retrieval tools and finding aids, and transfer of the submitted information and its associated metadata to archival storage.[40] *See also* archival information package (AIP); submission information package (SIP).

institutional repository. A "digital collection capturing and preserving the intellectual output of a single or multi-university community."[41]

integrity. The "quality of being whole and unaltered through loss, tampering or corruption."[42] Format identification and validation are key indicators of file integrity. Software, like JHOVE, can verify that a format is what its file extension claims, as well as determine the level of compliance to a particular format specification.[43] "This does not mean that the record must be precisely the same as it was when first created for its integrity to exist and be demonstrated. When we refer to an electronic record, we consider it essentially complete and uncorrupted if the message that it is meant to communicate in order to achieve its purpose is unaltered. This implies that its physical integrity, such as the proper number of bit strings, may be compromised, provided that the articulation of the content and any required elements of form remain the same. The integrity of a record may be demonstrated by evidence found on the face of the record, in metadata related to the record, or in one or more of its various contexts."[44] One of four qualities essential for preserving digital records, files, or objects.[45] *See also* authenticity; reliability; usability.

intellectual arrangement. Arrangement of archival records in a hierarchical manner based on provenance and reflecting their original order within a record-keeping system. The arrangement is reflected in description or metadata about the records. There is no physical expression of an intellectual arrangement, whether for analog or digital records. In the latter case, the original files and directory are not moved or modified in any way.[46]

Internet. The global system of interconnected computer networks (private, public, academic, business, and government) that use the Internet protocol (TCP/IP) to link devices worldwide. It uses a broad array of technologies, like telnet, file transfer protocol (FTP), and SMTF for e-mail, to enable communication or the transmission of information.[47] *See also* World Wide Web (WWW).

interoperability. The ability of one application or system to communicate or work with another.[48]

logs. See figure 5.3 for a sample electronic file structure for documenting information stored in the preservation description information (PDI) component of a stabilized SIP or processed AIP as defined by the OAIS reference model. The "logs" folder contains text files documenting actions performed on files in the AIP, particularly system actions like migration, file renaming, and file normalization.[49]

macroappraisal. Analysis and selection or rejection of archival records based on their information content and other qualities normally assessed for analog records. Macroappraisal is used for this stage of the appraisal process for digital records to contrast with microappraisal. *See also* microappraisal.

manifests. See figure 5.3 for a sample electronic file structure for documenting information stored in the preservation description information (PDI) component of a stabilized SIP or processed AIP as defined by the OAIS reference model. The "manifests" folder contains an inventory of all the files with last date modified, date created, and file directory; checksums; analysis or count of file types and file size; etc. This information is often automated or generated by a digital tool.[50]

media migration. A narrower term than migration. The "process of copying data from one type of storage material to another to ensure continued access to the information as the material becomes obsolete or degrades over time." Does not alter the bitstream. Examples of media migration include copying files from 5¼" floppy disks to 3½" floppy discs to CD to DVD."[51] *See also* reformat; refresh.

metadata. Structured information that characterizes or describes an information object, record, or archival resource. Metadata can be descriptive but differs from most description in that it frequently describes digital resources delivered via the web. Metadata is less narrative, more often transactional information about an interaction with technology.[52] There are a number of types of metadata. *See also* administrative metadata; descriptive metadata; preservation metadata; rights metadata; structural metadata; technical metadata.

microappraisal. The appraisal of the technical qualities of digital records as contrasted with and subsequent to macroappraisal. *See also* macroappraisal.

migration. The "process of converting records to newer formats in order to maintain their compatibility with a newer generation of hardware and/or software computer technology, while leaving intact their intellectual form."[53] Migration appears to be actions that must be taken to retain the ability to "read" (interpret and understand) a digital file or object with new technology when it is at risk because of the impending unavailability of the original hardware or software required to read it. Comparison of definitions for *reformat*, *migration*, *media migration*, and *format migration* yielded many that sound similar without clear distinctions between them. The words *system*, *carrier*, *storage medium*, and *structure* seem like equivalents of each other. Less succinct definitions that are clearer in meaning with examples would be more helpful, as different authors use different words while trying to define the same concept. Newer practitioners are unable to discern when a word is chosen for variety and when it signifies an actual difference in meaning between definitions. *See also* reformat.

normalization. In a preservation context, normalization refers to a preservation strategy for digital files that involves the imposition of a limited number of "standard" formats and rules to create preservable file formats.[54] Examples include changing a DOC file to PDF on ingest or standardizing the format for forming dates.

open archival information system (OAIS). Developed by the Consultative Committee for Space Data Systems (CCSDS) and accepted as ISO standard 14721:2012, the latest update was released in June 2012. The OAIS reference model is a "conceptual framework for an archival system dedicated to preserving and maintaining access to digital information over the long term."[55]

organic. "[G]enerated as the natural documentary byproduct of the activities or functions of corporate bodies or persons."[56]

personal (digital) archives. Personal papers or manuscripts has traditionally referred to the papers of private citizens and included materials they not only created but also received or acquired, but the term *personal archives* seeks to distinguish between digital and analog information rather than professional and personal and could include the written works of authors or poets. They are more likely to consist of digital records created by an individual.

preservation. Preservation tasks for digital records includes virus and malware checks, creating checksums and monitoring them over time, comparing the checksum of a SIP when received to the SIP when work commences for conversion to an AIP, and identification of obsolete and unknown file formats.

preservation description information (PDI). In the OAIS reference model, this is the information that is necessary for adequate preservation of the content information and that can be categorized as provenance, reference, fixity, context, and access rights information. Together with the content information, the PDI forms a SIP or AIP.[57] *See also* content information; submission information package (SIP).

preservation metadata. The "contextual information necessary to carry out, document, and evaluate the processes that support the long-term retention and accessibility of digital content. Preservation metadata documents the technical processes associated with preservation, specifies rights management information, establishes the authenticity of digital content, and records the chain of custody and provenance for a digital object."[58] *See also* structural metadata; technical metadata.

Preservation Metadata: Implementation Strategies(PREMIS). An international data structure standard used to record and manage digital preservation metadata about digital objects, preservation events and actions, agents, and rights statements.

processing. According to the OAIS reference model, archival processing is all the actions taken to transform digital records from the condition in which they are received from the producer (SIP) to the state they are in once they are in long-term storage (AIP) and ready to disseminate.[59] To be clear, this is not the point at which SIPs are stabilized and can be temporarily set aside until processing can be completed later on; this is after the processing has been performed.

producer. In the OAIS reference model, this is the person, office, or unit that creates the digital file(s) and metadata transferred or submitted for preservation in an OAIS-compliant system. *See also* open archival information system (OAIS); submission information package (SIP).

provenance. In the OAIS reference model, this is a component of the preservation description information (PDI).[60] Information that documents the history of the content information, including the origin or source of the content information, any changes that may have taken place since it was created, and the chain of custody since its creation. The archives is responsible for creating and preserving provenance information from the point of ingest; however, the producer should provide provenance information from creation until ingest. Provenance information adds to the evidence to support authenticity.[61] *See also* content information; preservation description information (PDI).

record. "[D]ata or information that has been fixed on some medium; that has content, context and structure; and that is used as an extension of human memory or to demonstrate accountability."[62]

record copy. The single copy of a document, often the original, that is designated as the official copy for legal, reference, and preservation purposes.[63]

reference. In the OAIS reference model, this is a component of the preservation description information (PDI). It is a unique identifier (numeric or numeric-alphabetic combination) assigned to each individual SIP or AIP and links it to externally stored information, like description. *See also* content information; preservation description information (PDI).

reformat. "[T]o create a copy with a format or structure different from the original, especially for preservation or access" or "to migrate information from one carrier [or storage medium] to another." Reformatting can cause some loss of data by changing from one format to a different one.[64] *See also* media migration; migration; refresh.

refresh. "[C]opying digital content from one digital medium to the same medium or another without any alteration."[65] *See also* media migration; migration; reformat.

reliability. One of four qualities essential for preserving digital records, files, or objects.[66] The "trustworthiness of a record as a statement of fact. It exists when a record can stand for the fact it is about."[67] The "degree to which a record can be considered reliable is dependent upon the level of procedural and technical control exercised during its creation and management in its active life."[68] *See also* authenticity; integrity; usability.

representation. Yakel uses *representation* in lieu of *arrangement and description* or *processing*. She says it refers both to the activity and products of that activity (i.e., description).[69] Information that stands in for, represents, or describes in a more succinct manner other information in the form of a document, photo, oral history, object, or other information source in a system that provides access to archival materials. *See also* surrogate.

representation information. In the OAIS reference model, this is the information necessary to render and view the content data object; information about the hardware and software used to create the content data object; any added information that may be required to ensure the information will be understood by future users of the designated community for which it is being preserved; for example, the meaning of acronyms or column headings that may be lost over time. "The standard representation information reported by JHOVE includes: file pathname or URI, last modification date, byte size, format, format version, MIME type, format profiles," and optional checksums. Representation information and the content data object together form the content information.[70]

resource description framework (RDF). An XML-based language for representing information about resources in the World Wide Web. It is particularly intended for representing metadata about web resources, such as the title, author, and modification date of a web page; copyright and licensing information about a web document; or the availability schedule for some shared resource.[71] *See also* Semantic Web.

rights metadata. One of several types of metadata, some authors include it as part of administrative metadata. Rights metadata documents copyrights, user restrictions, and license agreements that might constrain the end use of digital content (including metadata files).[72]

Semantic Web. Tim Berners-Lee defines the Semantic Web as a web of data that can be processed directly and indirectly by machines. Two important technologies for developing the Semantic Web are extensible Markup Language (XML) and the resource description framework (RDF). Also known as Web 3.0, the Semantic Web uses linked (open) data to connect structured data, not just documents.[73] *See also* resource description framework (RDF).

serialization. "[M]achine readable encoding of metadata structure and values for the purpose of storage, machine processing or sharing/exchange"; for example, XML, JavaScript Object Notation (JSON), and CSV. Some data structure standards only work with one serialization; for example, MODS in XML.[74]

standard. A "document that provides requirements, specifications, guidelines or characteristics that can be used consistently to ensure that materials, products, processes and services [like metadata] are fit for their purpose." Types of metadata standards include "conceptual models/frameworks; data structure, data content and data value standards; and serializations."[75]

structural metadata. "[D]escribes the internal structure of digital resources and the relationships between their parts. It is used to enable navigation and presentation." Path and folder structure (file directories) are an example. "Structural metadata is often used by software programs."

Helps ensure authenticity, a subset of preservation metadata, along with technical metadata.[76] *See also* authenticity; preservation metadata; technical metadata.

structured data. Any data that resides in a fixed field within a record or file. Structured data is predictive and repetitive; easily entered, stored, queried, and analyzed; and often resides in a database-type business information system. Examples include data contained in databases, spreadsheets, document management and imaging systems, or created by geographic information systems (GIS) and computer-aided design (CAD) software.[77] *See also* unstructured data.

submission agreement. An agreement between an OAIS system and an information creator that specifies information and content to be submitted, its file format, description, and any other specifics of the data to be transferred and its transfer method. *See also* open archival information system (OAIS); submission information package (SIP).

submission information package (SIP). The data and metadata transferred or submitted by a records creator to an OAIS at accessioning as part of the ingest process for use in the construction of an AIP.[78] *See also* archival information package (AIP); dissemination information package (DIP).

surrogate. Description of a document or item that is sufficiently detailed to substitute for the original; for example, an archival calendar. The use of description as a surrogate declined in the twentieth century, but digitization and technology have increased the creation of surrogates in the form of digital copies of originals rather than through description. *See also* representation.

technical metadata. "Information describing physical (as opposed to intellectual) attributes or properties of Digital Objects." "Metadata that describes the technical state of and process used to create a file. Often closely related either to its file format or the original software used to create the file, e.g. scanning equipment and settings used to create or modify a digital object." Helps ensure authenticity and integrity, a subset of preservation metadata, along with structural metadata.[79] *See also* authenticity; preservation metadata; structural metadata.

trustworthiness. The "accuracy, reliability and authenticity of a record."[80] This is established digitally by use of consistent processes, checksums, write blockers, and other methods that make it more difficult to change a file. *See also* authenticity.

unstructured data. The opposite of structured data. Loosely speaking, unstructured data is usually for humans, while computers are more able to manipulate and interpret structured data. E-mail and word-processed documents are examples of unstructured data.[81] *See also* structured data.

usability. One of four qualities essential for preserving digital records, files, or objects.[82] Digital records that have been preserved need to continue to meet their original purpose. *See also* authenticity; integrity; reliability.

World Wide Web (WWW). One of many Internet services. It sits on top of the Internet and is a significant portion of the Internet, but the two are different. A collection of interconnected documents (web pages) and other web resources linked by hyperlinks and URLs. It uses the hypertext transfer protocol (HTTP) language to transfer information, one of many languages or protocols used to communicate on the Internet.[83] *See also* Internet.

Xforms. An XML formatted web form used for data entry. It is generic and can be used in a standalone manner.[84]

Notes

1. International Council on Archives, *ISAD(G): General International Standard Archival Description*, 2nd ed. (Ottawa: International Council on Archives, 2000), 10, s.v. "access point," accessed January 10, 2017, http://www.ica.org/sites/default/files/CBPS_2000_Guidelines_ISAD(G)_Second-edition_EN.pdf. See also Society of American Archivists, *Describing Archives: A Content Standard*, 2nd ed. (Chicago: Society of American Archivists, 2013), xxi–xxiv, on access points.

2. Consultative Committee for Space Data Systems (CCSDS), *Reference Model for an Open Archival Information System (OAIS), Magenta Book*, no. 2, CCSDS 650.0-M-2 (Washington, DC: CCSDS Secretariat, June 2012), 1–14, "preservation description information (PDI)".

3. Richard Pearce-Moses, *A Glossary of Archival and Records Terminology* (Chicago: Society of American Archivists, 2005), s.v. "administrative metadata," accessed December 16, 2016, http://www2.archivists.org/glossary/terms/a/administrative-metadata; Shawn Averkamp, "Overview of Metadata for Archivists," Society of American Archivists Digital Archives Specialist webinar, June 19, 2015, slide 16; Seth E. Shaw, "Arrangement and Description of Electronic Records, Part I," Society of American Archivists Digital Archives Specialist workshop, Chapel Hill, NC, June 11, 2015, course booklet, 36.

4. CCSDS, *Reference Model*, 1–9 "archival information package (AIP)"; AIMS Work Group, appendix A, s.v. "AIP," in *AIMS Born-Digital Collections: An Inter-Institutional Model for Stewardship*, 2012, accessed August 6, 2016, http://dcs.library.virginia.edu/files/2013/02/AIMS_final.pdf.

5. Pearce-Moses, *Glossary*, s.v. "record," accessed May 8, 2016, http://www2.archivists.org/glossary/terms/r/record.

6. Elizabeth Yakel, "Archival Representation," *Archival Science* 3 (2003): 2.

7. Pearce-Moses, *Glossary*, s.v. "archives," accessed January 3, 2017, http://www2.archivists.org/glossary/terms/a/archives.

8. Society of American Archivists, *Describing Archives: A Content Standard*, 2nd ed. (Chicago: Society of American Archivists, 2013), xvii.

9. International Council on Archives, *ISAD(G): General International Standard Archival Description*, 2nd ed. (Ottawa: International Council on Archives, 2000), s.v. "collection," accessed January 10, 2017, http://www.ica.org/sites/default/files/CBPS_2000_Guidelines_ISAD(G)_Second-edition_EN.pdf.

10. Mark J. Myers, "Appraisal of Electronic Records," Society of American Archivists, Digital Archives Specialist workshop, Richmond, KY, June 21, 2013, course booklet, 3; Pearce-Moses, *Glossary*, s.v. "authenticity," accessed January 11, 2017, http://www2.archivists.org/glossary/terms/a/authenticity; Mark J. Myers, "Electronic Records: The Next Step," Society of American Archivists Digital Archives Specialist webinar, April 13, 2015, PowerPoint, 2; Shaw, "Arrangement and Description, Part II," course booklet, 36.

11. *National Digital Stewardship Alliance (NDSA) Glossary*, s.v. "bag," accessed January 14, 2017, http://ndsa.org/glossary.

12. *NDSA Glossary*, s.v. "bagger."

13. *NDSA Glossary*, s.v. "BagIt Specification."

14. Matthew Hutchins, *Testing Software Tools of Potential Interest for Digital Preservation Activities at the National Library of Australia* (Parkes Place, Canberra: Information Technology Division National Library of

Australia, 2012), 8, accessed January 11, 2017, http://openpreservation.org/system/files/Digital%20Pres ervation%20Project%20Report%20-%20Testing%20Software%20Tools.pdf.

15. Pearce-Moses, *Glossary*, s.v. "classification," accessed January 13, 2017, http://www2.archivists.org/ glossary/terms/c/classification.

16. Brian F. Lavoie, *The Open Archival Information System Reference Model: An Introductory Guide* (Dublin, OH: Office of Research, OCLC, January 2004), 12, accessed September 27, 2016, http://www.dpconline.org/ docman/technology-watch-reports/91-introduction-to-oais/file.

17. Lavoie, *Open Archival Information System*, 12.

18. Lavoie, *Open Archival Information System*, 12; AIMS Work Group, appendix A, s.v. "context," in *AIMS Born-Digital Collections*; Shaw, "Arrangement and Description, Part I," course booklet, 102.

19. Carole L. Palmer, Nicholas M. Weber, Trevor Muñoz, and Allen H. Renear, "Foundations of Data Curation: The Pedagogy and Practice of 'Purposeful Work' with Research Data," *Archive Journal* 3 (Summer 2013), accessed January 1, 2017, http://www.archivejournal.net/issue/3/archives-remixed/foundations-of-data -curation-the-pedagogy-and-practice-of-purposeful-work-with-research-data.

20. "InterPARES 2 Project Glossary," s.v. "data element," *International Research on Permanent Authentic Records in Electronic Systems (InterPARES)*, last modified January 20, 2017, http://www.interpares.org/ip2/ display_file.cfm?doc=ip2_glossary.pdf&CFID=10608648&CFTOKEN=76523578.

21. Palmer et al., "Foundations of Data Curation."

22. Sibyl Schaefer and Janet M. Bunde, "Module 1: Standards for Archival Description," in *Archival Arrange- ment and Description*, Trends in Archives Practice series (Chicago: Society of American Archivists, 2013), 20.

23. Schaefer and Bunde, "Module 1," 44; Pearce-Moses, *Glossary*, s.v. "data value standard."

24. Saikat Basu, "How to Convert Delimited Text Files to Excel Spreadsheets," accessed December 17, 2016, http://www.makeuseof.com/tag/how-to-convert-delimited-text-files-into-excel-spreadsheets.

25. Pearce-Moses, *Glossary*, s.v. "archival description," particularly the 1999 citation to Daniel Pitti; Univer- sity of Minnesota, Digital Preservation, *Glossary*, s.v. "description," accessed January 13, 2017, https://www .lib.umn.edu/dp/glossary.

26. *NDSA Glossary*, s.v. "metadata:descriptive"; Shaw, "Arrangement and Description, Part II," course book- let, 36.

27. Elizabeth Yakel, "Digital Curation," *OCLC Systems and Services: International Digital Library Perspectives* 23 (2007): 335; University of Minnesota, *Glossary*, s.v. "digital curation"; Palmer et al., "Foundations of Data Curation."

28. University of Minnesota, *Glossary*, s.v. "digital forensics."

29. *NDSA Glossary*, s.v. "digital object."

30. University of Minnesota, *Glossary*, s.v. "digital preservation."

31. Patricia B. Condon, "Digital Curation: Fundamentals for Success," Society of American Archivists Digital Archives Specialist workshop, Cambridge, MA, October 6, 2014, course booklet, "Course Definitions."

32. AIMS Work Group, appendix A, s.v. "DIP (Dissemination Information Package)," in *AIMS Born-Digital Collections*; Council of State Archivists (CoSA), PERTTS Portal, *Glossary*, s.v. "Dissemination Information Package (DIP)," accessed January 14, 2017, https://www.statearchivists.org/pertts/glossary/#C.

33. AIMS Work Group, appendix A, s.v. "disk image," in *AIMS Born-Digital Collections*.

34. *NDSA Glossary*, s.v. "emulation"; Pearce-Moses, *Glossary*, s.v. "emulation," accessed January 14, 2017, http://www2.archivists.org/glossary/terms/e/emulation; Jeffrey van der Hoeven, Bram Lohman, and Remco Verdegem, "Emulation for Digital Preservation in Practice: The Results," *International Journal of Digital Curation* 2 (2007): 124, accessed January 14, 2017, http://www.ijdc.net/index.php/ijdc/article/view/50/35; "Digital preservation," *Wikipedia*, accessed August 6, 2016, https://en.wikipedia.org/wiki/Digital_preservation.

35. "Definition: Extensible," *TechTarget*, accessed January 14, 2017, http://searchsoa.techtarget.com/definition/extensible.

36. Lavoie, *Open Archival Information System*, 12; PREMIS Editorial Committee, *PREMIS Data Dictionary for Preservation Metadata*, ver. 3.0, "Glossary," s.v. "fixity," accessed December 29, 2016. http://www.loc.gov/standards/premis/v3/premis-3-0-final.pdf.

37. *NDSA Glossary*, s.v. "fixity check."

38. AIMS Work Group, appendix A, s.v. "forensic disk image," in *AIMS Born-Digital Collections*.

39. Pearce-Moses, *Glossary*, s.v. "migration," accessed November 23, 2015, http://www2.archivists.org/glossary/terms/m/media-migration.

40. Lavoie, *Open Archival Information System*, 9.

41. Condon, "Digital Curation," course booklet, "Course Definitions."

42. Pearce-Moses, *Glossary*, s.v. "integrity."

43. PREMIS Editorial Committee, *PREMIS Data Dictionary*, s.v. "integrity."

44. Pearce-Moses, *Glossary*, s.v. "integrity."

45. Myers, "Electronic Records," PowerPoint, 2.

46. AIMS Work Group, *AIMS Born-Digital Collections*, 136.

47. "Internet," *Wikipedia*, accessed January 15, 2017, https://en.wikipedia.org/wiki/Internet; "The difference between the internet and the world wide web," *Webopedia*, last updated December 22, 2016, http://www.webopedia.com/DidYouKnow/Internet/Web_vs_Internet.asp.

48. "InterPARES 2 Project Glossary," s.v. "interoperability."

49. Shaw, "Arrangement and Description, Part I," course booklet, 114.

50. Shaw, "Arrangement and Description, Part I," course booklet, 114.

51. Pearce-Moses, *Glossary*, s.v. "migration," accessed November 23, 2015, http://www2.archivists.org/glossary/terms/m/media-migration.

52. Averkamp, "Overview of Metadata," slide 8; Schaefer and Bunde, "Module 1," 48; Averkamp, "Overview of Metadata," slide 6.

53. AIMS Work Group, appendix A, s.v. "migration," in *AIMS Born-Digital Collections*.

54. University of Minnesota, *Glossary*, s.v. "normalization"; "InterPARES 2 Project Glossary," s.v. "normalization."

55. OCLC/RLG Working Group on Preservation Metadata, *Preservation Metadata and the OAIS Information Model: A Metadata Framework to Support the Preservation of Digital Objects* (Dublin, OH: OCLC/RLG Working Group on Preservation Metadata, 2002), 5, accessed May 12, 2016, http://www.oclc.org/content/dam/research/activities/pmwg/pm_framework.pdf.

56. Steven L. Hensen, "NISTF II and EAD: The Evolution of Archival Description," *American Archivist* 60 (Summer 1997): 287.

57. CCSDS, *Reference Model*, 1–14, "preservation description information (PDI)," accessed January 15, 2017, https://public.ccsds.org/Pubs/650x0m2.pdf; Lavoie, *Open Archival Information System*, 12.

58. *NDSA Glossary*, s.v. "metadata: preservation."

59. Shaw, "Arrangement and Description, Part I," course booklet, 66.

60. Lavoie, *Open Archival Information System*, 12.

61. CCSDS, *Reference Model*, 1–14, "provenance information," accessed November 19, 2016, https://public.ccsds.org/Pubs/650x0m2.pdf.

62. Shaw, "Arrangement and Description, Part II," course booklet, 34.

63. Pearce-Moses, *Glossary*, s.v. "record copy," accessed January 18, 2017, http://www2.archivists.org/glossary/terms/r/record-copy.

64. Pearce-Moses, *Glossary*, s.v. "reformat," accessed November 23, 2015, http://www2.archivists.org/glossary/terms/r/reformat; CoSA, *Glossary*, "refresh/refreshing," "reformatting."

65. Pearce-Moses, *Glossary*, s.v. "migration," accessed January 13, 2017, http://www2.archivists.org/glossary/terms/m/migration; "InterPARES 2 Project Glossary," s.v. "refreshing."

66. Myers, "Electronic Records," PowerPoint, 2.

67. "InterPARES 2 Project Glossary," s.v. "reliability."

68. Anne J. Gilliland-Swetland and Phillip B. Eppard, "Preserving the Authenticity of Contingent Digital Objects," *D-Lib Magazine* 6 (July/August 2000), accessed January 17, 2017, http://www.dlib.org/dlib/july00/eppard/07eppard.html.

69. Yakel, "Archival Representation," 2, 1; Luciana Duranti, "Origin and Development of Archival Description," *Archivaria* 35 (Spring 1993): 51, states that "description . . . begins to act as a 'representation' rather than a surrogate." This suggests that a surrogate provides more information than a "representation."

70. "JHOVE—JSTOR/Harvard Object Validation Environment," *JSTOR and the President and Fellows of Harvard College*, accessed November 5, 2016, http://jhove.sourceforge.net/; Lavoie, *Open Archival Information System*, 12.

71. "InterPARES 2 Project Glossary," s.v. "resource description framework."

72. *NDSA Glossary*, s.v. "metadata:rights management."

73. "Semantic web," *Wikipedia*, accessed December 18, 2016, https://en.wikipedia.org/wiki/Semantic _Web; Tim Berners-Lee, James Hendler, and Ora Lassila, "The Semantic Web," *Scientific American* (May 2001): 1-4; Michele Combs, Mark A. Matienzo, Merrilee Proffitt, and Lisa Spiro, *Over, Under, Around, and Through: Getting around Barriers to EAD Implementation* (Dublin, OH: OCLC, 2010), 10 accessed December 17, 2016, www.oclc.org/research/publications/library/2010/2010-04.pdf; "Introduction to the Semantic Web," *Cambridge Semantics*, accessed December 18, 2016, http://www.cambridgesemantics.com/semantic -university/introduction-semantic-web.

74. Averkamp, "Overview of Metadata," slides 60, 39.

75. "Standards," *International Organization for Standardization*, accessed January 21, 2017, http://www.iso .org/iso/home/standards.html; Averkamp, "Overview of Metadata," slide 38.

76. National Initiative for a Networked Cultural Heritage (NINCH), *The NINCH Guide to Good Practice in the Digital Representation and Management of Cultural Heritage Materials* (Washington, DC: National Initiative for a Networked Cultural Heritage, 2003), 222, accessed January 21, 2017, http://www.ninch.org/guide .pdf; Shaw, "Arrangement and Description, Part I," course booklet, 104; CoSA, *Glossary*, s.v. "metadata:- structural"; Shaw, "Arrangement and Description, Part II," course booklet, 36; Shaw, "Arrangement and Description, Part I," course booklet, 40–41.

77. Vangie Beal, "Structured Data," *Webopedia*, accessed January 21, 2017, http://www.webopedia.com/ TERM/S/structured_data.html; CoSA, *Glossary*, "structured data"; Myers, "Appraisal of Electronic Records," course booklet, 22.

78. AIMS Work Group, appendix A, s.v. "SIP," in *AIMS Born-Digital Collections*; CCSDS, *Reference Model*, 1-15, "submission information package."

79. PREMIS Editorial Committee, *PREMIS Data Dictionary*, s.v. "technical metadata"; *NDSA Glossary*, s.v. "metadata:technical"; Shaw, "Arrangement and Description, Part II," course booklet, 36; Shaw, "Arrangement and Description, Part I," course booklet, 40–41.

80. "InterPARES 2 Project Glossary," s.v. "trustworthiness."

81. "Structured vs. Unstructured Data," *Bright Planet*, accessed January 21, 2017, https://brightplanet.com /2012/06/structured-vs-unstructured-data.

82. Myers, "Electronic Records," PowerPoint, 2.

83. "Internet"; *"The difference between."*

84. "XForms," *Wikipedia*, accessed December 17, 2016, https://en.wikipedia.org/wiki/XForms.

Bibliography

"64-Bit Computing." *Wikipedia*. Accessed January 24, 2017, https://en.wikipedia.org/wiki/64 -bit_computing.

"About DSpace." *DuraSpace*. Accessed March 5, 2017. http://www.dspace.org/introducing.

"Aid4Mail." *Fookes Holding*. Accessed March 6, 2017. http://www.aid4mail.com.

AIMS Work Group. *AIMS Born-Digital Collections: An Inter-Institutional Model for Stewardship*. AIMS, 2012. Accessed August 27, 2016. http://dcs.library.virginia.edu/files/2013/02/AIMS_final.pdf.

"Announcements: New Funding for the Social Networks and Archival Context Project." *Encoded Archival Context Corporate Bodies, Persons, and Families*. May 18, 2012. Accessed November 21, 2016. http://eac.staatsbibliothek-berlin.de/announcements.html.

"ArchivesSpace-Archivematica-DSpace Workflow Integration Project (April 2014–October 2016)." *Bentley Historical Library, University of Michigan*. Accessed December 31, 2016. http://archival-integration.blogspot.com.

"Archon (Software)." *Wikipedia*. Accessed December 18, 2016, https://en.wikipedia.org/wiki/Archon_(software).

Averkamp, Shawn. "Overview of Metadata for Archivists." Digital Archives Specialist webinar, Society of American Archivists. June 19, 2015.

Basu, Saikat. "How to Convert Delimited Text Files to Excel Spreadsheets." *MakeUseOf*. Accessed December 17, 2016. http://www.makeuseof.com/tag/how-to-convert-delimited-text-files -into-excel-spreadsheets.

Beagrie, Neil, ed. *Digital Preservation Handbook*. Rev. 2nd ed. Glasgow: Digital Preservation Coalition, 2015. Accessed June 19, 2016. http://handbook.dpconline.org/organisational-activities/acquisition-and-appraisal.

Beal, Vangie. "The Difference between the Internet and the World Wide Web." *Webopedia*. June 24, 2010. Accessed December 22, 2016. http://www.webopedia.com/DidYouKnow/Internet/Web_vs_Internet.asp.

———. "Structured Data." *Webopedia*. Accessed January 21, 2017, http://www.webopedia.com/TERM/S/structured_data.html.

Bearman, David. *Towards National Information Systems for Archives and Manuscript Repositories: The National Information Systems Task Force (NISTF) Papers 1981–1984.* Chicago: Society of American Archivists, 1987.

Becker, Christoph, Günther Kolar, Josef Küng, and Andreas Rauber. "Preserving Interactive Multimedia Art: A Case Study in Preservation Planning." Paper presented at International Conference on Asian Digital Libraries, Hanoi, Vietnam, December 10–13, 2007. Accessed July 16, 2016. http://www.planets-project.eu/docs/presentations/ICADL_2007_Christoph Becker_Interactiveart.pdf.

Berner, Richard C. *Archival Theory and Practice in the United States: A Historical Analysis.* Seattle: University of Washington Press, 1983.

———. "Arrangement and Description: Some Historical Observations." *American Archivist* 41 (April 1978): 169–81.

———. "Historical Development of Archival Theory and Practices in the United States." *Midwestern Archivist* 7, no. 2 (1982): 103–17.

Berners-Lee, Tim. "Linked Data." Last revised June 18, 2009. https://www.w3.org/DesignIssues/LinkedData.html.

Berners-Lee, Tim, James Hendler, and Ora Lassila. "The Semantic Web." *Scientific American* (May 2001): 1–4.

Birdsall, William F. "The American Archivists' Search for Professional Identity, 1909–1936." PhD diss., University of Wisconsin, Madison, 1973. ProQuest (7407456).

"BitCurator." *University of North Carolina School of Information and Library Science.* Accessed August 27, 2016. http://www.bitcurator.net/bitcurator.

Bizer, Christian, Tom Heath, and Tim Berners-Lee. "Linked Data: The Story So Far." *International Journal on Semantic Web and Information Systems* 5 (2009): 3. Accessed December 4, 2016. doi:10.4018/jswis.2009081901.

Brichford, Maynard. "The Provenance of Provenance in Germanic Areas." *Provenance* 7 (Fall 1989): 54–70.

Cappon, Lester J. "Historical Manuscripts as Archives: Some Definitions and Their Application." *American Archivist* 19 (April 1956): 101–10.

"ClamAV." *Cisco.* Accessed March 6, 2017. http://www.clamav.net/index.html.

"CollectiveAccess." *CollectiveAccess.* Accessed December 22, 2016. http://www.collectiveaccess.org.

Combs, Michele, Mark A. Matienzo, Merrilee Proffitt, and Lisa Spiro. *Over, Under, Around, and Through: Getting around Barriers to EAD Implementation.* Dublin, OH: OCLC Research, 2010. Accessed December 4, 2016. http://www.oclc.org/content/dam/research/publications/library/2010/2010-04.pdf.

Condon, Patricia B. "Digital Curation: Fundamentals for Success." Society of American Archivists, Digital Archives Specialist workshop, Cambridge, MA, October 6, 2014.

Consultative Committee for Space Data Systems (CCSDS). *Reference Model for an Open Archival Information System (OAIS) Recommended Practice CCSDS 650.0-M-2*. Washington, DC: CCSDS Secretariat, June 2012. Accessed January 15, 2017. https://public.ccsds.org/Pubs/650x0m2 .pdf.

"Contentdm." *OCLC*. Accessed December 22, 2016. http://www.oclc.org/en-US/contentdm.html.

"CuadraStar Information Management Solutions." *Lucidea*. Accessed December 22, 2016. http:// lucidea.com/cuadrastar.

"Curator's Workbench." *Community Owned Digital Preservation Tool Registry (COPTR)*. Last modi-fied April 7, 2016. http://coptr.digipres.org/Curator%27s_Workbench.

Daines, J. Gordon, III. "Module 2: Processing Digital Records and Manuscripts." In *Archival Ar-rangement and Description*, Edited and introduced by Christopher J. Prom and Thomas J. Frus-ciano, 100–110. Trends in Archives Practice series. Chicago: Society of American Archivists, 2013.

Daniels, Morgan G., and Elizabeth Yakel. "Seek and You May Find: Successful Search in Online Finding Aid Systems." *American Archivist* 73 (Fall/Winter 2010): 535–68.

"Dashboard/Administration." *University of California, California Digital Library*. Accessed December 23, 2016. http://www.cdlib.org/services/access_publishing/dsc/contribute/administration .html.

Data Accessioner. Accessed August 14, 2016. http://dataaccessioner.org.

Desnoyers, Megan Floyd. "When Is a Collection Processed?" *Midwestern Archivist* 7 (1982): 5–23.

Digital Collections and Archives, Tufts University, and Manuscripts and Archives, Yale University. *Fedora and the Preservation of University Records Project: 2.1 Ingest Guide*. Version 1.0. Medford, MA: Tufts University and Yale University, September 2006. Accessed September 29, 2016. http://dl.tufts.edu/catalog/tufts:UA069.004.001.00006.

"Digital Preservation." *Wikipedia*. Accessed August 6, 2016, https://en.wikipedia.org/wiki/ Digital_preservation.

"Digital Preservation: Glossary." *University of Minnesota*. Accessed January 13, 2017. https://www .lib.umn.edu/dp/glossary.

"Document Management System." *Wikipedia*. Accessed December 18, 2016. https://en.wikipedia .org/wiki/Document_management_system.

"Documentation." *Ohio EAD Task Force*. Accessed December 23, 2016. https://sites.google.com/ site/ohioead/s.

Dollar, Charles. *Archival Theory and Information Technologies: The Impact of Information Technologies on Archival Principles and Methods.* Edited by Oddo Bucci. Macerata, Italy: University of Macerata, 1992.

Dooley, Jackie. *The Archival Advantage: Integrating Archival Expertise into Management of Born-Digital Library Materials.* Dublin, OH: Online Computer Library Center, 2015.

Dooley, Jackie, and Katherine Luce. *Taking Our Pulse: The OCLC Research Survey of Special Collections and Archives.* Dublin, OH: Online Computer Library Center, 2010. Accessed May 27, 2016. http://www.oclc.org/content/dam/research/publications/library/2010/2010-11.pdf.

"Download DROID: File Format Identification Tool." *National Archives.* Accessed November 4, 2016. http://www.nationalarchives.gov.uk/information-management/manage-information/preserving-digital-records/droid.

"DSpace." *Wikipedia.* Accessed January 24, 2017. https://en.wikipedia.org/wiki/DSpace.

Duchein, Michel. "The History of European Archives and the Development of the Archival Profession in Europe." *American Archivist* 55 (Winter 1992): 14–24.

Duranti, Luciana. "Origin and Development of the Concept of Archival Description." *Archivaria* 35 (Spring 1993): 47–54.

DuraSpace. *Managing Digital Collections Survey Results Summary.* Winchester, MA: DuraSpace, 2014.

"EAD3 1.0 Is Available!" *Society of American Archivists.* Accessed December 19, 2016. http://www2.archivists.org/groups/technical-subcommittee-on-encoded-archival-description-ead/ead3-10-is-available.

"EAD Toolkit." *University of California, California Digital Library.* Accessed December 23, 2016. http://www.cdlib.org/services/access_publishing/dsc/tools/ead_toolkit.html.

"Electronic Records Archives (ERA): About ERA." *National Archives and Records Administration.* Accessed November 8, 2016. https://www.archives.gov/era/about.

"EnCase Forensic." *Guidance Software.* Accessed November 12, 2016. https://www.guidancesoftware.com/encase-forensic.

"Encoded Archival Context—Corporate Bodies, Persons, and Families (EAC-CPF)." *Society of American Archivists.* Accessed December 8, 2016. http://www2.archivists.org/groups/technical-subcommittee-on-eac-cpf/encoded-archival-context-corporate-bodies-persons-and-families-eac-cpf.

Encoded Archival Context Working Group of the Society of American Archivists and the Staatsbibliothek zu Berlin. *Encoded Archival Context—Corporate Bodies, Persons, and Families (EAC-CPF) Tag Library.* Version 2010 (initial release). Accessed December 29, 2016. http://www3.iath.virginia.edu/eac/cpf/tagLibrary/cpfTagLibrary.html.

"Encoded Archival Description Tag Library." Version 2002. *Encoded Archival Description Official Site*. Accessed January 6, 2017. https://www.loc.gov/ead/tglib/element_index.html.

"ExifTool." *Community Owned Digital Preservation Tool Registry (COPTR)*. Last modified October 6, 2015. http://coptr.digipres.org/ExifTool.

Faulder, Erin. "Accessioning and Ingest of Electronic Records." Society of American Archivists, Digital Archives Specialist workshop. Lexington, KY, May 6, 2015.

"Features." *BePress*. Accessed March 5, 2017. https://www.bepress.com/products/digital-commons/features.

"Fedora Commons." *Wikipedia*. Accessed May 27, 2016. https://en.wikipedia.org/wiki/Fedora_Commons.

"File-Analyzer: File Analyzer and Metadata Harvester." *Georgetown University Libraries*. Accessed March 7, 2017. https://georgetown-university-libraries.github.io/File-Analyzer.

"File Identification Tool Set (FITS)." *Harvard University*. Accessed August 27, 2016. http://projects.iq.harvard.edu/fits.

"Filemaker." *Wikipedia*. Accessed December 17, 2017. https://en.wikipedia.org/wiki/FileMaker.

"First Steps for Managing Born-Digital Content Report Inspires SAA Jump In Initiative." *OCLC Research.* Last modified June 12, 2013. http://www.oclc.org/research/news/2013/06-12.html.

"Floppy Disk." *Wikipedia*. Accessed April 5, 2016. https://en.wikipedia.org/wiki/Floppy_disk.

"Forensic Toolkit (FTK)." *Access Data*. Accessed November 12, 2016. http://accessdata.com/solutions/digital-forensics/forensic-toolkit-ftk.

Frauenfelder, Mark. "Computing Sir Tim Berners-Lee." *MIT Technology Review* (October 1, 2004). Accessed December 18, 2016. https://www.technologyreview.com/s/403095/sir-tim-berners-lee.

"Functions." *GASHE: Gateway to Archives of Scottish Higher Education*. Last updated January 24, 2006. Accessed December 2, 2016. http://www.gashe.ac.uk/heicolls/functions.html.

Gilliland-Swetland, Anne J., and Phillip B. Eppard. "Preserving the Authenticity of Contingent Digital Objects." *D-Lib Magazine* 6 (July/August 2000). Accessed January 17, 2017. http://www.dlib.org/dlib/july00/eppard/07eppard.html.

"Glossary." s.v. "metadata." *Federal Agencies Digitization Guidelines Initiative*. 2015. Accessed December 11, 2016. http://www.digitizationguidelines.gov/results.php?gltext=technical+metadata&x=0&y=0.

"Glossary." *National Digital Stewardship Alliance*. Accessed January 14, 2017. http://ndsa.org/glossary.

Gracy, David B., II. *Archives and Manuscripts: Arrangement and Description*. Basic Manual Series. Chicago: Society of American Archivists, 1977.

Greene, Mark A., and Dennis Meissner. "More Product, Less Process: Revamping Traditional Archival Processing." *American Archivist* 68 (Fall 2005): 208–63.

Gueguen, Gretchen, Vitor Manoel Marques da Fonsecs, Daniel V. Pitti, and Claire Sibille-de Gri-moüard. "Toward an International Conceptual Model for Archival Description: A Preliminary Report from the International Council on Archives' Experts Group on Archival Description." *American Archivist* 76 (Fall/Winter 2013): 567–84.

"Guide to Archives Consortia." *Society of American Archivists*. Accessed December 23, 2016. http://www2.archivists.org/groups/regional-archival-associations-consortium-raac/guide-to -archives-consortia.

Gustainis, Emily Novak. "Center for the History of Medicine Metrics Project Documentation." *Harvard Medical School Wiki*. Last revised October 23, 2012. https://wiki.med.harvard.edu/ Countway/ArchivalCollaboratives/CHoMMetricsDocumentation.

Ham, F. Gerald. *Selecting and Appraising Archives and Manuscripts*. Archival Fundamentals Series. Chicago: Society of American Archivists, 1993.

Hamill, Lois D. *Archives for the Lay Person: A Guide to Managing Cultural Collections*. Lanham, MD: AltaMira Press, 2013.

———. "Provenance and Original Order: The Evolution of Their Acceptance as Principles of Arrangement and Description." Master's thesis, University of Massachusetts, Boston, 1997. ProQuest (UMI 1395725).

Harvey, Ross. "Keeping, Forgetting, and Misreading Digital Material: Libraries Learning from Ar-chives and Recordkeeping Practice." Whyte memorial lecture, Monash University, Melbourne, Australia, September 15, 2015. Accessed January 1, 2016. https://rossharveynet2016.files. wordpress.com/2016/01/harvey_whyte_lecture_2015.pdf.

Hensen, Steven L., comp. *Archives, Personal Papers, and Manuscripts*. Chicago: Society of American Archivists, 1989.

———. "NISTF II and EAD: The Evolution of Archival Description." *American Archivist* 60 (Summer 1997): 284–96.

Hobert, Karen A., Gavin Tay, and Joe Mariano. *Magic Quadrant for Enterprise Content Management*. Stamford, CT: Gartner, October 31, 2016. Accessed December 18, 2016. https://www.gartner .com/doc/reprints?id=1-3KZPGDB&ct=161031&st=sb.

Holmes, Oliver W. "Archival Arrangement: Five Different Operations at Five Different Levels." *American Archivist* 27 (January 1964): 21–41.

"How Preservica Works." *Preservica*. Accessed March 5, 2017. http://preservica.com/preservica -works.

Humanities Advanced Technology and Information Institute, University of Glasgow, and National Initiative for a Networked Cultural Heritage. *The NINCH Guide to Good Practice in the Digital Representation and Management of Cultural Heritage Materials.* Washington, DC: National Initiative for a Networked Cultural Heritage, 2003. Accessed January 21, 2017. http://www.ninch.org/guide.pdf.

Hunter, Gregory S. *Developing and Maintaining Practical Archives: A How-to-Do-It Manual.* New York: Neal-Schuman, 2003.

Hutchins, Matthew. *Testing Software Tools of Potential Interest for Digital Preservation Activities at the National Library of Australia.* Parkes Place, Canberra: Information Technology Division National Library of Australia, 2012. Accessed January 11, 2017. http://openpreservation.org/system/files/Digital%20Preservation%20Project%20Report%20-%20Testing%20Software%20Tools.pdf.

"Hydra Is a Repository Solution." *Hydra.* Accessed March 5, 2017. https://projecthydra.org.

"ICA-AtoM." *Artefactual.* Accessed December 22, 2016. https://www.ica-atom.org.

International Council on Archives. *ISAD(G): General International Standard Archival Description.* 2nd ed. Stockholm: International Council on Archives, 1999. Accessed January 10, 2017. http://www.icacds.org.uk/eng/ISAD(G).pdf.

International Council on Archives, Experts Group on Archival Description (EGAD). *Records in Contexts: A Conceptual Model for Archival Description.* Consultation draft v0.1. Paris: International Council on Archives, September 2016. Accessed November 23, 2016. http://www.ica.org/sites/default/files/RiC-CM-0.1.pdf.

International Standard Organization. *ISO 15489-1 Information and Documentation—Records Management: Part 1: General.* Geneva: International Standard Organization, 2001. Accessed October 15, 2016. http://www.wgarm.net/ccarm/docs-repository/doc/doc402817.PDF.

"Internet." *Wikipedia.* Accessed January 15, 2017. https://en.wikipedia.org/wiki/Internet.

"InterPARES 2 Project Glossary." *International Research on Permanent Authentic Records in Electronic Systems (InterPARES).* Last Modified January 20, 2017. http://www.interpares.org/ip2/display_file.cfm?doc=ip2_glossary.pdf&CFID=10608648&CFTOKEN=76523578.

"Introduction to the Semantic Web." *Cambridge Semantics.* Accessed December 18, 2016. http://www.cambridgesemantics.com/semantic-university/introduction-semantic-web.

"JHOVE." *Open Preservation Foundation.* Accessed March 6, 2017. http://jhove.openpreservation.org.

"JHOVE—JSTOR/Harvard Object Validation Environment." *JSTOR and the President and Fellows of Harvard College.* Accessed November 5, 2016. http://jhove.sourceforge.net.

"Karen's Directory Printer 5.3.2." *MajorGeeks.* Accessed November 4, 2016. http://www.majorgeeks.com/files/details/karens_directory_printer.html.

Land, Robert H. "The National Union Catalog of Manuscript Collections." *American Archivist* 17 (April 1954): 195–207.

Landis, William E. "Overcoming the Bibliographic Conundrum in Archival Description." *American Archivist* 74 (2011 Supplement): 11–19.

Lavoie, Brian F. "Meeting the Challenges of Digital Preservation: The OAIS Reference Model." *OCLC Newsletter*, no. 243 (January/February 2000). Accessed September 27, 2016. http://www.oclc.org/research/publications/library/2000/lavoie-oais.html.

———. *The Open Archival Information System Reference Model: An Introductory Guide*. Dublin, OH: Office of Research, Online Computer Library Center, January 2004. Accessed September 27, 2016. http://www.dpconline.org/docman/technology-watch-reports/91-introduction-to-oais/file.

Leland, Waldo G. "American Archival Problems." In *Annual Report of the American Historical Association for the Year 1909, Tenth Report of the Public Archives Commission, Report of the First Annual Conference of Archivists*, 342–48. Washington, DC: Government Printing Office, 1911.

———. "Some Fundamental Principles in Relation to Archives." In *Annual Report of the American Historical Association for the Year 1912, Thirteenth Report of the Public Archives Commission, Appendix B Proceedings of the Fourth Annual Conference of Archivists*, 264–68. Washington, DC: Government Printing Office, 1914.

Library of Congress. *Departmental and Divisional Manuals No. 17 Manuscripts Division*. Washington, DC: Library of Congress, 1950.

"Linked Data." *Wikipedia*. Accessed December 4, 2016. https://en.wikipedia.org/wiki/Linked_data.

Lynch, Karen T., and Helen W. Slotkin. *Processing Manual for the Institute Archives and Special Collections, MIT Libraries*. Cambridge: Massachusetts Institute of Technology, 1981.

Lyons, Bertram, and Josh Ranger. "Hard Skills for Managing Digital Collections in Archives." Midwest Archives Conference's Fall Symposium, Minneapolis, MN, September 18–19, 2015.

MacNeil, Heather. "Archival Theory and Practice: Between Two Paradigms." *Archivaria* 37 (1994): 6–20.

McCoy, Donald R. *The National Archives: America's Ministry of Documents, 1934–1968*. Chapel Hill: University of North Carolina, 1978.

Millar, Laura A. *Archives: Principles and Practice*. London: Facet, 2010.

Miller, Fredric M. *Arranging and Describing Archives and Manuscripts*. Archival Fundamentals Series. Chicago: Society of American Archivists, 1990.

Minisis. Accessed December 22, 2016. http://www.minisisinc.com/index.html.

"Mission and History." *ArchivesSpace*. Accessed December 18, 2016. http://archivesspace.org/about/mission-and-history.

Mitchell, Thornton W. Introduction to *Norton on Archives: The Writings of Margaret Cross Norton on Archival and Records Management*, by Margaret Cross Norton, xv–xxi. Carbondale: Southern Illinois Press, 1975.

Mount St. Mary's University (Los Angeles, CA). *Procedure Manual for Cuadra Star Knowledge Center for Archives*, ix. Los Angeles: Mount St. Mary's University, March 21, 2015. Accessed December 22, 2016. http://www2.archivists.org/sites/all/files/msmu_001.pdf.

Myers, Mark J. "Appraisal of Electronic Records." Society of American Archivists, Digital Archives Specialist workshop, Richmond, KY, June 21, 2013.

——. "Electronic Records: The Next Step." Society of American Archivists Digital Archives Specialist webinar, April 13, 2015.

National Archives and Records Administration. *Appraisal Policy of the National Archives and Records Administration*. Washington, DC: National Archives and Records Administration, n.d. Accessed June 26, 2016. https://www.archives.gov/records-mgmt/publications/appraisal-policy.pdf.

"The National Archives on GitHub." *National Archives and Records Administration*. Accessed March 7, 2017. https://www.archives.gov/social-media/github.html.

National Information Standards Organization. *Understanding Metadata*. Bethesda, MD: National Information Standards Organization, 2004. Accessed May 12, 2016. http://www.niso.org/publications/press/UnderstandingMetadata.pdf.

Nelson, Naomi L., Seth Shaw, Nancy Deromedi, Michael Shallcross, Cynthia Ghering, Lisa Schmidt, Michelle Belden, Jackie R. Esposito, Ben Goldman, and Tim Pyatt. *Managing Born-Digital Special Collections and Archival Materials*. SPEC Kit 329. Washington, DC: Association of Research Libraries, 2012.

NUCMC: National Union Catalog of Manuscript Collections. Accessed December 18, 2016. http://www.loc.gov/coll/nucmc.

"NUCMC History Timeline: 1947–Present." *NUCMC: National Union Catalog of Manuscript Collections*. Accessed December 18, 2016. http://www.loc.gov/coll/nucmc/timeline.html.

OAC Working Group, Metadata Standards Subcommittee. *OAC Best Practice Guidelines for EAD*. Oakland: University of California, 2005. Accessed December 23, 2016. http://www.cdlib.org/services/access_publishing/dsc/contribute/docs/oacbpgead_v2-0.pdf.

OCLC/RLG Working Group on Preservation Metadata. *Preservation Metadata and the OAIS Information Model: A Metadata Framework to Support the Preservation of Digital Objects*. Dublin, OH: OCLC/RLG Working Group on Preservation Metadata, 2002. Accessed May 12, 2016. http://www.oclc.org/content/dam/research/activities/pmwg/pm_framework.pdf.

"OhioLINK EAD Finding Aid Creation Tool." Version 1.7. *Kent State University*. Accessed December 23, 2016. https://ead.library.kent.edu/login.php.

"Omeka: Serious Web Publishing." *Roy Rosenzweig Center for History and New Media, George Mason University*. Accessed December 23, 2016. https://omeka.org/about.

"OpenRefine." *Wikipedia*. Accessed December 17, 2016. https://en.wikipedia.org/wiki/OpenRefine.

O'Toole, James M. *Understanding Archives and Manuscripts*. Archival Fundamentals Series. Chicago: Society of American Archivists, 1990.

Owens, Trevor. "NDSA Levels of Digital Preservation: Release Candidate One." *The Signal*. November 20, 2012. http://blogs.loc.gov/thesignal/2012/11/ndsa-levels-of-digital-preservation-release-candidate-one.

Palmer, Carole L., Nicholas M. Weber, Trevor Muñoz, and Allen H. Renear. "Foundations of Data Curation: The Pedagogy and Practice of 'Purposeful Work' with Research Data." *Archives Journal* 3 (Summer 2013). Accessed January 1, 2015. http://www.archivejournal.net/issue/3/archives-remixed/foundations-of-data-curation-the-pedagogy-and-practice-of-purposeful-work-with-research-data.

Palmer, Russell. "Lyrasis Islandora Hosting Services Demonstration." Live web presentation viewed October 20, 2015.

"Pass the Word." *Kentucky Oral History Commission*. Accessed December 23, 2016. http://passtheword.ky.gov.

Pearce-Moses, Richard. "Accession." In *A Glossary of Archival and Records Terminology*. Chicago: Society of American Archivists, 2005. Accessed August 2, 2016. http://www2.archivists.org/glossary/terms/a/accession.

———. "Administrative Metadata." In *A Glossary of Archival and Records Terminology*. Chicago: Society of American Archivists, 2005. Accessed December 16, 2016, http://www2.archivists.org/glossary/terms/a/administrative-metadata.

———. "Archival Description." In *A Glossary of Archival and Records Terminology*. Chicago: Society of American Archivists, 2005. Accessed January 13, 2017, http://www2.archivists.org/glossary/terms/a/archival-description.

———. "Archives." In *A Glossary of Archival and Records Terminology*. Chicago: Society of American Archivists, 2005. Accessed January 6, 2016, http://www2.archivists.org/search/saasearch_glossary/archives.

———. "Archives, Personal Papers, and Manuscripts." In *A Glossary of Archival and Records Terminology*. Chicago: Society of American Archivists, 2005. Accessed January 3, 2017, http://www2.archivists.org/glossary/terms/a/archives-personal-papers-and-manuscripts.

———. *Archives in the Digital Era*. Accessed July 8, 2016. http://archivesinthedigitalera.blogspot.com.

———. "Authenticity." In *A Glossary of Archival and Records Terminology*. Chicago: Society of American Archivists, 2005. Accessed January 11, 2017, http://www2.archivists.org/glossary/terms/a/authenticity.

———. "Canadian-United States Task Force on Archival Description." In *A Glossary of Archival and Records Terminology*. Chicago: Society of American Archivists, 2005. Accessed December 1, 2015. http://www2.archivists.org/glossary/terms/c/canadian-united-states-task-force-on-archival-description.

———. "Classification." In *A Glossary of Archival and Records Terminology*. Chicago: Society of American Archivists, 2005. Accessed January 13, 2017, http://www2.archivists.org/glossary/terms/c/classificaton.

———. "Data Value Standard." In *A Glossary of Archival and Records Terminology*. Chicago: Society of American Archivists, 2005. Accessed January 13, 2017, http://www2.archivists.org/glossary/terms/d/data-value-standard.

———. "Describing Archives: A Content Standard." In *A Glossary of Archival and Records Terminology*. Chicago: Society of American Archivists, 2005. Accessed April 14, 2016, http://www2.archivists.org/glossary/terms/d/describing-archives-a-content-standard.

———. "Description." In *A Glossary of Archival and Records Terminology*. Chicago: Society of American Archivists, 2005. Accessed April 12, 2016, http://www2.archivists.org/glossary/terms/d/description.

———. "File." In *A Glossary of Archival and Records Terminology*. Chicago: Society of American Archivists, 2005. Accessed January 12, 2016, http://www2.archivists.org/glossary/terms/f/file.

———. "Integrity." In *A Glossary of Archival and Records Terminology*. Chicago: Society of American Archivists, 2005. Accessed January 11, 2017, http://www2.archivists.org/glossary/terms/i/integrity.

———. "Item." In *A Glossary of Archival and Records Terminology*. Chicago: Society of American Archivists, 2005. Accessed January 12, 2016, http://www2.archivists.org/glossary/terms/i/item.

———. "Macroappraisal." In *A Glossary of Archival and Records Terminology*. Chicago: Society of American Archivists, 2005. Accessed July 8, 2016, http://www2.archivists.org/glossary/terms/m/macro-appraisal.

———. "Migration." In *A Glossary of Archival and Records Terminology*. Chicago: Society of American Archivists, 2005. Accessed January 13, 2017, http://www2.archivists.org/glossary/terms/m/migration.

———. "Record." In *A Glossary of Archival and Records Terminology*. Chicago: Society of American Archivists, 2005. Accessed June 8, 2016. http://www2.archivists.org/glossary/terms/r/record.

———. "Record Copy." In *A Glossary of Archival and Records Terminology*. Chicago: Society of American Archivists, 2005. Accessed July 8, 2016. http://www2.archivists.org/glossary/terms/r/record-copy#.V3_XVKIYFHo.

———. "Reformat." In *A Glossary of Archival and Records Terminology*. Chicago: Society of American Archivists, 2005. Accessed November 23, 2015, http://www2.archivists.org/ glossary/ terms/r/reformat

"PERTTS Portal: Glossary." *Council of State Archivists (CoSA)*. Accessed July 9, 2016. https://www .statearchivists.org/pertts/glossary.

Pitti, Daniel V. "Encoded Archival Description: The Development of an Encoding Standard for Archival Finding Aids." *American Archivist* 60 (Summer 1997): 268–83.

———. "Technology and the Transformation of Archival Description." *Journal of Archival Organization* 3 (2006): 9–22. http://dx.doi.org/10.1300/J201v03n02_02.

Planning Committee on Descriptive Standards. Preface to *Canadian Archival Standard Rules for Archival Description*, xiii–xiv. Rev. ed. Ottawa: Bureau of Canadian Archivists, 2008. Accessed December 1, 2015, http://www.cdncouncilarchives.ca/rad/radcomplete_july2008.pdf.

Posner, Ernst. "Some Aspects of Archival Development Since the French Revolution." *American Archivist* 3 (July 1940): 159–72.

PREMIS: Preservation Metadata Maintenance Activity. Last modified January 15, 2016. http://www .loc.gov/standards/premis.

PREMIS Editorial Committee. *PREMIS Data Dictionary for Preservation Metadata*. Ver. 3.0. November 2015. Accessed December 29, 2016. http://www.loc.gov/standards/premis/v3/premis-3 -0-final.pdf.

Prom, Christopher J. "Making Digital Curation a Systematic Institutional Function." *International Journal of Digital Curation* 6 (2011): 139–52.

———. "Optimum Access? Processing in College and University Archives." *American Archivist* 73 (Spring/Summer 2010): 146–74.

———. "Using Web Analytics to Improve Online Access to Archival Resources." *American Archivist* 74 (Spring/Summer 2011): 158–84.

"Quick View Plus Standard Edition." *Avantstar*. Accessed August 27, 2016. http://www.avantstar .com/quick-view-plus-standard-edition#fndtn-overview.

"ReNamer." *Den4B*. Accessed March 6, 2017. http://www.den4b.com/products/renamer.

"Report of the Working Group on Standards for Archival Description." *American Archivist* 52 (Fall 1989): 440–61.

"A Rising Tide Lifts All the Boats." *Wikipedia*. Accessed January 7, 2017. https://en.wikipedia.org/ wiki/A_rising_tide_lifts_all_boats.

Roe, Kathleen D. *Arranging and Describing Archives and Manuscripts*. Archival Fundamentals Series II. Chicago: Society of American Archivists, 2005.

Rouse, Margaret. "Data Governance (DG)." *TechTarget*. Accessed December 31, 2016. http:// searchdatamanagement.techtarget.com/definition/data-governance.

———. "Extensible." *TechTarget*. Accessed January 14, 2017. http://searchsoa.techtarget.com/ definition/extensible.

"SAA Core Values Statement and Code of Ethics." *Society of American Archivists*. Accessed June 11, 2016. http://www2.archivists.org/statements/saa-core-values-statement-and-code-of -ethics#.V1yFs6IYFHo.

Santamaria, Abelardo. *Report on the Work of CNEDA (2007–2012): Toward a Conceptual Model for Archival Description in Spain*. Seville, Spain: Ministerio de Educación, Cultura, y De- porte, July 11, 2012. Accessed November 23, 2016. http://www.mecd.gob.es/cultura-mecd/ dms/mecd/cultura-mecd/areas-cultura/archivos/mc/cneda/documentacion/ReportC NEDA_11_07_2012-pdf/ReportCNEDA_11_07_2012.pdf.

Santamaria, Daniel A. "Module 3: Designing Descriptive and Access Systems." In *Archival Ar- rangement and Description*, edited by Christopher J. Prom and Thomas J. Frusciano, 145–215. Trends in Archives Practice. Chicago: Society of American Archivists, 2013.

Schaefer, Sibyl, and Janet M. Bunde. "Module 1: Standards for Archival Description." In *Archival Arrangement and Description*, edited by Christopher J. Prom and Thomas J. Frusciano, 7–85. Trends in Archives Practice. Chicago: Society of American Archivists, 2013.

Schellenberg, T. R. *The Management of Archives*. New York: Columbia University Press, 1965.

Schmitt, Bob. "Collections Management Systems/Software." Ver. 1.2. 2014. Accessed December 22, 2016. http://carlibrary.org/CMS-Table.htm.

"Semantic Web." *Wikipedia*. Accessed December 18, 2016. https://en.wikipedia.org/wiki/ Semantic_Web.

Shallcross, Mike. "Archivematica Users Group @ SAA." *ArchivesSpace-Archivematica-DSpace Workflow Integration*. August 9, 2016. Accessed August 27, 2016. http://archival-integration .blogspot.com.

Shaw, Seth E. "Arrangement and Description of Electronic Records, Part I." Society of American Archivists, Digital Archives Specialist workshop, Chapel Hill, NC, June 11, 2015.

———. "Arrangement and Description of Electronic Records, Part II." Society of American Archi- vists, Digital Archives Specialist workshop, Chapel Hill, NC, June 12, 2015.

Skiljan, Irfan. *Irfanview*. Accessed November 5, 2016. http://www.irfanview.com.

Smith, MacKenzie, Mary Barton, Mick Bass, Margret Branschofsky, Greg McClellan, Dave Stuve, Robert Tansley, and Julie Harford Walker. "DSpace: An Open Source Dynamic Digital Repos- itory." *D-Lib Magazine* 9 (January 2003). Accessed May 27, 2016. http://www.dlib.org/dlib/ january03/smith/01smith.html.

Society of American Archivists. *Describing Archives: A Content Standard.* 2nd ed. Chicago: Society of American Archivists, 2013.

Spiro, Lisa. *Archival Management Software.* Washington, DC: Council on Library and Information Resources, 2009.

"Standards Development and Review." *Society of American Archivists.* Last modified January, 2012. http://www2.archivists.org/governance/handbook/section7/groups/Standards/Development-and-Review#.Vy-dhXoYFHo.

"Structured vs. Unstructured Data." BrightPlanet. June 28, 2012. Accessed January 21, 2017. https://brightplanet.com/2012/06/structured-vs-unstructured-data.

Technical Subcommittee for Encoded Archival Context of the Society of American Archivists and Staatsbibliothek zu Berlin. *Encoded Archival Context–Corporate Bodies, Persons, and Families (EAC-CPF) Tag Library.* 2014. Accessed May 15, 2016. http://eac.staatsbibliothek-berlin.de/fileadmin/user_upload/schema/cpfTagLibrary.html.

"TeraCopy." *Code Sector.* Accessed November 19, 2016. http://www.codesector.com/teracopy.

"Thunar File Manager." *Xfce Development Team.* Accessed November 4, 2016. http://docs.xfce.org/xfce/thunar/start.

"Timeline of Computer History: Networking and the Web." *Computer History Museum.* Accessed May 31, 2016. http://www.computerhistory.org/timeline/networking-the-web.

"Timeline of Computer History: Computers." *Computer History Museum.* Accessed May 30, 2016. http://www.computerhistory.org/timeline/computers/.

"Timeline of Computer History: Memory & Storage." *Computer History Museum.* Accessed May 30, 2016. http://www.computerhistory.org/timeline/memory-storage/.

"Timeline of Computer History: Networking and the Web." *Computer History Museum.* Accessed May 31, 2016. http://www.computerhistory.org/timeline/networking-the-web/.

"Timeline of Computer History: Software & Languages." *Computer History Museum.* Accessed May 31, 2016. http://www.computerhistory.org/timeline//software-languages.

"Tools." *Library of Congress.* Accessed August 27, 2016. http://www.digitalpreservation.gov/tools.

"Tools: Exactly." *AudioVisual Preservation Solutions.* Accessed March 6, 2017. https://www.avpreserve.com/avpsresources/tools.

"Tools for Preservation Metadata Implementation." *PREMIS: Preservation Metadata Maintenance Activity.* Accessed December 31, 2016. https://www.loc.gov/standards/premis/tools_for_premis.php.

"TreeSize Professional." *Jam Software.* Accessed August 27, 2016. https://www.jam-software.com/treesize.

University of Oxford and University of Manchester. "Appraisal and Disposal." Chap. 4 in *Paradigm: Workbook on Digital Private Papers*. Last modified January 2, 2008. http://www.paradigm.ac.uk/workbook/appraisal/appraisal-approaches.html.

———. "Arranging and Cataloguing Digital and Hybrid Archives." Chap. 6 in *Paradigm: Workbook on Digital Private Papers*. Last modified January 2, 2008. Accessed November 26, 2016. http://www.paradigm.ac.uk/workbook/cataloguing/index.html.

"USB Flash Drive." *Wikipedia*. Accessed May 30, 2016. https://en.wikipedia.org/wiki/USB_flash_drive.

van der Hoeven, Jeffrey, Bram Lohman, and Remco Verdegem. "Emulation for Digital Preservation in Practice: The Results." *International Journal of Digital Curation* 2 (2007): 123–32. Accessed January 14, 2017. http://www.ijdc.net/index.php/ijdc/article/view/50/35.

Virtue, Ethel B. "Principles of Classification for Archives." In *Annual Report of the American Historical Association for the Year 1914: In Two Volumes, Vol. 1*, 373–84. Washington, DC: Government Printing Office, 1916.

Walch, Victoria Irons, comp. *Standards for Archival Description: A Handbook*. Chicago: Society of American Archivists, 1994. Accessed November 24, 2015. http://www.archivists.org/catalog/stds99/index.html.

"Web 2.0." *Wikipedia*. Accessed December 18, 2016. https://en.wikipedia.org/wiki/Web_2.0.

"What Is Enterprise Content Management (ECM)?" *Association for Information and Image Management*. Accessed December 18, 2016. http://www.aiim.org/What-is-ECM-Enterprise-Content-Management.aspx#.

"WinDirStat: Windows Directory Statistics." *WinDirStat*. Last updated June 28, 2016. http://windirstat.info.

Wisser, Katherine M., and Jackie Dean. "EAD Tag Usage: Community Analysis of the Use of Encoded Archival Description Elements." *American Archivist* 75 (Fall/Winter 2013): 542–66.

Working Group on Standards for Archival Description. "Recommendations of the Working Group on Standards for Archival Description." *American Archivist* 52 (Fall 1989): 462–77.

Work Projects Administration, Historical Records Survey. *Preparation of Inventories of Manuscripts: A Circular of Instructions for the Use of the Historical Records Survey Projects*. Preliminary ed. Washington, DC: Federal Works Agency, Work Projects Administration, Division of Professional and Service Projects, Research and Records Projects Subdivision, 1940.

Work Projects Administration, Survey of the Federal Archives. *The Manual of the Survey of Federal Archives*. Washington, DC: February 1936.

"World Wide Web." *Wikipedia*. Last modified September 3, 2016. https://en.wikipedia.org/wiki/World_Wide_Web.

"Xerography." *Wikipedia*. Last modified August 4, 2016. https://en.wikipedia.org/wiki/Xerography.

Yaco, Sonia. "It's Complicated: Barriers to EAD Implementation." *American Archivist* 71 (Fall/Winter 2008): 456–75.

Yakel, Elizabeth. "Archival Representation." *Archival Science* 3 (2003): 1–25.

———. "Digital Curation." *OCLC Systems and Services: International Digital Library Perspectives* 23 (2007): 335–40.

———. "Encoded Archival Description: Are Finding Aids Boundary Spanners or Barriers for Users?" *Journal of Archival Organization* 2, nos. 1–2 (2004): 63–77. Accessed December 28, 2016. doi:10.1300/J201v02n01_0663.

Yakel, Elizabeth, and Deborah A. Torres. "AI: Archival Intelligence and User Expertise." *American Archivist* 66 (Spring/Summer 2003): 51–78.

Zach, Lisl, and Marcia Peri. "Desperately Seeking Solutions: College and University E-Records Management (ERM) Programs." Paper presented at Mid-Atlantic Regional Archives Conference, Morristown, NJ, October 27, 2006.

Index

Note: *Page references for figures, tables, and text boxes are italicized.*

Landis, William E., 10, 14n44, 29
Library of Congress Name Authority File. *See* standards
Library of Congress reorganization (1940), 4
library profession, 1–2, 9; bibliographic influence on archival standards, 10; manages manuscript collections, 2; national cataloging code, 3, 4
linked (open) data (LOD), 117–118, 128

manuscript collections: bibliographic influence, 4–5; definition, 17; dominates public records tradition, 4; examples of, 23; influence of Library of Congress on, 2; origin of, 1; personal digital records, 17, 167. *See also* appraisal
markup languages, 116, 117, 127
Meissner, Dennis. *See* More Product, Less Process
metadata, 92, 108; administrative, 40, *80*, *95*, 161; definition, 40, 166; descriptive, 40, *80*, 164; preservation, *80*, 82–83, 167–168; rights management, 40, *80*, 83, *83*, *111*, 113, 169; structural, 40, *80*, 92, *95*, 169; technical, 40, *78–80*, *95*, 107, 170
More Product, Less Process (MPLP), 25–26, 28. *See also* processing, backlogs

National Archives, 3, 6
National Union Catalog of Manuscript Collections, 41, 123, 135
Norton, Margaret Cross, 3, 5

OhioLINK, 41, 127
Online Archive of California, 41, 126
Open Archival Information System (OAIS) framework, 75, 76, *77*, 107, 167; archival information package (AIP), *82*, 82, 84, 93, 99, 108, *110–112*, 113, 161; ingest function, 76, 81–82, 165; preservation description information (PDI), *82*, *83*, 84, 82–84, 167; representation information, *79*, *82*, 82, *95*, 111, 113, 169; stabilized SIP, *78–81*, 82, 84, 93, 97; submission information package (SIP), 75, *82*, 82–83, *83*, 85, 93, 97, 108, 170. *See also Describing Archives*, unique identifier
organizational records. *See* arrangement of records
original order, 44n4, 91, 92; *Strukturprinzip*, 1, 44n4

Paradigm (Personal ARchives Accessible in DIGital Media) project, 98
Pass the Word, 41, 127
personal papers. *See* manuscript collections
Pitti, Daniel, 8, 116, 117

preservation, 167; assessment of digital records, 76; assessment during microappraisal, 65; performance during records processing, 27–28; physical review of new acquisitions, 20–21; tasks for digital records, *78–80*, 84, *94-97*, 100, 111–113
preservation copy, 60
preservation metadata. *See* metadata
processing, 107, 168; backlogs, 27, 41; comparison of workflow for analog records to digital records, *54–55*, 56; digital photos, 85; manuals, 25, 26, 27; plans, 23, 43–44, *95*, 98; rates, 26–27. *See also* More Product, Less Process
Prom, Christopher J., 27, 41, 114, 133, 136–137, 138
provenance, *81*, *95*, 115; component of preservation description information (PDI), *82*, 83, *83*, *84*, 91; definition, 18, 44n4. *See also respect des fonds*
public records tradition: differences with manuscript collections, 3, 9–10; Dutch influence, 2; origin, 1

record, definition, 17–18, 91, 161, 168
record copy, 60, 168
record group, 4, 6, 18; level, 6, 19
Records in Context: A Conceptual Model for Archival Description, 117
records management, 52, 59, 60, 66, 101, 124–125, 138. *See also* data governance
reference (preservation description information [PDI]). *See Describing Archives*, unique identifier
reliability, 168. *See also* authenticity; digital records, four essential characteristics
representation, 118n1, 161, 169
respect des fonds, 1, 18, 44n4. *See also* provenance
rights management metadata. *See* metadata, rights management

Santamaria, Daniel A., 127
Schellenberg, T. R., 6, 19, 59
semantic web, 128, 169
series, definition, 19. *See also* arrangement
standardized general markup language (SGML), 8
standards, 39–41, 108–109, 110; Anglo-American Cataloging Rules (AACR), 5, 7; Anglo-American Cataloging Rules, 2nd ed. (AACR2), 5, 8; *Archives, Personal Papers, and Manuscripts* (APPM), 5, 8; benefits of use, 40–41, 109, 110, 127; bibliographic influence on standards development, 10; data content standards, 8–9, 39, 110, 163; data structure standards, 8–9, 39, 110, 163; data value, 39, 163; definition,

39; *Describing Archives: A Content Standard*
(DACS), 9, 39, 40, 44n4, *80, 96,* 108-111,
113, 115; development, 7-9; Dublin Core,
39, 109; *Encoded Archival Content-Corporate
Bodies, Persons, and Families* (EAC-CPF), 9,
39, 40, *112,* 113, 115, 116–117; encoded archival
description (EAD), 8-9, 39, 110, 114, 115,
116–117, 118; encoded archival description 3
(EAD3), 128; *General International Standard
Archival Description* (ISAD[G]), 9, 39, 44n4;
*International Standard Archival Authority Record
for Corporate Bodies, Persons, and Families
(ISAAR*[CPF]), 9, 39, 40, 116; *International
Standard for Describing Functions* (ISDF),
39, 117; *International Standard for Describing
Institutions with Archival Holdings* (ISDIAH),
39; Library of Congress Name Authority File,
39–40; Preservation Metadata Implementation
Strategies (PREMIS), 40, *80, 96, 111,* 113;
USMARC, 5, 7, 8, 123-124; USMARC AMC, 5,
8, 115. *See also Describing Archives: A Content
Standard* (DACS)

standards implementation, 128, 130, 134, 135, *137,*
137, 140

standards interoperability, 127

Society of American Archivists (SAA): Committee
on Finding Aids, 6; National Information
Systems Task Force (NISTF), 7–8; Standards
Committee, 39

structural metadata. *See* metadata

structured query languages (SQL), 116

subgroup, 14, 45n9; level, 19, 108

technical appraisal. *See* appraisal, micro

technical metadata. *See* metadata, technical

thesauri. *See* standards, data value

unique identifier (UID). *See Describing Archives,*
unique identifier

U.S. machine-readable cataloging (USMARC). *See*
standards

U.S. machine-readable cataloging for archives and
manuscripts control (USMARC AMC). *See*
standards

usability, 170. *See also* authenticity; digital records,
four essential characteristics

Van Laer, Arnold, 2

Yaco, Sonia, 128

Yakel, Elizabeth, 30, 118n1, 133

About the Author

Lois Hamill is the university archivist and an associate professor at Northern Kentucky University's Steely Library. She manages the university archives, the regional and local history collections, and the records and information management program. A practicing archivist for more than seventeen years, Ms. Hamill's last book, *Archives for the Lay Person*, was well received, winning a 2013 Kentucky History Award. Ms. Hamill is a certified archivist, holds the SAA Digital Archives Specialist certificate, and is a successful grant writer.

She is professionally active nationally, in the Midwest region, and in Kentucky and speaks on archival topics at archives, library, and history conferences.